From all over the world come these easily prepared

Fabulous Foods For People You Love

to help you cook with flair—entertain with elegance and ease—at a small buffet or a formal dinner.

Japanese Shrimp Tempura, Swedish Pot Roast, Chinese Sub-Gum-Gai-Pen, Irish Gingerbread Cake, Chicken Mexicaine, French Coq au Vin, Vermont Baked Apples, and many more fabulous foods, from tempting hors d-oeuvres to dramatic desserts—with this book these, and many more fascinating and exotic recipes can become your own specialities!

"A superb guidebook to good eating."
—Stamford (Conn.) Advocate

THE
COOKBOOK
of fabulous foods for people you love

by Carolyn Coggins

Decorations by Dave Lyons

PYRAMID BOOKS, 444 Madison Avenue, New York 22, New York

FABULOUS FOODS FOR PEOPLE YOU LOVE,
by Carolyn Coggins

for
Willard and Lorraine Simpson
which is the best way I know to
take them with me from Spain to Denmark

A Pyramid Book, published by arrangement with the author

Pyramid Books edition: first printing, November 1959

Copyright, © 1955, by Carolyn Coggins
All Rights Reserved

Printed in the United States of America

Table of Contents

Cooking . . . From Kansas to Paris	3
1. Serve Yourself Appetizers	5
The Fine Flair of Serving with Ease	5
Hors d'Oeuvres	8
Canapés	13
Unusual Ideas for the Hors d'Oeuvres Tray	17
2. Delicious Soups	19
The Fine Flair of Soup Making	20
Bisques	22
Colorful Soups	27
3. Unusual Supper Dishes	34
4. The "Foundation Garments" for Fine Meals	46
Rice	46
Pasta	53
5. Seafood . . . Exotic but Easy	60
Interesting Recipes	
6. Vegetables and Sauces	72
How to Cook and Flavor Vegetables	72
Herb Flavoring for Vegetables	97
Sauces for Vegetables	99
7. Fine Meat Dishes . . . Beautifully Presented	104
Beef	104
Veal	113
Lamb	116
Pork	119
Ham	124
Meat Platter Garnishes	133
8. Poultry and Game	141
Chicken	142
Turkey	155
Stuffings for Chicken or Turkey	157
Duck	159
Notes on Game Birds	162
9. Salad Secrets	169
What There Is to Choose From	169
Do You Serve Salads in All These Ways?	170

Green Salads	170
Mixed Vegetable Tossed Salads	173
Ring Molded Salads	175
Soufflé Salads	181
Fruit Salads	183
Salads with an International Reputation	186
Frozen Salads	191
Salad Dressings	192
10. Party Pies	**197**
Pie Crusts, Shells and Meringues	197
Parfait Liqueur Pies	204
Colorful Pies	206
To Freeze Pies	215
11. Cakes from Many Lands	**217**
Cakes	217
Teatime Cakes	227
Frostings	233
12. Dramatic Desserts	**240**
Chocolate and Wonderful Flambés	240
Ambrosias—the Food of the Gods	252
Frozen Desserts, Ice Creams and Ices	258
Cheeses from All Over the World Offer Delectable Dessert	267
13. Planning Fabulous Meals	**271**
Serving Buffet	271
Interesting International Dinners	272
Meals Your Guests Will Like	274
Men in the Kitchen	279
14. When It's a Party	**282**

To Answer Your Questions

You who sit in the audience when I am speaking, often ask questions about the equipment used in my kitchen, about the type I would recommend for yours. So here I put it down for you—along with my blessings for the people who make these kitchen slaves do our work—the timing, temperature controlling, beating, blending, freezing, chilling, serving and toting.

These duties are achieved at my house through an electric blender at each end of the kitchen, and a timer on the gas range in addition to one which can be carried to the other end of the house. The gas range does it own temperature controlling too, once I set it correctly. The electric mixer saves your breath and mine, although a large wire whisk is within reach for beating meringue. My two "Mermaids," complete the picture. Each of these are half refrigerator, half freezer.

The warmers heated by candles, fluid or alcohol carry on with daily duty in the dining room keeping food hot. The large serving cart totes everything except its owner back and forth! On it, the infrared broiler, miracle portable cooker, goes everywhere in the house—or patio. All this—and the heaven they provide—is available to you.

Carolyn Coggins

Cooking ... From Kansas to Paris

When I was a little girl in Kansas I thought there were only three places for any right thinking person to spend any time: on a horse ... in a tree ... or in my mother's kitchen. The kitchen was always warm, but day in and day out the year-round it was fragrant as a berry patch in summer.

Then, as now, a homemaker prepared about 3500 meals in ten years. The test of a good cook then was to make something out of what you had. This was nothing to speak of compared to the supplies we have now, but of course the cellar was filled to its slanted door. Part of the kitchen fragrance came from the work of filling it, putting sausage cakes in lard at butchering time, digging potatoes (that wasn't so much fun) or pulling onions to store away. But the apples were a pleasure to collect. How we loved the tedious work of picking more cherries and peaches than we ate, so that there would be fruit for preserving. The garden and the orchard and autumn butchering to prepare food for other seasons went along with cooking much of it for consuming right then. The *then* part held fascination for each of us.

To grow up and spend a year in Europe on a food writing tour has been as extraordinary as to have the gas range replace the wood-burning stove. The modern refrigerators, the freezers, the electric beaters, the abundance of year-round supplies in our markets make us the envy of women all over the world. These American luxuries make preparing family and party meals less dreary than necessary cooking can sometimes become, and less time consuming than for the good cooks in Europe.

And what devoted and skillful cooks they are, achieving miracles of beauty and flavor, in almost everything they prepare. The kitchens they work in are as devoid of conveniences as the childhood kitchen we remember; but their creative love of cooking long ago elevated what they do to an art. Many of the great chefs are men, and the almost saint-like expressions on their faces reveal the happiness they find in working with food.

Cooking can be great fun—as many men in this country have discovered. They, and the women who prepare the 3500 meals, know that cooking with *flair* makes the job fascinating, absorbing, rewarding. Part of this knack of preparing food and serving it attractively develops from trying new dishes and serving them in new ways, discovering some of the recipes so beloved that they become "regulars" at your table.

The recipes included here offer novelty, superb flavor, interesting menus, and fun cooking which is reasonably time consuming or downright quick to prepare. In all of them, international recipes have been presented in a practical way for us Americans to use. For, while remaining in countries long enough to replace surprise by understanding, I also realized that there was a great difference between interesting recipes and those which are as practical as they are good when made in my modern home and in your efficiently equipped kitchens.

The food in this book is "American" in that it represents many famous meals and recipes and customs from Europe, mingled with our own. Together, they represent the fabulous food from countries whose men and women brought their dreams halfway around the world to create our fabulous land.

1

Serve Yourself Appetizers

The Fine Flair of Serving with Ease

There are three approaches to appetizers—those you make in a hurry, those you fuss over, those you made and stored for the hour they are needed. The type you favor will depend upon whether or not you are always pressed for time, and upon whether or not you have a freezer where flavorful pots and petite sandwiches and spreads can be stored away.

A collection of these appetizers is tantalizing enough to compose complete party fare. An assortment can also fill the decorative hors d'oeuvres tray at a buffet party or be a convenient first course, served in the living room, before a sit-down dinner.

Hors d'oeuvres are a colorful conversation-provoking picture. Assemble dips, canapés, a marinated array of vegetables, bowls of mushroom buttons (*page 89*), olives, and spreads. The effect is festive. Have a tray filled for small gatherings; a table full for big crowds. Whichever it is, select them so that flavors, textures, colors, will be contrasted for a grand effect.

APPETIZER CRISPS

Depending upon the number of guests, use a small or large round bowl—copper, ceramic, wooden or glass. Fill it with crushed ice and top it with an assortment of your favorite raw vegetables. Choose from radish roses, celery curls, carrot sticks, green pepper strips, cauliflowerets, turnip slices. Add olives, pickles and cooked shrimp or lobster chunks, for attractive contrast.

In a small bowl in the center of the ice, place a dunking sauce.

DUNKING SAUCE

Makes 1½ cups

- 1 cup mayonnaise
- ½ cup chili sauce
- 1 tablespoon horseradish
- ¼ teaspoon dry mustard
- ¼ teaspoon salt
- ¼ teaspoon paprika
- ¼ teaspoon freshly ground black pepper

Combine all ingredients, mix well and pile into an attractive bowl.

APPETIZER DIPS

All these dips can be made ahead and stored in the refrigerator until ready to serve or they can be left there over night.

A variety of seasoned, savory dips, in small bowls on a tray or, each bowl reigning supreme on a platter of its own, want crisp dippers for company. Surround the bowls with potato chips, cheese or wheat or corn wafers, round or square saltines, or melba toast slices.

Makes about 1 cup each

EGG-PARSLEY DIP:—Mix together 4 hard-cooked eggs (shelled and chopped), 1 tablespoon minced parsley, 2 tablespoons lemon juice, 1 teaspoon minced onion, ¾ teaspoon salt, a pinch of mixed dried herbs and ½ cup mayonnaise. Garnish with sprig of fresh parsley.

DEVILED CRAB DIP:—Drain, bone and flake 1 (6½ oz.) can of crabmeat. Mash with 2 hard-cooked eggs, shelled and chopped. Add ½ teaspoon prepared mustard, ½ cup mayonnaise and 1 tablespoon lemon juice. Mix well.

GUACAMOLE DIP:—Mash pulp of 1 small, peeled avocado. Stir in 2 tablespoons lemon juice immediately to prevent discoloration. Add 1 teaspoon minced onion, ½ teaspoon salt, 2 teaspoons Worcestershire sauce, ⅛ teaspoon cayenne pepper, a sprinkling of freshly ground black pepper and 1 clove garlic, mashed, if you and everyone else likes it. Mix well. Cover with thin layer of mayonnaise to prevent discoloration. Just before serving, stir in mayonnaise. This is a good time to add a little cooked, crumbled bacon and fresh, diced tomato if you wish. Smooth top of mixture, then make circle in center with a spoon and garnish with pimiento circle, or radish rose.

Makes about 2 cups each

TOMATO—SOUR CREAM DIP:—Mix together 1 (8-oz.) can tomato sauce, 1 cup thick sour cream, 1 teaspoon salt, 2 teaspoons minced onion, ⅓ cup prepared white horseradish. Garnish with sprinkling of paprika.

COTTAGE CHEESE DIP:—Mix together 1 pint creamed cottage cheese, 1 small triangle Roquefort or Blue cheese (sieved), 3 tablespoons prepared horseradish, 3 tablespoons mayonnaise, 1 teaspoon salt, 2 teaspoons finely chopped chives and ⅛ teaspoon freshly ground black pepper. Combine all ingredients, stir until well blended. Garnish with ring of chopped chives around the edges of the serving bowl.

Makes about 5 cups.

MILL REEF CLUB DIP:—1 avocado (peeled), ½ teaspoon garlic salt, 1 cup chopped pecans, ¼ cup orange juice, 2 tablespoons coarsely grated orange peel, 1 cup chopped cooked chicken or minced ham, and ½ cup lemon mayonnaise. Mash pulp of avocade and stir in all other ingredients except mayonnaise. Sprinkle with lemon juice and spread lemon mayonnaise over top. Chill until ready to serve. Stir mayonnaise into mixture and pile into bowl.

SPICY CHILI DIP:—1 can (No. 2) chili con carne, 1 cup chutney (chopped), 1 cup chopped apple (peeled and cored), ½ cup raisins (chopped), 1 tablespoon lemon juice, and 1 teaspoon Angostura bitters. The idea is to chop the chutney and apple so that each ingredient is about the size of the beans, or a bit smaller. Mix with a fork, cover and chill overnight or longer before serving.

Putting everything except the beans through the food chopper is a quick way to do it.

Hors D'Oeuvres

FRESH VEGETABLE HORS D'OEUVRES

Fresh vegetables cut in strips: Young green peppers, small tender carrots, firm tomatoes, cauliflower cut to eat with fingers. Chill in ice water before serving. Add celery hearts. Radishes and water cress for color. Arrange on platter with a dip for the cauliflower made of cream cheese thinned with a little cream flavored with anchovy paste, onion juice and salt to taste. Add a little paprika on top before serving.

When the Scandinavians arrange banquet-laden table effects with their famous assortment of fishes, vegetables, seafoods, cheese and meats; it is an eye stopper . . . a palate tantalizer.

At a dinner in Göteborg, Sweden, I was not surprised to find my six-course dinner beginning with what they called a "small assorted smörgåsbord."

This "small" assortment consisted of eight small bowls filled with a variety which began with pickled herring served with a spray of fresh dill and a slice of lemon. In another bowl were small boiled potatoes. This pair is always the beginning. Any Scandinavian eats these two first. From there on choice is rampant.

The eye-catching bowl held a yellow rose, dewfresh and half open as it might be in the garden while still untouched by the sun. It was made of the delicious golden Danish butter!

Danish butter and the dark whole-grain, thinly sliced fresh bread, make the smörgåsbord a wonderful experience. For these you have to go to Denmark, Sweden or Norway. But for the rest of the dishes composing a fine smörgåsbord, the restaurants in New York City or in Stowe, Ohio, where one hundred and twenty-five dishes await your choice, will make you a convert to the food and train your eye for serving it. As with a Scandinavian smörgåsbord, pickled vegetables and salads on trays are on the same table with smoked fish and open tins of sardines, cheeses, thin crisp breads, and an abundant variety of desserts. Everything is beautifully garnished from a whole fish to a cold fowl, and both savories and sweets are colorful.

SWEDISH FISH HORS D'OEUVRES

Up in Göteborg last year, where the fishing fleet comes in, a woman told me she had gone to a party where there were 29 different dishes on the smörgåsbord table, each made with the same type of fish. Fish canapés are so extraordinary, so inexpensive, so good for you without ruining the figure.

Well—usually. Depends upon how much sour cream and such is added.

These combinations are for dips, or to fill chunks of celery. Fish is its Sunday best surrounded by thin slices of pumpernickle, ice box rye bread, or rye or whole wheat crisps.

HOW TO MAKE FISH DIPS

Combine creamed cottage cheese with any flaked, seasoned and cooked fish you like. Make it about half and half, but so long as the mixture holds together for spreading and dipping the proportion does not matter. Add 1 tablespoon lemon juice for each cup of mixture, then stir in seasonings. And what about them?

Add 1 tablespoon chopped sweet pickle per cup to the smoky ones, to the salty ones.

Stir ½ teaspoon dry mustard into shrimp or crabmeat ones, and add a teaspoon of Worcestershire sauce.

Add ½ teaspoon Angostura bitters to each cup of chopped, boned sardines and the cheese. Stir in a couple spoonfuls of chopped pimiento just for looks.

Sprinkle the pale dips with paprika for style, or with finely chopped parsley.

Provide every sliced fish, be it freshly cooked and cooled or the salted and smoked variety you bought from the store, with a wedge or two of lemon.

Stuff green seeded olives with snips of anchovy or with anchovy paste. Pack back in bottle, cover with its own juice, seal and let stand overnight. Eating these makes you wonder what you've been doing all your life. It's a Spanish trick, really.

Pickled herring in sour cream—you better buy that, but don't forget to. Provide thin slices of sweet onion if it is missing.

Ah... and smoked salmon. Serve small thin slices on buttered toasted squares. Sprinkle with freshly ground black pepper. Must be fresh or don't use pepper.

Swedish caviar (thinned with cream) and thin slices of smoked eel are both delicious on buttered bread rounds.

WELSH RABBIT SPREAD

Makes 5 cups

- 1 (12 oz.) bottle or can of ale or beer
- 1½ pounds aged Cheddar cheese, grated
- ¼ pound Roquefort cheese, crumbled
- ½ teaspoon salt
- 1 teaspoon dry mustard
- 2 tablespoons soft butter
- 1 teaspoon Worcestershire sauce
- ⅛ teaspoon Tabasco sauce
- 2 teaspoons grated onion or chopped chives

Open ale or beer and let stand until foaming stops. Mix together remaining ingredients. Gradually add ale or beer, stirring until smooth and creamy. Serve immediately or store in tightly covered container in refrigerator or freezer.

POTTED DUCKLING SPREAD

As you will discover, this is a recipe to treasure. Make a lot so that you can eat some, freeze a pot or two. This keeps 6 to 8 weeks in the freezer.

Makes about 5 cups

- 1 duckling, 4 to 5 pounds, ready to cook weight
- 1 (3 oz.) can chopped broiled mushrooms (or ½ cup chopped cooked fresh mushrooms)
- 1 (12 oz.) package cream cheese
- 1 (5 oz.) can toasted diced almonds
- 1 teaspoon Kitchen Bouquet
- ¾ cup duck fat
- 1 teaspoon Worcestershire sauce
- ¼ teaspoon Tabasco sauce
- 1 teaspoon salt
- 1 tablespoon grated onion
- ½ cup sour cream

Cut duckling in quarters. Place duckling, including neck and giblets in Dutch oven. Add 3 cups water, 2 teaspoons salt, 10 peppercorns, 1 small bay leaf and 4 whole cloves. Cover and bring to boil. Cook gently until duck is tender, about 45 minutes. Remove from heat. Cool duck in broth for half an hour, then strain off broth. Chill skin fat off to use later. Take meat from bones, discarding skin and bones. Put duck meat and giblets through food chopper, using fine cutter. There should be about 4 cups of the ground duck meat. Drain mushrooms, saving broth for future use in soup or gravy and chop fine. Soften cream cheese at room temperature, then blend in the chopped mushrooms, almonds and Kitchen Bouquet. Add ½ cup of the soft duck fat, Worcestershire, Tabasco, salt and onion. Mix thoroughly, then add and blend in duck meat and sour cream, stirring lightly until well mixed. Place canapé mixture in small casseroles. Pour the remaining ¼ cup of duck fat melted, over top of the spread. Chill well before serving. Or fill two 3-cup casseroles and freeze one.

EDAM CHEESE BOWL

1 Edam cheese, 3 to 3½ pounds	¾ cup beer
	Dash of Tabasco sauce
1 tablespoon Worcestershire sauce	Few grains salt
	Paprika

Hollow out cheese from center leaving a 1-inch. Let soften at room temperature. Using an electric mixer, mix cheese until smooth and fluffy. Gradually add beer and continue to mix until thoroughly blended. Mix in seasonings. Heap spread into cheese shell. Let soften at room temperature. Using an electric mixer, mix cheese until smooth and fluffy. Gradually add beer and continue to mix until thoroughly blended. Mix in seasonings. Heap spread into cheese shell and sprinkle top with paprika. (There will be enough cheese spread for a refill.)

To make even more festive, mark a circle at the top of the cheese with a sharp knife to indicate the portion that will be hollowed out later. Then, make star, tree or other designs on the sides of the cheese by cutting into the crimson wax coating and peeling it off to let the natural creamy color of the cheese show. Then fill the cheese. Serve within the week.

Canapés

Canapés are the little rounds and slices you broil or spread or decorate. Their advantage is that odds and ends used on top of toasted bread rounds produce a flower-garden effect on a platter, taste as good as they look. Besides—it empties the ice box. You can use any of your Dips on these, you know.

However, some of them can only be made by the broiler route and are truly wonderful. Remember those Cheese Puffs? Abbie's Cheese Puffs* they were. Well, you may think Abbie is always turning up in my recipes; but so does seafood. Those Puffs, for example, can also be created with minced clams. From a can. You don't have to dig and clean and chop the little devils, as I've done with enough bushels of clams to appreciate the canned ones. Can't tell the difference. Here is how you make the puffs.

CLAM PUFFS

Makes 24 puffs

- 4 ounces cream cheese
- ¼ cup melted butter or heavy cream
- 2 cans minced clams, drained
- ¼ teaspoon rosemary
- 1 teaspoon Worcestershire sauce
- ½ teaspoon salt
- 1 teaspoon grated lemon peel
- 24 rounds of thin bread or saltines
- ¼ cup finely chopped parsley

* *Successful Entertaining At Home,* by Carolyn Coggins. Prentice-Hall, 1951.

Combine cheese with butter, stir until blended and add remaining ingredients except the bread rounds. Toast them on one side, pile mixture on the toasted side and arrange on a cooky sheet. Place in broiler 4 inches from medium heat, and broil until puffy. Sprinkle with parsley and serve instantly.

It is a good idea to do these in two pans for a small group, so that the puffs will appear, hot as the tropical sun, fresh from the oven.

PEANUT BUTTER DREAMS

Makes about 50

1¼ cups peanut butter   ¼ cup mayonnaise

Combine until easy to spread. Pile spoonful on unpeeled but cored and sliced apple wedges. Spread some on toasted bread rounds or on saltines and sprinkle with crushed crisped bacon or salami bits. Put some between white bread, thinly sliced, and cut into small shapes for tea size sandwiches. Or, spread a thin slice of bread cut horizontally, giving you a slice the size of your loaf. Sprinkle with finely chopped gherkins. Trim crusts and roll up as if it were a jelly roll. Wrap and chill before slicing very thin.

STUFFED MUSHROOM CAPS

Makes 32 caps

- 32 fresh mushrooms
- ½ package frozen flounder filets, thawed
- 1 stick (¼ pound) butter or margarine, melted
- ¼ cup finely chopped parsley
- ¼ teaspoon oregano
- 1 teaspoon salt
- 1 teaspoon Bovril
- 1 tablespoon finely chopped onion
- 1 teaspoon garlic salt
- ½ teaspoon freshly ground black pepper
- ½ teaspoon thyme
- 2 eggs, beaten
- ½ cup crushed prepared bread stuffing

Select mushrooms which are similar in size for the best effect. Remove stems, being careful not to break the caps. Wash and chop stems, add to the melted fat and sauté over very low heat 20 minutes, stirring occasionally. Add flaked fish, and cook another 10 minutes. Combine all other ingredients, stir and pile into the mushroom cap cavities making a mound pressed firmly into place with the spoon. Place stuffed side up on a baking sheet which has been well greased with cooking oil, *no butter*. Bake in moderate (375°) oven 15 minutes. Remove and serve on toasted bread rounds, or plain on the canapé tray, or alone in a chafing dish to keep them warm.

MUSHROOM DEVILED EGGS

Makes 12 halves

- 6 hard-cooked eggs
- ¼ teaspoon salt
- ½ teaspoon prepared mustard
- ½ teaspoon vinegar
- 1 tablespoon diet mayonnaise
- A dash of pepper
- A dash of Worcestershire sauce
- 1 (3 oz.) can sliced broiled mushrooms

Cut hard-cooked eggs in half lengthwise. Remove yolks and force through a coarse sieve, or mash until smooth. Add salt, mustard, vinegar, mayonnaise, pepper and Worcestershire sauce, blending well. Drain mushrooms, saving broth for future use in soup or gravy, and reserve 12 slices. Chop remaining mushrooms until fairly fine and add to egg yolk mixture, stirring gently. Fill egg whites lightly, do not pack. Garnish tops with sliced mushrooms. Cover, to keep from drying, and chill. Serve on cold plate garnished with water cress.

SWISS CHEESE CARAWAY SQUARES

Makes 15 dozen 1-inch squares

- 1 cup sifted enriched flour
- 2 teaspoons dry mustard
- 1 teaspoon salt
- ½ cup Swiss cheese, grated
- 4 drops Tabasco sauce
- ½ teaspoon Worcestershire sauce
- ½ teaspoon paprika
- 2 teaspoons caraway seeds
- ⅓ cup butter or homogenized shortening
- 3 tablespoons cold water

Combine sifted flour, dry mustard and salt and sift together once. Add the grated cheese, seasonings and caraway seeds, then cut in the shortening until mixture is coarsely blended with particles the size of a small pea. Sprinkle with the cold water and toss lightly with a fork until the dough is moist enough to hold together. Form into a ball to roll out on floured pastry board and cut into 1-inch fluted squares with a pastry wheel. Place on ungreased baking sheet and sprinkle with a little paprika. Bake in preheated hot oven (450°) until brown, about 9 minutes.

PARTY MIX

Makes about 4½ quarts

- 3 bars (1½ cups) butter
- ¼ cup Worcestershire sauce
- 2 teaspoons garlic salt
- 2 teaspoons onion salt
- 2 teaspoons celery salt
- 1 pound mixed salted nuts, pecans or peanuts
- 1 (12 oz.) package shredded wheat squares
- 1 (6 oz.) package crisp rice cereal
- 1 (7 oz.) package crisp doughnut-shaped oat cereal
- 1 (6 oz.) package tiny pretzel twist, thin pretzel sticks or pretzel nuggets

In a small saucepan, melt butter. Stir in Worcestershire sauce and seasoned salts. Remove from heat and let stand. Meanwhile, in a large roasting pan, combine nuts, cereals and pretzels. Pour butter sauce over cereal mixture. Mix lightly. Bake uncovered at 225° for 2 hours, stirring lightly about every 20 minutes. Spread out on absorbent or heavy brown paper to cool. Keep crisp by storing in an airtight container.

SAVORY MELBA TOAST

Add 1 teaspoon celery, poppy or caraway seeds to ¼ pound softened butter. Mix until blended and brush onto Melba toast. Spread additional Melba toast with softened butter to which you have added ½ teaspoon mayonnaise or 1 teaspoon chili powder for each ¼ pound butter. Arrange close together on a large flat platter as if they formed spokes in a wheel.

Unusual Ideas for the Hors D'Oeuvres Tray

Select small onions of uniform size, prepare for stuffing, cook, drain and cool—or use already cooked, small canned onions. Fill with minced ham, chicken liver, chicken—any cold, finely chopped meat which has been cooked and seasoned and mixed with enough mayonnaise to hold it together.

Make Puff Shells, as for dessert (*page 229*) only make them very small. Fill with mixture of any cooked seafood, chicken, game which has been seasoned and chopped and mixed with mayonnaise. Shrimp is especially good in these shells.

At the seashore, use clam shells for filling with dips. Sometimes you'll want to sprinkle the dip-filled shells with cheese and slide under the broiler for browning.

If you have an electric automatically controlled deep fryer, you will not put it away after making these cheese squares or balls you prepare for hors d'oeuvres. Mix up a few fritter batters, drop very small spoonfuls into the fat, fish them out after a few minutes for draining to serve hot. Mighty good on a cold winter day.

Serve Fondue Neuchâteloise (*page 35*) from Switzerland. It is a marvelous supper, but it can also be the highlight of a cocktail party.

Always remember to add a few radishes, carrot or celery crisps, a few sprigs of water cress or parsley to make your food trays look as beautiful as they are good.

One of the best canapés in the world—when there is money in the bank and it's yours—is the hot buttered toast rounds, spread with chilled caviar, topped by a blob of cold sour cream. Russians would have a fit, but I froze some of these without the cream, shoved them into a preheated oven to thaw, added the cream and they were good.

2

Delicious Soups

Your soups are delicious, your soup bowls are attractive but the presentation depends upon how you serve it, how you garnish it, what you float on the top. Pale soups are beautifully garnished with chopped fresh chives or finely chopped parsley, with a sprinkling of paprika or with fresh chopped mint, depending upon the flavor of the soup.

The Onion Soup (*page 31*) requires specific garnishing of grated cheese just as Vichyssoise (*page 23*) must be sprinkled with paprika and garnished with fresh chopped chives. But occasionally you have a choice. Try some of these:

Avocado cubes are velvety and delicious. They are also rich. Try them floated on the top of hot consommé, on cream of chicken or mushroom soup.

Thin slices of dill pickle or sweet gherkins can be floated on the top of cream soups for a wonderful contrast.

Make Croutons for soup with all your left-over bread. Chop into dainty or ½ inch squares or cut into rounds and toast as you would Melba toast in an oven that is barely warm until pieces are dried out and browned clear through. Save these to serve in the bottom of the bowls. Flavor the croutons by rolling the small cubes in olive oil or butter stirring them over low heat until brown and crisp. Sprinkle with garlic salt during the cooking to make garlic croutons. These are wonderful sprinkled over salads too, or over plain stewed tomatoes being served as soup.

Give the croutons a cheese flavor by grating cheese over them as they brown. Sprinkle with freshly ground nutmeg and use these on top of pea soup. These toasted croutons should be drained on paper towels before serving.

Sour cream or whipped cream is a delicious addition to many soups especially Borsch (*page 28*) or Gazpacho (*page 30*).

How much soup do you serve as a "serving"? Three-quarters of a measuring cup or 6 ounces is considered appropriate for a first course soup. If it becomes the main dish at a luncheon or supper or a filling midnight snack this is considerably larger, but almost any recipe you see which says makes 4 Serving means 4 Servings of ¾ cup each, which means that the recipe when finished totals 3 measuring cups.

These recipes are given in measuring cup quantities so that you can decide whether or not you want the ¾ measuring cup portions for a first course or a much larger one for a main course.

The Fine Flair of Soup Making

Gourmets all over the world regard soups as a superb delicacy, a fragrant tantalizer for the beginning of a meal. In royal households, hot soups are part of the daily breakfast menus, particularly in the cold northern countries. Soup is so highly regarded that the finest cooks in the world consider making it an art worth cultivating during a whole lifetime; and much of the world believes a large bowl of good

DELICIOUS SOUPS

soup—and they would have nothing less than *good* soup unless they are willing to throw away the good name of the family—is as fine an evening meal for the family as can be devised.

Of course THEY know how to make it. Do you? Soup, like a child waiting to lick the platter, begs for bits of all the flavorful things cooked in your kitchen, for all the juices left from steamed or boiled vegetables, for the juices drained from cans, for the extra leaves spared when tossing a green salad, for small quantities of meat or fowl you can spare from the main course.

In Europe, every woman prides herself on the soup pot. It is a large and roomy affair, simmering on the back of the stove, the liquid bubbling over beef bones and a knuckle or two from veal. To the pot, which never boils but is ever steaming hot, she would add all these bits I've mentioned. You can do the same, or save the juices—except strong-flavored ones from spinach or kale—in jars, covered and refrigerated. Use them for thinning canned soups, or combine to make a soup. Whatever you do, if you are a good cook, you will never underestimate the worthiness of soups. Before the recipes for some you may enjoy, here are:

A Few Ideas for the Soup Maker:

Add 1 tablespoon sherry to each cup of almost any canned soup to achieve mystery and flavor.
Combine several canned soups to compose unusual flavors.
Thin any canned soup you would serve with sour cream—such as Black Bean, Tomato, Beef Bouillon—with buttermilk. Serve hot or cold.
Buy the best quality canned soups, flavor with your favorite herbs.
Add oregano to Minestrone, tarragon or curry to

Creamed Chicken, nutmeg to Cream of Pea, as a starter.

Serve croutons, icy sour cream, freshly grated cheese, to enhance and beautify your soups.

CREAM OF VEGETABLE SOUP

Makes 3 cups

2½ cups milk or cream	1 cup cooked vegetable, coarsely diced
1 tablespoon flour	
2 tablespoons butter	Seasoning which favors the vegetable
1 teaspoon salt	
⅛ teaspoon pepper	

If using an electric blender combine milk, flour, butter, salt and pepper with the vegetable and seasoning in the container. Turn on blender and run until smoothly blended, from 1 to 3 minutes. Cooked vegetables blend more quickly than raw, and give a smoother texture. Pour into saucepan and bring to a boil over low heat, stirring constantly until soup is slightly thick and tastes full-flavored.

If making without a blender, heat milk in top of double boiler. Melt butter in a large saucepan and stir in the flour, salt and pepper. Stir constantly as the hot milk is slowly added, add cooked vegetables (raw cannot be used until cooked) and special seasonings. Continue cooking over low heat until thickened slightly and put through a strainer into the top of the double boiler in which the milk heated. Cover until ready to serve.

Bisques

Bisques are definitely top drawer when it comes to soups. With their velvet texture, their delicate flavor, they are a "tongue-luxury." They also fall into the department of hard work if the chopping and blending must be done by hand. In case you have an electric blender, however, bisques are for you as easy as for a man to look at a pretty girl.

First what flavor shall it be? Choose from any cooked boneless fish you like, or use shrimps, crabs, clams or lobster or those rare but delicious black mussels. Meat or chicken can be used too, but seafood bisques are excessively superb.

Now, having selected the fish, use 2/3 cup of the cooked seafood or meat in place of the 1 cup of vegetables in the Cream of Vegetable Soup recipe. Cream is recommended too, or rich milk. And you have a bisque.

Here, again, your know-how with seasonings will make it extra good. With chicken or fish, try ¼ teaspoon curry powder and ⅛ teaspoon hot paprika for the amount of this recipe. Use ½ teaspoon oregano with tuna or white fish. Try ½ teaspoon nutmeg and ⅛ teaspoon thyme with chicken. Use ¼ teaspoon curry and ⅛ teaspoon nutmeg in shrimp bisque. Or add ⅛ teaspoon dill to shrimp bisque. Add sherry to any of them, 1 tablespoon per cup, stir into finished bisque just long enough to heat it, and serve. Carry on as inspiration and your taste buds direct you!

BANANA VICHYSSOISE

Makes 5 cups

- 1 cup coarsely diced raw potato
- ½ cup coarsely diced onion
- 1 cup coarsely diced peeled apple
- ½ cup sliced tender celery
- 1 yellow banana, sliced
- 1½ cups well seasoned chicken broth, fresh or canned
- ½ teaspoon salt
- 1 tablespoon butter
- ½ teaspoon curry powder
- 1 cup heavy cream

Place potato, onion, apple, celery, banana and chicken broth in saucepan. Cover and bring to boil. Simmer over low heat until vegetables are tender, about 15 minutes. Pour slowly into container of blender. Add salt, butter and curry powder. Cover container and turn on blender. Run until contents are smooth, about 30 seconds. Stir in cream and chill thoroughly. Serve topped with minced chives or grated lemon peel.

COCONUT SOUP

Makes 3 cups

- 1 cup shredded coconut, finely chopped
- 2 cups chicken broth, fresh or canned
- ⅛ teaspoon curry powder
- ½ teaspoon salt
- 1 tablespoon butter
- 1 tablespoon cornstarch
- ½ cup light cream

Place coconut, chicken broth, seasonings, butter and cornstarch in container of electric blender. Cover container and turn on blender. Run until coconut is finely divided, about 2 minutes. Pour into saucepan. Add cream. Heat until soup comes to boil, stirring frequently. Lower heat and let simmer about 5 minutes. Serve immediately with crisp croutons. Also try chilling this soup to serve cold.

CHICKEN SOUP ORIENTAL

Makes 4 cups

- ¼ cup packaged precooked rice
- 2 cups hot seasoned chicken broth
- ⅛ teaspoon curry powder
- 1 cup diced cooked chicken
- 1 (3 oz.) can chopped broiled mushrooms
- 1 cup heavy cream

Place rice in container of blender. Add hot broth, cover and allow to stand for 10 minutes. Remove cover, add curry powder and cooked chicken. Cover container and blend until contents are smooth, about 1 minute. Stop blender, remove cover and add contents of can of mushrooms. Cover and blend until mushrooms are semi-fine about 3 seconds. Pour into quart jar, cover and chill. When ready to serve stir in cream and garnish each bowl with a sprinkle of paprika.

QUICK CRAB BISQUE

Makes 6 servings

- 1 (7½ oz.) can crabmeat, flaked
- 1 can mock turtle soup
- 1 (10½ oz.) can condensed tomato soup
- 1 (10½ oz.) can condensed pea soup
- 1 can beef bouillon
- 1 (14½ oz.) can evaporated milk, undiluted
- 1 teaspoon onion salt
- 6 thin slices lemon
- ½ cup sherry

Combine all ingredients in a large saucepan, except lemon slices and sherry. Place over heat and stir until blended and thoroughly hot. Add sherry, stir until blended and serve immediately with a lemon slice floating on top of each bowl.

CUCUMBER SOUP

Makes 3½ cups

- 3 cups rich milk
- 3 tablespoons flour
- 1½ teaspoons salt
- ½ teaspoon paprika
- Dash of black pepper
- 2 chicken bouillon cubes
- 1 tablespoon grated onion
- 1 medium-size unpeeled cucumber, shredded
- 1 tablespoon lemon juice

Sprinkle flour, salt, paprika and pepper over milk in top of double boiler; beat with rotary beater until blended. Add bouillon cubes, onion and cucumber. Cook over boiling water, stirring constantly, until thickened, 10 to 15 minutes. Remove from heat; gradually stir in lemon juice. Garnish each serving with finely chopped parsley. Serve hot or chilled.

SALMON SOUP

Makes 8 servings

- 1 (1 pound) can salmon
- 2 tablespoons grated onion
- 2 (10½ oz.) cans condensed cream of chicken soup
- 2 cups chicken broth, fresh or canned
- ½ teaspoon fresh ground black pepper
- 2 tablespoons chopped chives
- 4 sweet gherkins

Drain and flake salmon, discarding skin and bones. put flaked salmon and liquid in a large saucepan. Add all other ingredients except the sweet gherkins. Place over heat and beat with a rotary beater until thoroughly hot. Serve in bowls on which thin slices of the sweet gherkins are floated as garnish.

CHILLED SHRIMP SOUP

Makes 12 (¾-cup) servings

- 2 (11 oz.) cans condensed cream of celery soup
- 2 (5 oz.) cans shrimp, drained
- 2 cups undiluted evaporated milk
- 1 teaspoon prepared mustard
- 1 teaspoon oregano
- 3 cups tomato juice

Place 1 can soup, 1 can shrimp and 1 cup milk in container of electric blender. Blend until nearly smooth, about 5 seconds. Repeat, adding mustard and oregano. Combine mixtures with tomato juice. Chill thoroughly before serving.

PINK VELVET SOUP

Makes 3 cups

- 1 thin slice onion
- 1 (8 oz.) can diced beets
- ¼ cup tomato catsup
- 1 tablespoon Bovril
- 1 cup light sour cream
- 1 (3 oz.) package cream cheese

Place all ingredients in container of blender in order indicated. Cover container and turn on blender. Run until Bovril is smoothly blended in, or about 30 seconds. Chill blended mixture. Serve in chilled soup cups, granished with a sprinkle of minced parsley.

Colorful Soups

HOT APPLE SOUP

Makes 3 cups

- 2 tablespoons butter
- 2 tablespoons diced onion
- 1 pound McIntosh apples, unpeeled
- 1 cup water
- ⅛ teaspoon ginger
- ⅛ teaspoon mace
- 1 tablespoon flour
- 1 cup pineapple juice

Melt butter in saucepan. Add onion and let cook 2 minutes. Core and cut up apples. Place in saucepan and add water, ginger and mace. Cover and bring to boil. Cook 5 minutes. Pour into container of blender. Add flour. Cover, turn on blender, run until contents are smooth, about 30 seconds. Pour blended mixture into saucepan. Add pineapple juice and bring to boil again. Let simmer for 5 minutes, stirring frequently. Correct seasoning if necessary. Serve with crisp cheese croutons.

BORSCH

Makes 12 6-ounce servings

- 1 (8 oz.) can tomato sauce
- 1 cup water
- ¼ cup diced onion
- 2 (No. 2) cans sliced beets
- 1 tablespoon sugar
- 1 teaspoon salt
- ⅛ teaspoon pepper
- 2 tablespoons lemon juice
- 2½ cups chicken broth
- 1½ cups sour cream

Bring tomato sauce, water and onion to boil in saucepan, cover and cook until onion is tender, about 5 minutes. Meanwhile chop or blend beets in electric blender, can at a time, until smooth, about 15 seconds, and pour into large saucepan. Place tomato sauce and onion mixture in container, add seasonings and lemon juice and blend until smooth, about 30 seconds. Add to beets. Stir in chicken broth. Serve hot or cold topped with sour cream.

CHERRY SOUP
Danis Kirsebaersuppe

Make 3 cups

- 1 package frozen red, pitted sweetened cherries
- 4 cups water
- 1 stick whole cinnamon
- 4 slices lemon
- 1 tablespoon cornstarch
- ¼ cup sugar

Reserve a few of the red cherries before combining with the water and cinnamon in a saucepan. Place over medium heat and simmer until cherries are very tender, about 20 minutes. Strain through a sieve and return to saucepan. Add the cherries which were reserved to the strained juice, add lemon slices and the cornstarch which has been made into a paste with some of the cherry juice. Add sugar, bring to a boil over medium heat and continue to cook, stirring constantly, until sugar is dissolved and juice slightly thickened. Remove from heat and serve hot or cold. Serve zwieback with the soup hot; if cold, a blob of icy cold, slightly sweetened whipped cream is delicious and beautiful with this soup.

Replace cornstarch with tapioca for a brighter colored soup, being sure the last cooking is at least 8 minutes.

CHINESE DUCK SOUP

Makes 4 cups

Bones left from roast duck, broken or crushed
Pieces of skin from the roast; Neck, wing tips and giblets
½ chopped carrot
1 cup shredded celery leaves
1 onion, halved
2 sprigs parsley
1 bay leaf
2 peppercorns
1 cup pork rind cut into cubes or strips
2 tablespoons Soya sauce
Water to cover
4 raw unbroken egg yolks

In a large kettle with a tight fitting cover place all the broken roast duck bones and pieces of skin, wing tips, neck and giblets. Add the vegetables, seasonings and pork rind, cover tightly and bring to a boil. Reduce heat and simmer for at least 2 hours, adding water if necessary to keep the ingredients well covered. Strain to secure the clear broth and remove the giblets and a few pieces of the pork rind to use in the soup. Reheat to be sure it is piping hot and serve in bowls into which you have broken the egg yolks.

GAZPACHO

Spanish

Makes 4 cups

- 1½ cups fresh tomatoes, chopped (or use canned tomatoes)
- ¼ cup cooked beets, chopped
- ¼ cup celery, chopped
- ¼ cup cucumber, chopped
- 2 tablespoons chopped sweet onion
- 1 clove garlic, minced
- ⅓ cup coarse bread crumbs
- ½ green pepper, chopped
- 1 teaspoon paprika
- ½ teaspoon basil
- ¼ teaspoon freshly ground pepper
- ¼ teaspoon cloves
- ½ cup wine vinegar
- ½ cup beef bouillon
- 2 tablespoons olive oil
- Salt to taste

Chop vegetables very fine, add liquid ingredients, blend thoroughly and taste for seasoning. Cover and chill to icy cold before serving. If you make this in a blender, add all ingredients to container and blend about 30 seconds.

QUICK GAZPACHO

Spanish

Makes 3 cups

- 1 can condensed tomato soup, undiluted
- ⅓ cup finely chopped celery
- 1 tablespoon grated onion
- 1 tablespoon vinegar
- ½ clove garlic, minced
- ¼ teaspoon basil

Chill the canned tomato soup before opening. When ready to blend combine all ingredients, mix well, cover and chill to icy coldness before serving.

ONION SOUP

French

Makes 4 cups

- 2 cups red onion slices (½ pound)
- 2 tablespoons bacon fat
- 2 tablespoons flour
- 4 cups rich beef bouillon
- 4 slices French bread
- 4 rounds of toasted bread (French preferably)
- ½ cup grated Gruyere cheese

Cook onions in bacon fat until translucent. Sprinkle with flour, stir until browned lightly. Add rest of flour, stirring constantly. Add bread and bouillon; cover, reduce heat and simmer 25 minutes. Place toast rounds in individual heated soup pots, fill with onion soup, sprinkle with cheese and cover 2 minutes before serving. Don't worry when the soup is "stringy." Gruyere cheese gives that effect but the flavor is worth it.

PUMPKIN SOUP

English

"What is this wonderful soup?" I asked the chef at the Atheneum Court in London as I was consuming a second portion. Never had I tasted anything like this before and I had to know how to make it. It is one of the recipes which will vanquish the idea that the English never have anything good to eat. This recipe is given in quantity so that you will make some, eat some and freeze some.

Makes 10 cups

3½ cups (No. 2½ can) cooked, mashed, sieved pumpkin	1 tablespoon Worcestershire sauce
7 cups rich ham broth	1 large clove garlic, minced
	1 tablespoon Bovril

Combine all ingredients in large saucepan. Place over medium heat and stir until blended and steaming. Taste for saltiness from that ham broth. You may need to add salt now but don't add it before as you may ruin the soup. If your ham broth is not rich enough to suit you add another tablespoon of Bovril. The English serve this hot but you can serve it cold if you are fond of cold soups.

CREAM OF PUMPKIN SOUP:—Omit last three ingredients and for liquid use only 4 cups very rich ham broth in which 1 cup quick-cooking tapioca has heated until broth comes to a boil. Combine 1 cup heavy cream with 2 cups milk, scald, add 1 tablespoon brown sugar and combine sieved hot pumpkin with cream and ham liquids. Blend well and serve with sprinkling of nutmeg.

HUNGARIAN TOMATO SOUP

Makes 1½ cups

1¼ cups tomato juice, chilled	Few grains dried marjoram
½ teaspoon salt	¼ cup thick sour cream
⅛ teaspoon cayenne	4 teaspoons chopped chives
⅛ teaspoon basil	

For this soup the tomato juice must be icy cold; the sour cream thick; and if you put more than a few grains, about 1/16 of a teaspoon but how can you measure that, of marjoram into the soup you may spoil it. This recipe is just perfect as it is. Combine everything except the chives in a jar or electric blender, shake or mix madly until the ingredients are blended. A jar does nicely for this because you can put it back into the refrigerator and chill until serving time, when you pour it into 2 chilled cups and sprinkle with chives. This recipe is small, so that you will try it. After that you will make it often.

3

Unusual Supper Dishes

PAELLA RISCAL

Makes 6 (2-cup) servings

- 2 cups cooked lobster meat, fresh-cooked, canned or frozen
- 2 cups scallops, browned
- 2 pounds pork or veal, cubed and cooked
- 1 cup green peas, cooked
- 6 chicken legs, or breasts, browned and cooked
- 2 (4½ oz.) cans artichoke hearts, drained
- 5 cups cooked Saffron Rice (page 50)
- 12 ripe olives
- 1 piece pimiento

This selection of seafood and cooked meat composes my favorite *Paella*, the dish from Spain which always creates a sensation. It is so good and twice as beautiful. Its "presentation" is important. Lacking the flat black iron pans of Spain, settle for a big ceramic ovenware bowl—anything big enough to hold the Paella attractively.

Cook pork and chicken until brown and very tender. Cut the lobster into chunks. Sauté the scallops, and cook any seafood you want to add, for you do not have to stick to the recipe for this. Fill the bottom of the bowl with Saffron Rice, dot the top with the cooked seafood, vegetables and meat. Put into 400° oven 5 minutes to be sure it's hot. Garnish with ripe olives and pimiento and serve the gorgeous thing.

The 2-cup servings are given from experience, knowing that people never eat less—maybe more.

JAPANESE RICE A LA LUISE

Makes 8 cups

- 1 cup long grain rice, toasted
- ½ cup onions, sliced
- 2 tablespoons butter
- 1 cup sliced celery
- 1 (3 oz.) can broiled mushrooms, drained
- 1 large bell pepper, slivered
- 1 cup blanched almonds, shredded
- 1 can water chestnuts, drained
- 1 can bamboo sprouts, drained
- 3 cups chicken broth, fresh or canned
- 3 tablespoons Soy sauce
- 1½ teaspoons salt
- ½ teaspoon pepper

Place rice in shallow pan, toast in a preheated 350° oven until lightly browned, stirring occasionally. Melt butter in a large saucepan and sauté onions until translucent. Add all other ingredients and stir over medium heat until hot but not boiling. Add salt to taste, if necessary. Place browned dry rice in 3-quart or larger casserole, and pour contents of saucepan over it. Cover and bake in 350° oven until liquid is absorbed, about 45 minutes.

SWISS CHEESE FONDUE
Fondue Neuchâteloise

This is a famous dish of Switzerland where Swiss

cheese is made in the Emmentaler Valley. Here the bitter cold recommends warm food, and skiers— Swiss or not—find Fondue their favorite feast. Eaten indoors beside the fire, it can be yours too, ready to enjoy about 5 minutes from the time you put low heat under the pan.

The Swiss prepare this Fondue in an earthenware casserole which has a handle, and this is the best thing to use providing you do not expose it to direct heat and crack it. A chafing dish or attractive skillet can be used as well. This recipe is for a chafing dish. Because the cooking moves rapidly, it is a good idea to surround yourself with the necessary ingredients before you actually begin the cooking.

When the Fondue is ready to eat each person sits around the dish and with a fork spears up chunks of white bread, preferably with the crust on one side. These are about 1½ inches square. Each person dips the bread into the hot melted cheese, gives it a twist to coat it thoroughly and eats it. He continues taking his turn until the last drop is consumed down to the brown crust formed on the bottom of the pan.

Serves 4

- 1 pound (2 cups) Switzerland Swiss cheese, coarsely grated or finely chopped
- 3 tablespoons flour
- 1 clove garlic
- 2 cups dry white wine
- 1 teaspoon salt
- ¼ teaspoon freshly ground pepper
- Sprinkling of nutmeg
- ½ cup Kirsch, light rum or applejack
- 1 loaf crusty French bread, cubed

Place the cheese in a bowl, sprinkle with the flour and mix lightly. Nip the end off the garlic clove and rub the inside of the dish in which you intend to cook the Fondue, until it is well flavored with garlic, then discard the garlic clove. Pour the white wine into the chafing dish, place over low heat, watch carefully for air bubbles coming to the surface. When they are rising—*you don't want this to boil*—stir with a fork as you add handfuls of the floured cheese. Be sure that each handful is melted before adding another. Stir vigorously until the mixture begins to bubble and the last handful of cheese has been added. Then quickly add salt, pepper, nutmeg and Kirsch. Stir to mix thoroughly, reduce heat. Although you don't want the mixture to continue cooking too much, it should be kept hot and lightly bubbling.

This is the point where everyone begins to eat. The Swiss take a small glass of Kirsch halfway through eating this Fondue or at the end of eating it, depending upon which part of Switzerland they live in. This is such a famous dish that the procedure is a rite. Hot coffee or tea is always the finale.

When the Swiss make this they use Neuchâtel wine, but any dry white wine of the Rhine, Riesling or Chablis types will do nicely.

SPIEDENO ROMANO

Makes 2 servings

2 small loaves French bread	½ cup butter
1½ cups milk	2 whole eggs, well beaten
½ pound Mozarella cheese	½ teaspoon salt
	4 anchovies, chopped

Remove crusts from bread, making oval oblongs or squared lengths for each serving. Slice without cutting through base, into ¼-inch slices. Pour milk into bowl, turn bread until drenched. Remove to greased cooky sheet and place slice of cheese between each bread slice.

Add beaten eggs and salt to milk, blend thoroughly and hold each bread loaf firmly as you turn it in the egg mixture to coat heavily. Return to cooky sheet, sprinkle tops with anchovies and bake in preheated 350° oven until browned and crisp, about 15 minutes.

This, served with a green salad, wine, and a fruit concoction or flambé dessert, is a meal for the gods.

HAM IN VERMOUTH SAUCE

Makes 8 servings

1 (8 oz.) package green spinach noodles	2 tablespoons margarine or butter
4 quarts rapidly boiling water	2 tablespoons poppy seeds
	4 cups cooked ham, cubed
2 tablespoons salt	2 cups Vermouth Sauce

Place noodles in rapidly boiling water. Add salt. Boil 12 minutes or until *al dente*. Drain. Toss with margarine or butter and poppy seeds. Arrange in a ring on a serving plate. Fill center with sauced ham.

VERMOUTH SAUCE

Makes 2 cups

¾ cup butter	1 cup dry vermouth or sherry
¼ cup flour	1 cup chicken broth

Melt the butter in a skillet and stir over medium heat until it is lightly browned but not burned. Add the flour and stir until blended. Slowly add the vermouth (or sherry) and broth, reduce heat, and stir until the mixture is thickened. Add the ham cubes, continue stirring over low heat until they have been heated through and pour the whole mixture into the center of the green noodle ring.

Smoked turkey, chopped or cubed, is delicious served in this Vermouth Sauce inside the noodle ring.

ROAST BEEF AND SHERRIED MUSHROOMS

Makes 4 servings

- 4 slices cold roast beef, 1½ inches thick
- ½ cup butter
- ½ pound mushrooms
- 2 cups thick gravy
- ½ cup orange juice
- 1 cup dry sherry

Melt the butter in a heavy skillet and brown the beef slices lightly in the butter. This also reheats the beef. When browned remove to a hot serving platter and keep hot while making the sauce.

Sauté mushrooms in the butter, add the brown gravy (which was also left from the roast), orange juice and sherry. Stir over low heat until very smooth and simmer gently for about 5 minutes. Pour over the beef and serve.

CHICKEN OR TURKEY MORNAY

Makes 6 servings

- 1 pound asparagus, cooked (fresh, frozen or 1 No. 2 can)
- 6 generous slices cooked chicken or turkey breast
- 1 can (1¼ cups) condensed cream of chicken soup
- ½ teaspoon marjoram
- ½ cup shredded American cheese

Place asparagus in the flat baking dish or pan from which you will serve this delightful main course. Arrange the chicken or turkey slices over the asparagus stalks. In a saucepan combine the soup, marjoram and cheese. Stir until blended, pour over the meat slices and place under moderately hot preheated broiler 3 inches from the flame, until lightly browned. Sprinkle with paprika and serve.

SAUSAGE GASTRONOME

Makes 4 servings

- 1 package frozen whipped potatoes
- 1 pound link sausages
- 1 can brown gravy
- 1 teaspoon Bovril
- ¼ cup thick sour cream (optional)
- 1 cup coarsely grated Cheddar or Parmesan cheese

This is a delicious and fragrant dish quickly made and best served in 4 shirred egg ovenware dishes. Prepare the potatoes as directed on the package while sautéing the sausages over low heat, turning to cook thoroughly and brown evenly on all sides. Pour the canned brown gravy into a saucepan, add the Bovril and stir over low heat until thoroughly hot. Remove from heat. Lightly grease the shirred egg dishes, fill with a layer of the whipped potatoes. Arrange the browned link sausages on top of the potatoes. Return the brown gravy to heat and add the sour cream stirring it until it begins to bubble; then pour it over the sausages. Sprinkle the tops with grated cheese and slide under a hot broiler to brown until the cheese is crusty, about 5 minutes.

LOBSTER AU CHAMPAGNE

Makes 2 servings

- 1½ cups cooked lobster meat (fresh, frozen or canned)
- ¼ cup butter
- ¼ cup onions, chopped
- ¼ cup carrots, chopped
- ¼ cup parsley, chopped
- 3 egg yolks, beaten
- 1½ cups heavy cream or undiluted evaporated milk
- 1 teaspoon salt
- ⅛ teaspoon cayenne
- ¾ cup champagne

At Prunier's in Paris, the restaurant closes when

the great delicacies from the sea are out of season. There the chef prepares this lobster in cream and champagne.

Melt the butter in a large saucepan, add onions, carrots and parsley. Simmer over low heat until vegetables can be mashed with back of spoon. Combine egg yolks with some of the cream, mix well and pour slowly into the pan stirring constantly. Add lobster pieces, remaining cream, salt and cayenne. When sauce thickens, add champagne and cook 1 minute longer.

SPICED TONGUE WITH CURRY SAUCE

Makes 8 to 10 servings

4 pounds smoked tongue Cold water to cover	1 medium-sized onion, sliced
2 tablespoons mixed pickling spice	3 stalks celery
	3 sprigs parsley

Place tongue in a 4-quart kettle. Cover with cold water. Tie spice in a bag and add to the water along with remaining ingredients. Cover. Cook slowly until tongue is tender (about 2 hours). Cool in the water. Remove skin from the tongue, slice and serve with Curry Sauce and potato salad, or with potato or rice and a vegetable.

CURRIED TONGUE SAUCE

Makes 2 cups

1 tablespoon chopped onion	2 teaspoons curry powder
2 tablespoons margarine or butter	½ teaspoon salt
	¼ teaspoon sugar
3 tablespoons flour	1/16 teaspoon ground black pepper
2 cups spicy tongue broth	1/16 teaspoon garlic powder

Sauté onion in margarine or butter. Blend in flour. Gradually stir in tongue broth. Add seasonings. Cook until medium thickness, stirring constantly. Serve hot over sliced tongue.

CHICKEN LIVERS IN SOUR CREAM

Makes 4 servings

- ¼ cup chicken fat
- 2 teaspoons kitchen bouquet
- ½ cup onion, thinly sliced
- 1 pound chicken livers
- 1½ teaspoons salt
- ¼ teaspoon pepper
- ⅛ teaspoon rosemary
- 1 (3 oz.) can broiled sliced mushrooms
- 2 teaspoons cornstarch
- 1 cup thick sour cream
- Cooked rice or noodles

Heat fat in large frying pan. Add kitchen bouquet and onions. Cook over moderate heat about 5 minutes, stirring frequently. Add chicken livers and sprinkle with salt, pepper and rosemary. Cook, stirring occasionally, until the livers are well browned, about 15 minutes. Drain mushrooms, reserving broth. Combine cornstarch and mushroom broth and add to livers, stirring constantly until thickened. Add mushrooms and sour cream, stirring until smoothly blended. Cover and simmer over low heat until thoroughly hot, about 15 minutes. Serve immediately over hot cooked rice or noodles.

SWEETBREADS AND HAM

Makes 4 servings

- 1 pair calf sweetbreads
- 3 tablespoons butter
- 1 tablespoon minced onion
- 3 tablespoons flour
- ¾ cup dry white wine or chicken broth
- ½ cup light cream
- ½ teaspoon Kitchen Bouquet

UNUSUAL SUPPER DISHES

1 (3 oz.) can sliced broiled mushrooms	½ teaspoon salt
	1/12 teaspoon pepper
1 cup julienne sliced cooked ham	⅛ teaspoon dry mustard

Cover sweetbreads with cold water and let stand 15 minutes. Carefully remove thin outer membrane. Place in saucepan and cover with cold water, adding 1 teaspoon salt and 1 tablespoon vinegar per quart. Bring to boil and let simmer for 15 minutes. Drain, then plunge sweetbreads into ice water. Meanwhile melt butter in saucepan. Add onion and cook 1 minute over moderate heat. Stir in flour. Add wine, cream, Kitchen Bouquet and contents of the can of mushrooms. Cook, stirring constantly, until sauce thickens. Add ham and seasonings. Cut sweetbreads in quarters and add to sauce. Heat thoroughly.

SALMON LOAF

Makes 6 servings

1 (1 pound) can (2 cups) salmon with juice, flaked	2 eggs, slightly beaten
	1 can (1¼ cups) condensed cream of celery soup
1½ cups dried bread crumbs	
½ cup minced green pepper	¼ teaspoon marjoram

Combine ingredients as listed and mix. Pack lightly into a small greased loaf pan. Bake in a moderate oven (350°) about 1 hour, or until done. Pour off extra juice and turn loaf out on a warm platter. Serve with Celery Sauce.

CELERY SAUCE

Makes 1¾ cups

1 can (1¼ cups) condensed cream of celery soup	1 teaspoon prepared mustard
	½ teaspoon tarragon

¼ cup milk or cream
1 hard-cooked egg, chopped

3 tablespoons sweet pickle relish

Empty soup into a saucepan, blend in mustard, tarragon and milk. Add relish and egg, place over low heat and stir till thoroughly hot.

This is not only very good over the Salmon Loaf but is delicious with Fish Cakes.

HAM LOAF WITH TOMATO HORSERADISH SAUCE

Makes 8 servings

1 pound ground veal
1 pound ground smoked ham
1 cup fine dry bread crumbs
½ teaspoon salt
¼ teaspoon pepper
½ teaspoon thyme or basil

3 tablespoons minced onion
3 tablespoons minced green pepper
2 eggs, beaten
¼ cup catsup
¼ cup water
1 can (1¼ cups) condensed tomato soup

Combine ingredients in the order given and mix thoroughly. Pack lightly into a greased loaf pan and bake in a moderate oven (350°) for 1 hour. Pour off juice, loosen edges, and invert on platter. Garnish if you like with green pepper, pimiento or sliced stuffed olives and sprigs of parsley, or gash top in diamond pattern and stud the loaf with cloves.

TOMATO HORSERADISH SAUCE

Makes 1½ cups

1 can (1¼ cups) condensed tomato soup
2 tablespoons prepared horseradish

2 teaspoons prepared mustard
¼ teaspoon ground cloves
½ teaspoon freshly ground black pepper

Mix all ingredients well. Serve hot or cold with the ham loaf.

CANADIAN BACON WITH SHERRY

Makes 4 servings

1 pound Canadian bacon thinly sliced	1½ cups dry sherry

Place bacon in skillet, cover with the sherry and let it marinate for 30 minutes to 1 hour. Place over low heat and cover. Simmer for 20 to 25 minutes until the sherry has almost disappeared.

4

The "Foundation Garments" for Fine Meals

Rice

Someone told me the other day about a man who had written down two hundred ways to prepare rice. Personally I like rice of every type cooked in every way that it has ever been presented before me. Brown rice, white rice, wild rice, rice with saffron, rice with chopped parsley, rice cooked in orange juice, rice with beguiling slices of mushrooms sliced into it, herb rice, parsley rice. They are all worth knowing about and I am going to give you as many as I think you would like for a starter, but first maybe we had better clear up the various names given to the rice recipes you will read.

In the Near Eastern countries and in some parts of the United States rice is called *Pilau*. Again you will meet it in various parts of the world as *Pilas*. *Risotto* is rice in Italy; *Paella* refers to the saffron rice of Spain. These are the *noms de plume* most often used but each means rice, flavored and cooked according to the custom of the country.

THE "FOUNDATION GARMENTS" FOR FINE MEALS 47

Rice is one of the most deliciously flavorful foods on earth. Each type has one thing in common—it provides a substantial background for any meat, fish, vegetables, sauces you want to serve on it, in it, or with it. Even fruit, spices or sugar and cream are delicious on rice. It is also—as millions of people could tell you—a fine dish when served alone.

Each type of rice, flavored as you wish, can also be pressed lightly into a buttered ring mold then later unmolded on a platter where it can hold creamed seafood and any number of good things which are piled in the center of the rice ring.

WHITE RICE

Whether short- or long-grained, precooked or plain, rice should be cooked according to the directions on the package, using the amount of seasoning and liquid indicated. You can, however, do a number of additional things to it so far as seasoning:

FRENCH RICE:—Melt ¼ cup butter in a saucepan and add 1 cup dry rice. Sauté over low heat for about 5 minutes, stirring occasionally. Add chicken or beef broth in place of the liquid indicated for the rice you are using, and continue cooking according to directions on the package.

ROSY RICE.—Can be made by using tomato juice for the liquid in which the rice cooks.

ORANGE RICE:—Can be made with orange juice as a liquid in which the rice is cooked.

CHEESE RICE:—Is delicious. Begin by boiling 2 cups rice in chicken or beef broth and when the liquid is nearly absorbed add 1 cup grated Swiss cheese, ½ teaspoon paprika and a few drops of Tabasco. Stir over low heat only until the cheese is melted and the liquid absorbed.

ROSY CHEESE RICE:—Cook the rice with tomato

juice and then add the cheese as indicated for Cheese Rice.

PARSLEY RICE:—Make this and serve plain or fill a ring mold. To fill a 9-inch mold combine 2 beaten eggs with 2 cups rich milk and 1 cup finely chopped parsley. Add 2 tablespoons minced onion and 1 teaspoon garlic salt. Add 4 cups rice which has been cooked and stir until thoroughly mixed. Turn into a buttered baking dish and bake in a moderate oven (325°) until liquid has been absorbed, about 25 minutes.

CHIVES RICE:—Make rice pretty and piquant by stirring in 2 tablespoons finely chopped fresh chives before serving.

CHILI RICE:—Add 1 teaspoon chili powder to cooked rice and stir in with fork.

BROWN RICE

Brown rice is even more delicious, in many people's opinions, than white rice. In any case, you cook it according to package directions or use any of the flavorings you like which was suggested for white rice. However, there is one time when it should be handled with special attention to browning as for the way it is cooked in France.

BROWN RICE FRENCH FASHION:—Melt ¼ cup butter in a saucepan for each 1 cup dry rice. Add the rice when the butter is melted and stir over medium heat until the butter is absorbed and the rice a beautiful deep brown. Add 1 cup chicken or beef broth for each cup of rice used. Cover, reduce heat and cook until the liquid is absorbed and the rice tender. Add garlic button to this during the cooking if you are fond of garlic, and remove it when the rice is served.

RICE RING

Fills a 5-cup ring mold

- 1 egg
- ½ teaspoon salt
- 1 teaspoon grated onion
- 1 cup evaporated or rich milk, undiluted
- ½ cup chicken broth
- 3 cups cooked rice

Beat egg and add the remaining ingredients. Stir until thoroughly mixed and pour into a well buttered ring mold. Set in a pan of hot water and bake in a preheated moderate oven (350°) until set, about 45 minutes.

Freshly cooked rice can be turned into a ring mold if packed down ever so gently, being careful not to mash the grain. Leave it for a few minutes and place a serving platter over the top, invert the mold and the rice will retain its shape. To insure a perfect mold on the platter the ring mold should be filled to the brim.

1 cup of uncooked rice makes about 3½ cups of cooked rice.

Sauté 1 pound of sliced mushrooms in a little butter for a minute or two and fold them into the rice. Canned, drained mushrooms can be used for this too and the quantity does not matter. Use a few or a lot.

Any of the following recipes can be molded into a ring or served plain.

HERBED WILD RICE

Makes 3½ cups

- 1 cup wild rice
- 3 cups cold water
- 1 teaspoon salt
- ¼ cup butter
- 1 teaspoon fresh parsley, finely chopped
- 1 teaspoon grated onion
- ½ teaspoon basil

Wash the rice thoroughly in cold water changing

the water until it becomes clear. Drain and cover the rice with 3 cups of fresh cold water to which salt has been added. Place over high heat and bring to a boil, but do not stir. Lower heat sufficiently to keep it bubbling until tender, 15 to 40 minutes. Prevent sticking by shaking the kettle now and then, but do not cover and do not stir and cook the rice the minimum time. Drain and sprinkle with herbs, place in a buttered ovenproof serving dish, dot with lumps of butter and place in the oven tightly covered. Keep hot and encourage grains to absorb any additional moisture at 375° for 15 minutes.

SAFFRON RICE

Spanish

Makes 6 servings

- 1¼ cups long grain white rice
- 2 tablespoons olive oil
- 2 tablespoons butter
- 2 tablespoons finely chopped onion
- 1 clove garlic, minced
- 1 bay leaf
- 1 teaspoon thyme
- ⅛ teaspoon rosemary
- ½ teaspoon salt
- ¼ teaspoon freshly ground black pepper
- ⅛ teaspoon cayenne
- 1¼ cups chicken broth
- ½ to 1 teaspoon shredded saffron, diluted in broth and strained out

Heat the olive oil and butter in a heavy skillet which has a tight-fitting lid. Add the onion, garlic and seasonings and the dry rice and cook over medium heat until the rice is a light golden color. (In some parts of Spain the rice is cooked to a deep rich brown.) Add the chicken broth and stir until contents of skillet are thoroughly mixed. Cover tightly and simmer over low heat until liquid is absorbed and the rice tender, about 25 minutes.

The trick in making Saffron Rice is to get it delicately gold without being revoltingly gold. Add the shredded saffron to some of the chicken broth as long as the night before or merely an hour before you prepare the rice. Strain before adding the tinted chicken broth to the skillet.

BAKED PINEAPPLE RICE

Makes 5 cups

- 1¼ cups white or brown rice
- 1¼ cups water
- ¼ cup pineapple juice
- ½ teaspoon salt
- 1 cup drained crushed pineapple
- ⅓ cup light brown sugar, firmly packed
- 3 tablespoons butter
- 2 teaspoons grated lemon rind
- ¼ teaspoon nutmeg

Combine the rice, water, pineapple juice and salt and cook according to directions on package for the rice you are using. When the liquid is absorbed and the rice is tender add remaining ingredients and stir lightly with a fork. Turn into a buttered 1 quart casserole and bake in a preheated moderate oven (400°) for 20 minutes.

COCONUT RICE

Makes 4 servings

- 1 cup canned coconut, chopped
- 2 cups rich milk, scalded
- 1 tablespoon butter or margarine
- ¼ cup finely chopped onion
- 1 small clove garlic, minced
- ¼ teaspoon ground ginger
- ½ cup chicken broth
- 1 tablespoon quick cooking tapioca
- 1 cup rice, cooked
- 1 cup chicken broth
- 2 cups cooked shrimp, chopped (or you may use veal or sweetbreads)

The first and last two acts in this little drama can be done any time you want and combined 2 or 3 hours later when it is about to be served, for then you will have it hot. Combine the canned, chopped coconut with the milk and allow it to stand for a few hours. Sauté the onion and seasonings in a saucepan in the butter over very low heat stirring constantly. Add the chicken broth and the coconut and milk mixture. Add the tapioca and stir over medium heat in the top of a double boiler over boiling water, stirring constantly until it thickens. Strain the sauce or put it in an electric blender and turn on the machine until is is fine and creamy. Return to saucepan, add the seafood or sweetbreads (any number of things can be used for this). Serve the rice and this mixture in separate bowls, passing the rice first. This can be served with a tray of condiments just as for Curried Chicken (*page 146*) or any other curried dish.

BRAZILIAN RICE

Makes 4 servings

- ½ cup onions, diced
- ½ cup carrots, diced
- ½ cup celery, diced
- ¼ cup green pepper, diced
- 1 cup water
- 1 cup tomato sauce
- 1 (3 oz.) can chopped, broiled mushrooms
- ½ teaspoon salt
- ½ teaspoon sugar
- ⅛ teaspoon pepper
- 1 cup converted rice

Place uncooked, diced onions, carrots, celery, green pepper and water in container of electric blender. Cover container and run blender until vegetables are finely chopped about 3 seconds. Pour blended mixture into saucepan and add tomato sauce, contents of can of mushrooms, seasonings and rice. Cover and bring to boil. Reduce heat and cook slowly until rice is tender and most of liquid is absorbed, about 20 minutes.

PEANUT LOAF

Makes 4 servings

- ⅔ cup cooked oatmeal, wheat cereal, rice or pasta
- ¼ cup chopped green pepper
- 3 tablespoons minced onion
- 1 teaspoon salt
- 2 teaspoons lemon juice
- 1 cup chopped salted peanuts
- ⅔ cup fine bread crumbs
- 1 cup (¼ pound) grated Cheddar cheese
- 1 egg, beaten
- ⅓ cup rich milk
- ¼ cup peanut butter, softened and blended with the milk

Combine all ingredients for mixture and milk until blended. Turn into buttered loaf pan. Bake in moderate oven (350°) 1 hour. Serve hot with Mushroom Sauce (*page 69*) and cranberry relish.

Pasta

The macaroni family is a big one. The Italian *pasta* has been a soul satisfying dish for so many hundred years that there are now said to be 500 different names for it across the world. There are 200 sizes and shapes of these egg noodles to choose from; and some of our big markets carry 75 shapes and sizes of macaroni, spaghetti, noodles—whatever name you care to give those you like. Don't let the name delay your trying out some new shapes or sizes. You will also find two colors, for the spinach and parsley noodles currently on the market are a moss green in the package, a come-hither green when steaming on the platter. For dieters, the green variety comes in no-starch artichoke-flour noodles, with very few calories.

If you imagine that spaghetti or macaroni has no taste, it is because you do not cook it correctly. In that you have plenty of company, for this jewel of an egg noodle dish, cooked *al dente*—meaning tender but not soft—knowingly sauced, seasoned or served with Swedish meat balls or in any combination you cherish, should be cooked in a big pot of well salted water. Generous amounts of water and salt avoid blandness, stickiness. Its cooking should be timed to the minute to avoid softness and loss of character. Follow the split second timing recommended in this cooking chart, cooking 2 minutes less, you'll notice, when the pasta is to be exposed to heat a second time in a combination dish.

Cooking Macaroni ... Spaghetti ... Noodles

To cook 4 ounces macaroni, spaghetti, noodles or any pasta put 2 to 3 quarts boiling water and 1 tablespoon salt into a large pan, about 4-quart size. When cooking 6 to 8 ounces macaroni products, 3 to 4 quarts boiling water and 2 tablespoons salt give most satisfactory results.

With water at bubbling boil, gradually add the pasta so as to keep water actively boiling. Leave the pan uncovered. Pasta is done when a piece pressed gently with a spoon against the side of the pan cuts cleanly. Cooking time varies with the size and on whether the pasta is to be served plain or combined with other foods with which it will cook a bit more. For *al dente*, use least time indicated on the Time Chart (*page 55*).

When done, drain the pasta by pouring into colander or large coarse sieve. Rinse, or "blanch" by letting water run gently over macaroni, spaghetti or noodles. If to be served hot, use hot water. If it is to be used in cold dishes, such as salads, use cold water.

Because of the many varied shapes of macaroni products, the simplest method for measuring the products is by weight. In most recipes, macaroni, spaghetti or noodles may be used interchangeably. A satisfactory guide is to allow 1 ounce macaroni produce per serving when used in combination dishes, and 1½ ounces when served plain, with a sauce.

TIME CHART FOR COOKING

Product	For serving plain
Elbow Macaroni	10 to 12 minutes
Long Macaroni	12 to 15 minutes
Macaroni Shells	8 to 10 minutes
Elbow Spaghetti	5 to 8 minutes
Long Spaghetti	12 to 15 minutes
Vermicelli	10 to 12 minutes
Fine Noodles	4 to 6 minutes
Medium Noodles	4 to 6 minutes
Broad Noodles	6 to 8 minutes

PASTA
Italian

Makes 4 servings

- 1 (8 oz.) package pasta shells
- ¼ cup olive oil
- ¼ cup butter
- 4 cloves garlic, minced
- 1 cup chopped onion
- 1 (No. 2) can tiny French peas
- ⅓ cup finely chopped parsley
- ¼ teaspoon marjoram
- ½ to 1 teaspoon salt
- ¼ teaspoon freshly ground black pepper

Cook the pasta shells *al dente* (*page 54*) and set

aside until ready to combine this dish for heating just before serving. Heat the olive oil and butter in a heavy skillet and add the chopped garlic and onion to sauté, stirring constantly until delicately browned. Drain the liquid from the peas into the skillet and continue cooking until most of the liquid has disappeared. Remove from heat, stir in the peas, the parsley and seasonings. Add the cooked, drained pasta shells and mix lightly with a fork. Cover tightly, return to heat for 1 minute and remove to a place where it will keep warm until ready to serve. This dish can also be turned into a buttered casserole, tightly covered, and placed in a warm oven to keep hot. Or, if the dish has been prepared in advance, the casserole can be put into the refrigerator and later heated in a hot oven before serving.

MACARONI AND CHEESE WITH PEANUTS

Makes 4 servings

- 1 (8 oz.) package macaroni or spaghetti, broken into small pieces
- 3 tablespoons butter or margarine
- 2 tablespoons flour
- 1/8 teaspoon cayenne
- 1 teaspoon salt
- 1/2 teaspoon tarragon (optional)
- 1 1/2 cups rich milk
- 2/3 cup grated Cheddar cheese
- 3/4 cup chopped peanuts
- 1/4 cup toasted, buttered bread crumbs

Cook macaroni or spaghetti in boiling, salted water until tender. Drain. Melt butter or margarine. Blend in flour and seasonings. Add milk and cook slowly until thickened, stirring constantly. Arrange alternate layers of cooked macaroni or spaghetti, grated cheese, and the chopped peanuts in a greased baking dish saving some of the peanuts and cheese for the top. Cover with a White Sauce (*page 99*) flavored with ½ teaspoon tarragon. Sprinkle with crumbs, peanuts and cheese. Bake in moderate oven (375°) until brown, about 20 minutes.

RAISIN SPAGHETTI WITH HAM BALLS

Makes 4 servings

RAISIN SAUCE

- 2 tablespoons fat
- ¼ cup onion, chopped
- ¼ cup green pepper, chopped
- ¼ cup celery, chopped
- ½ cup seedless raisins
- ¼ cup tomato catsup
- 1 tablespoon vinegar
- 1 cup water
- 1 teaspoon salt
- ⅛ teaspoon pepper

Melt fat in skillet. Add onion, green pepper and celery. Cook 5 minutes. Add raisins, catsup, vinegar, water, salt and pepper. Cover and simmer 25 minutes. While sauce simmers, make Ham Balls.

HAM BALLS

- 1 pound ground ham
- ¼ cup onion, chopped
- 1 cup bread crumbs
- 1 teaspoon salt
- ¼ teaspoon pepper
- 1 egg, beaten
- ½ cup milk
- 1 tablespoon Worcestershire sauce
- ¼ cup fat
- 6 ounces spaghetti, cooked as directed (page 55)

Combine ham, onion, bread crumbs, salt, pepper, egg, milk and Worcestershire sauce. Mix well. Shape into balls, allowing ¼ cup for each. Melt fat in skillet. Brown ham balls in melted fat. Cook 20 minutes. While ham balls are cooking, cook spaghetti; fold into Raisin Sauce. Arrange on hot platter, and top with Ham Balls.

SALAMI MACARONI TOSS-UP

Makes 4 servings

- 4 ounces elbow macaroni, cooked (page 55)
- 3 tablespoons butter or margarine
- 3 tablespoons enriched flour
- 1 teaspoon salt
- ⅛ teaspoon pepper
- ½ teaspoon dry mustard
- 1 teaspoon Worcestershire sauce
- 1½ cups milk
- 1 tablespoon minced onion
- ½ cup grated American cheese
- 1 cup slivered salami
- ¼ cup slivered sweet pickle

While macaroni is cooking, melt butter or margarine in top of double boiler. Stir in flour, salt, pepper, mustard and Worcestershire sauce. Gradually add milk, stirring constantly until thickened. Fold in onion, cheese, salami and pickle. Mix lightly. Fold in macaroni. Pour into 4 greased individual casseroles. Bake in moderate oven (350°) 25 minutes.

SALMON PUFF

Makes 8 servings

- 8 ounces elbow macaroni, cooked (page 55)
- 2 (1 pound) cans flaked salmon—4 cups
- 2 cups milk
- 2 eggs, beaten
- 2 teaspoons salt
- ¼ teaspoon cayenne
- 2 tablespoons melted butter or margarine
- ¼ teaspoon tarragon
- 2 teaspoons grated lemon rind
- 2 tablespoons minced onion
- 4 hard-cooked eggs

While macaroni is cooking, combine salmon, milk,

beaten eggs, 1 teaspoon salt and the cayenne, butter or margarine, tarragon, lemon rind and onion. Fold in macaroni. Pour half the macaroni mixture into greased loaf pan. Cut hard-cooked eggs into halves lengthwise, and arrange on macaroni mixture. Pour remaining macaroni over eggs. Bake in moderate oven (350°) 45 minutes. Turn out of pan. Serve in slices with prepared mustard, a tart green salad and hot green peas.

5

Seafood ... Exotic but Easy

Interesting Recipes

BAKED STRIPED BASS

Makes 6 to 8 servings

- 1 3 to 4 pound bass
- 12 green onions or scallions, sliced thin
- 2 tablespoons chopped parsley
- 2 tablespoons butter
- 2 cups dry white wine
- Salt
- Pepper

Select a baking dish as long as the fish or longer, and grease it. Line pan with aluminum foil and grease it. Put in the fish which has been prepared for cooking (cleaned and scales removed, with head left on). Add scallions using the white parts only, parsley, butter and sufficient wine to cover. Add the seasonings depending upon the size of your fish, and then bake uncovered in a moderate oven (375°) basting about every 10 minutes. Allow 10 minutes per pound if under 4 pounds, add 5 minutes to total cooking time for each pound over 4 pounds. If necessary place under broiler for last few minutes to brown the fish thoroughly. Lift up the aluminum foil and slide contents on a serving dish.

STUFFED BAKED STRIPED BASS:—Select and prepare bass exactly as above except that when you are stuffing a bass you often select a larger fish. Stuff before baking. Whatever the size use either of the stuffings (*pages 70 to 71*) packing the cavity loosely and closing the belly of the fish with skewers or a few stitches with a kitchen needle and heavy cord.

DEVILED CRABS IN SHELLS

Makes 8 servings

- 4 cups lump crabmeat
- 4 cups Swiss Cheese Sauce (page 100)
- ½ cup heavy cream, whipped
- 8 crab shells or ramekins

Place 3 cups Swiss Cheese Sauce in a saucepan, taste for seasoning and add more salt if necessary. Stir over medium heat until thoroughly hot. Remove from heat, add the crabmeat and toss lightly. Fill the shells with the creamy crab mixture. Then cover the mounds with the remaining 1 cup of Swiss Cheese Sauce which has been folded into the whipped cream. Sprinkle the tops with paprika and arrange on a baking sheet to slide under the hot broiler until the tops are delicately browned.

These shells can be prepared in the morning and refrigerated until ready to remove and place under broiler. For the chilled Deviled Crabs place in medium hot broiler 5 inches from the heat so that they will not brown before the crabmeat is heated clear through.

BEER-DED SHRIMP

Makes 6 servings

- 3 pounds fresh shrimp, left in shells
- 2 (12 oz.) cans beer
- 1 tablespoon dry mustard
- 2 tablespoons chopped parsley
- 1 tablespoon chives
- 2 cloves garlic, chopped
- 1 teaspoon thyme
- 1 teaspoon salt
- ½ teaspoon pepper

Remove tails from shrimp, slit and remove black vein, but leave in shells. Combine all other ingredients in large saucepan, place over high heat. When liquid begins to boil, add shrimp, reduce heat and simmer 5 minutes. Transfer shrimp and liquid to tureen. Serve immediately with individual bowls of Dunking Sauce.

DUNKING SAUCE

- ½ pound butter (2 sticks)
- ¼ cup lemon juice
- 1 tablespoon finely chopped celery leaves
- 1 tablespoon finely chopped chives
- 2 teaspoons salt
- 1 teaspoon Angostura bitters

Melt butter in saucepan, add all other ingredients. Stir and pour into 6 small bowls for "dunking."

Menu: Serve with mugs of beer, a bowl of tossed green salad or Vegetable Ring Mold (*page 180*). For dessert, fresh fruit and a Gouda or sharp Cheddar cheese with crisp saltines.

SHRIMP SCAMPI

Makes 2 servings

- 1 pound raw shrimp, or 1 (12 oz.) package frozen raw shrimp
- 1 clove garlic, minced
- ½ cup melted butter
- ½ teaspoon Kitchen Bouquet or 1 teaspoon Soya sauce

Remove outer shells and black vein from shrimp. Leave tails intact. Place shrimp in suitable bowl. Combine garlic, butter and Kitchen Bouquet. Sprinkle over shrimp and toss lightly with fork to coat all pieces evenly. Arrange shrimp on heatproof serving platter. Broil 5 inches from moderate heat for about 10 minutes, turning once at the end of 5 minutes. Serve immediately.

For frozen shelled, cooked shrimp, reduce broiling time to 2 minutes on each side.

SHRIMP TEMPURA

Japanese

Makes 4 servings

2 pounds jumbo shrimp in their shells	1 teaspoon tarragon
8 large lettuce leaves	½ teaspoon thyme
2 bay leaves	½ teaspoon basil
	2 tablespoons wine vinegar

Wash the shrimp but do not dry them. Place the rinsed lettuce leaves in the bottom of a heavy skillet and pile the shrimps on top of this green bed to be cooked very much as peas are cooked in France. Add the bay leaves, vinegar and sprinkle the herbs on top before covering tightly to steam, for 15 or 20 minutes over medium heat. The time for steaming depends upon the size of the shrimp, the largest ones need 20 minutes. Do not lift the lid until ready to remove from heat. Cool shrimps and remove shell without removing the tails.

BUTTERFLY SHRIMP:—The Japanese prepare these by peeling the body of the shrimp, drying them and slitting them, not quite through, down the back after they have been deveined. This separates the halves so that they can be pressed back to look like butterflies. Press these while still warm and when cool they will hold their shape. Dip in the batter and fry until golden brown in deep fat (375°) about 4 minutes.

BATTER

2 eggs, beaten
1 cup milk
1 cup flour
½ teaspoon salt
Fat for deep frying

SHRIMP AND HAM JAMBALAYA

Makes 6 to 8 servings

2 pounds shrimp
1 slice precooked smoked ham ½-inch thick, cubed
3 tablespoons olive oil
2 small white onions, chopped
1 green pepper, chopped
1 clove garlic, minced
1 bay leaf, crushed
1½ cups uncooked rice
2 cups water
1 (No. 2½) can whole tomatoes
½ teaspoon salt
½ teaspoon black pepper
½ teaspoon paprika

Cook shrimp in court bouillon (*page 65*). Shell and clean. In a large skillet, sauté ham in ham fat until lightly browned. Remove from skillet and set aside. Measure olive oil into skillet. Add onions, green pepper, garlic and bay leaf. Cook until onion is tender. Add rice and cook, stirring constantly, until browned. Add water, tomatoes and seasonings; mix well. Cover and cook, stirring occasionally until rice is tender, about 30 minutes. If mixture becomes too dry, add water. When rice is cooked, add shrimp and ham. Continue to cook until shrimp are heated, about 10 minutes. (If desired, transfer to a casserole and heat over a candle-lit warming stand or in a hot oven, 425°, until shrimp are heated.)

Serve immediately with a tossed green salad, French bread and beer.

COURT BOUILLON

- 2 quarts water
- 1 tablespoon mixed pickling spices
- 1 teaspoon salt
- ½ stalk celery, optional

Combine all ingredients in large saucepan. Bring water to boil. Add shrimp as indicated above. Return to boil, then reduce heat. Simmer 5 minutes. Drain shrimp. Cool quickly.

BROILED ROCK LOBSTER FLORIDIAN

Makes 4 servings

- 4 frozen rock lobster tails
- 2 quarts boiling water
- 3 tablespoons salt
- 1 teaspoon Kitchen Bouquet
- ¼ cup melted butter
- ¼ cup lemon or lime juice

Drop lobster tails into boiling water, add salt and bring to boil again. Lower heat, cover and simmer for about 10 minutes. Drain. With knives or shears, remove soft shell-like covering on underside of tail. Make a deep cut through center of flesh and remove dark vein. Combine Kitchen Bouquet, melted butter and lemon juice. Brush lobster meat generously with this mixture, then place on broiler rack about 5 inches from moderate heat. Broil about 6 minutes. Brush several times during the broiling period using all of the Kitchen Bouquet mixture. Serve immediately in the shell.

BROILED SAVORY SCALLOPS

Makes 4 to 6 servings

1½ pounds scallops	2 tablespoons grated onion
1 teaspoon Kitchen Bouquet or Worcestershire sauce	¼ cup melted butter
	2 tablespoons lemon or lime juice
½ teaspoon salt	Paprika
¼ teaspoon curry powder	Parsley, minced

Unless scallops are the small variety cut in ¾-inch pieces. Place scallops in a bowl and sprinkle with Kitchen Bouquet and salt. Toss lightly with fork to coat pieces evenly. Arrange on shallow heatproof serving platter. Combine curry powder, onion, butter and lemon juice and cook over moderate heat about 3 minutes. Pour over scallops. Broil 4 inches from moderate heat in preheated broiling compartment for about 20 minutes, stirring at the end of 10 minutes. Serve on toast. Sprinkle with paprika and minced parsley.

BARBECUED SWORDFISH

Makes 4 to 6 servings

2 pounds swordfish steak	¼ teaspoon pepper
1 teaspoon oregano	3 tablespoons lemon or lime juice
3 tablespoons melted butter	
½ teaspoon salt	

Arrange fish steaks on heatproof serving platter. Brush tops and sides with melted butter. Combine remaining ingredients and pour around fish. Bake in moderate oven (350°) until fish flakes easily, about 35 minutes, basting with the sauce about every 10 minutes. Serve immediately.

TUNA SOUFFLÉ

Makes 4 to 5 servings

- 3 tablespoons quick cooking tapioca
- ½ teaspoon salt
- 1 can condensed cream of celery soup
- ½ cup milk
- 1 (7 oz.) can tuna fish, drained and flaked
- 3 egg whites
- 3 egg yolks
- ⅓ cup milk

Combine tapioca, salt, ½ cup of the soup, and ½ cup of milk in saucepan. Cook and stir over medium heat until mixture comes to a boil. Remove from heat, add tuna fish, and allow to cool slightly while beating eggs. Beat egg whites until stiff. Beat egg yolks until thick and lemon colored. Add tapioca mixture to egg yolks and mix well. Fold into egg whites. Turn into 1½-quart baking dish. Place in pan of hot water and bake in moderate oven (350°) 50 minutes, or until soufflé is firm. Meanwhile make celery sauce by combining remaining soup and ⅓ cup milk. Heat, stirring occasionally. Add a little chopped parsley, if desired. Serve with the soufflé, or serve soufflé with a White Sauce (*page 99*) or Cheese Sauce (*page 99*).

SPICED NOODLES À LA NEPTUNE

Makes 6 to 8 servings

- 3 tablespoons margarine or butter
- ¼ cup onion, chopped
- ¼ cup green pepper, chopped
- ¼ cup celery, diced
- ½ teaspoon salt
- ¼ teaspoon ground black pepper
- ⅓ cup sliced fresh mushrooms
- 3 tablespoons flour
- 1 can condensed tomato soup

½ can water	⅛ teaspoon basil
1 (7 oz.) can tuna fish	½ package (4 oz.) fine noodles
¼ teaspoon whole oregano leaves, crumbled	

Melt margarine or butter in a saucepan. Add next 4 ingredients and sauté until limp. Stir in flour. Remove from heat and stir in tomato soup and water. Cook noodles as directed on package. (For perfectly cooked noodles see paragraph and time chart, *page 55.*) Drain, arrange in a ring around the edge of the serving plate, and fill center with the tuna fish mixture.

SEA FOOD TUREEN
Danish

Makes 8 cups

¼ cup butter	1 (6 oz.) can sliced broiled mushrooms
1 package frozen flounder filets	1½ cups evaporated milk, undiluted
1½ cups dry white wine	
1 package frozen shelled cooked shrimp	1 can cream of mushroom soup, undiluted
1 cup cooked lobster meat, canned or frozen	½ cup sherry
	Salt
Pepper	

Melt butter in large saucepan, add frozen thawed filets and wine. Cover and simmer 10 minutes. Add remaining ingredients except sherry and seasonings. Simmer another 5 minutes. Add sherry and seasonings to taste. Serve in large tureen with buttered toast.

Lobster and flounder should be in chunks or flakes. Shrimp should remain whole.

FISH PUDDING WITH MUSHROOM SAUCE
Scandinavian

Makes 6 servings

- 1½ pounds boneless cod or haddock
- 1 teaspoon salt
- ½ teaspoon oregano
- ½ teaspoon paprika
- 2 egg whites
- 2 tablespoons finely chopped parsley
- ¾ cup evaporated milk, undiluted
- ¼ cup cream of rice cereal

Put fish through food chopper, using finest knife. Add seasonings, parsley, evaporated milk and cream of rice cereal, mixing in well. Beat egg whites until stiff but not dry and carefully fold into fish mixture. Pour into greased loaf pan, about 8 x 4 inches. Bake in slow oven (325°) until set and lightly browned, about 1¼ hours.

MUSHROOM SAUCE

- 3 tablespoons butter or margarine
- ¼ cup minced onion
- 3 tablespoons flour
- 1¼ cups chicken broth
- ⅛ teaspoon pepper
- 1 (3 oz.) can sliced broiled mushrooms
- 1 tablespoon lemon juice

Melt butter in saucepan. Add onion and cook 1 minute. Stir in flour. Add chicken broth, pepper and contents of can of mushrooms. Cook, stirring constantly, until sauce thickens. Add lemon juice. Serve on top of Fish Pudding.

STUFFING FOR LARGE BAKED FISH
(For Lean Fish)

Makes about 3½ cups

- 1 dozen large chestnuts
- ½ teaspoon salt
- Boiling water
- 1 (6 oz.) can sliced broiled mushrooms
- 2 tablespoons green pepper
- ¼ cup thinly sliced celery
- ¼ cup thinly sliced carrots
- ¼ cup onions, chopped
- 1 cup Brussels sprouts
- Bread crumbs
- Sauterne
- 2 tablespoons melted butter
- 3 tablespoons lemon juice
- 1 teaspoon grated lemon peel
- 2 eggs, slightly beaten
- 1 tablespoon chopped parsley
- ¼ teaspoon marjoram

Cut a small gash forming a cross in the top of each chestnut shell. Place in a saucepan, add the salt and boiling water to barely cover. Cook until tender. Drain and shell the chestnuts and chop them coarsely. Add remaining ingredients in a large mixing bowl using only enough bread crumbs to make the dressing dry but manageable. Add dry sauterne to moisten.

CUCUMBER STUFFING
(For Fat Fish)

Makes about 3½ cups

- 1½ cups chopped cucumber
- ¼ cup onion, finely chopped
- 1 tablespoon chopped parsley
- 4 to 5 fresh mushrooms, sautéed and chopped
- 1 teaspoon salt
- ½ teaspoon pepper
- 2 cups coarse, dry bread crumbs
- 3 tablespoons bacon drippings
- 1 tablespoon butter
- 2 tablespoons lemon juice
- 1 egg, slightly beaten

Cucumbers can be used peeled or with the green peel left on. However, remove seeds, then chop and drain the moisture from the cucumbers. Mix with remaining ingredients in the order mentioned and toss until blended sufficiently to stuff any fat fish.

6

Vegetables and Sauces

How to Cook and Flavor Vegetables

Want the last drop of valuable flavor and goodness left in every vegetable you serve? They are filled with the good things from earth and sunshine which will be yours if you remember:

The outside leaves on that head of lettuce, on the firm hard head of cabbage, are older than the delicate leaves at the heart. Keep each one unless damaged—and you should not have bought it if they are—to benefit from the iron and calcium and vitamins these dark outside leaves contain.

Get the habit of cooking vegetables the least possible amount of time for tenderness, in the least possible amount of water.

If any liquid is unwanted with the served vegetables, pour it into a juice jar kept covered and in the refrigerator for this purpose. Keep juice from spinach and kale separately, for it overwhelms the milder flavored juices. Add juice to thin a canned soup, to a thick white sauce to be served over the vegetable, to the gravy pan when making gravy. Or toss it in the electric blender with cubed fresh vegetables to make a cold or hot blended vegetable soup.

Cook potatoes in their skins whenever possible. Eat the skins or remove them after potatoes are cooked.

Expose vegetables, fresh or frozen or canned, to as little heat and air and standing after being cooked as you can manage. The time between preparation, cooling and serving should be brief.

Use heavy pans with tight-fitting lids for almost waterless cooking.

Consider pressure sauce pans for cooking vegetables; then cook them the minimum time for highest flavor and texture for the vitamin content and color retained. Cool as directed. When directions advise it, be sure to submerge pan in cold water to quickly reduce steam.

VEGETABLE SOUFFLÉ

Makes 4 servings

- 2 tablespoons onion, finely chopped
- ½ tablespoon green pepper, finely chopped
- 1 tablespoon celery, finely chopped
- 2 tablespoons butter or baking fat, melted
- 2 tablespoons flour
- ½ cup chicken broth or liquefied nonfat dry milk
- ½ cup grated Cheddar cheese
- ½ teaspoon salt
- ¼ teaspoon freshly ground black pepper
- ¾ to 1 cup diced or mashed cooked vegetables
- 2 egg yolks, well beaten
- 2 egg whites, stiffly beaten

Brown the onion, green pepper and celery lightly in the fat. Blend in flour and add milk or broth. Cook over low heat, stirring constantly until thickened. Add cheese and stir only until blended. Season with salt and pepper. Stir vegetables into this sauce and add the hot mixture to the beaten egg yolks. Beat the egg whites until stiff but not dry and fold into the vegetable mixture. Pour into greased baking dish. Bake in slow oven (325°) until set, 40 to 50 minutes.

When making the soufflé use one of the herbs appropriate for the vegetables being used. For example, add ½ teaspoon basil if it is an eggplant soufflé— ¼ teaspoon marjoram for an onion soufflé.

VEGETABLE SHORTCAKES

Makes 6 servings

- 6 biscuit shortcakes, baked
- 2 (10½ oz.) cans condensed cream of asparagus or cream of mushroom soup
- 1½ cups milk
- 2 cups diced cooked meat (ham, chicken, beef or lamb or some of each)
- 3 hard-cooked eggs, sliced

Make shortcakes from packaged biscuit mix omitting the sugar. Bake, split and butter. Meanwhile, combine soup and milk in a saucepan, stir until blended, and place over medium heat. Add the cold diced meat and cook slowly 5 minutes stirring constantly. Add egg slices just before serving, saving several to garnish the shortcakes. Place half of the creamed meat filling between shortcakes and the other half over the top. Garnish with the remaining egg slices and serve hot.

A variety of vegetables can be stirred into the cream soup in place of the meat. Use peas, string beans or grated carrots—or a combination of vegetables can be used in these shortcakes. Add 1 cup cream and 4 tablespoons sherry in place of the milk for extra flavor. Try ¼ teaspoon nutmeg when using chicken soup, add ½ teaspoon thyme or ¼ teaspoon marjoram for the asparagus soup base.

VEGETABLE SUKIYAKI
Japanese

Makes 4 servings

- 2 tablespoons bacon drippings
- 2 tablespoons sugar
- 1 cup onions, thinly sliced
- ½ cup Shoyu or Soya sauce
- ½ cup chicken or beef bouillon
- 2 cups Chinese cabbage, sliced
- ¾ cup sliced mushrooms, canned or fresh
- ½ cup water
- 1 egg
- Cooked long grain rice

Melt the fat and sugar in a large skillet over low heat. Add the onions, stir until they begin to brown. Add all other ingredients except the egg. Cover and cook 2 minutes. Make a well in the center of the pan, break the egg into the center, stir to mix some of the egg through all the contents of the pan and serve immediately over cooked rice.

BAKED POTATOES

Select oblong potatoes of uniform size. Wash and dry them and bake in a hot oven (425°) about 1 hour or until tender when pierced with a fork. If you want the skin to be soft rub a little bacon drippings on the potato before baking and then place in a pan instead of on the rack.

Serve baked potatoes by cutting across the flat side of the potato with a sharp knife. Squeeze to force cut edges up a little, then sprinkle with paprika or place a cube of butter in the center of each opening.

If you want to bake the potatoes while baking something else in the oven, remember that the desirable mealy texture is sacrificed by low temperature and that they will require longer baking.

For variety, wrap potatoes in aluminum foil and

bake them. Then cut a cross in the top without removing the foil and serve them in their silver wrappings.

STUFFED POTATOES:—To stuff a potato which you have baked cut the baked potatoes in half and scoop out the insides. Mash until softened, then add seasonings and hot milk or hot cream as you would for mashed potatoes. Return the potato to the shell and sprinkle with paprika, chopped parsley, or grated cheese which can then be melted and browned under the broiler.

LUMPLESS MASHED POTATOES:—To make your mashed potatoes fluffy remember to do the mashing job thoroughly with every lump vanquished before adding any liquid. Then add your butter or margarine, seasonings and milk or cream and beat again to blend.

BOILED NEW POTATOES:—Can be seasoned any number of interesting ways. Since you don't want to waste any flavor or goodness you probably boil these babies with their jackets on. Cool just enough to remove skins unless you are going to eat them with the jackets, adding butter on the plate. When skins are removed, the potatoes can be reheated and seasoned by placing in a saucepan in which 4 tablespoons butter or margarine and 1 to 2 teaspoons caraway seeds have been blending. Or roll them in the melted butter over low heat to reheat and be coated with butter, then sprinkle with paprika or finely chopped parsley.

BOILED NEW POTATOES WITH SOUR CREAM:
—Heat 1 cup thick sour cream with ¼ teaspoon cracked peppercorns and 2 teaspoons caraway seeds, crushed or whole. Add the peeled, boiled potatoes to the saucepan, stir over low heat until thoroughly coated and served with bouquets of water cress or parsley on the serving dish.

Try adding ¼ teaspoon rosemary to the butter used in mashed or boiled potatoes.

GERMAN POTATO CAKES
Dr. Irving's

Makes 2 servings

- 6 raw potatoes, coarsely grated
- 1 egg, slightly beaten
- Pepper
- 1 tablespoon flour
- 3 tablespoons bacon drippings
- ½ cup water
- 3 teaspoons salt

Peel and grate the potatoes. Add the egg and pepper and stir until thoroughly mixed and sprinkle with the flour. Place a heavy iron skillet over a hot fire and when the skillet or griddle is very hot add a little of the bacon drippings and a tablespoon of the potato mixture, patting it down to flatten into a thin cake. When browned pick up the cake on a turner and dash a spoonful of salt mixture (made by combining 3 teaspoons salt with ½ cup water) onto the griddle. Place the cake on the griddle brown side up and cover instantly with a pot cover. Cook 2 more minutes, remove cake to hot serving platter and repeat until the potatoes have all been cooked.

FLUFFY BROWNED POTATO BALLS

Cook extra mashed potatoes so as to have some left for fluffy little potato balls. Frozen mashed potatoes are ideal for making these. Shape the balls, brush with beaten egg yolk, sprinkle with paprika and place on greased baking sheet. Bake in 375° oven until well heated through and browned, or deep fry them.

SCALLOPED POTATOES

Makes 4 servings

- 3 cups pared, thin sliced potatoes
- 3 tablespoons butter
- 1½ cups rich milk, heated
- 2 medium-sized onions, sliced
- 3 tablespoons flour
- 1¼ teaspoons salt
- ¼ teaspoon rosemary or basil
- ¼ teaspoon paprika

Place a layer of paper thin raw potato slices in the bottom of an 8-inch buttered casserole, sprinkle with ½ the flour and dot with ½ the butter. Make a layer of onions and cover with another of potatoes and sprinkle with the rest of the flour and dot with butter. Sprinkle with the herb you decided to use. Pour on the hot milk and sprinkle with paprika.

If you want to use more butter in making this it cannot hurt. Bake in a moderate oven (375°) for 1 hour or more until potatoes are tender and the top browned.

RÖSTI

Swiss Pan Browned Potatoes

Makes 6 servings

- 3 cups cold boiled potatoes, grated
- 3 tablespoons butter
- 1 tablespoon bacon drippings
- 1 teaspoon salt
- ½ teaspoon freshly ground pepper

This is a Swiss dish prepared from potatoes which have been boiled in their jackets, if possible on the day before you want to use them. Peel and grate the potatoes, add seasonings and stir lightly. Melt butter and bacon drippings in a heavy skillet, and when hot, dump the potatoes into the pan and press into a smooth cake with the back of a large spoon. Cover and cook over medium heat until heated through, about 8 minutes. Remove cover and continue cooking to form crisp brown crust on bottom, about 5 minutes. Loosen edges with spatula. Place plate over top of skillet and invert to transfer potato cake to serving plate browned side up. The cake should be crusty, brown, hot, and about an inch thick. Cut into wedges for serving.

Half this amount, in a small skillet, is even more easily made and served for two hungry people.

CARAMELIZED POTATOES

Makes 6 servings

- ¼ cup butter or margarine
- 2 tablespoons granulated sugar
- 2 pounds small potatoes, cooked and peeled

Melt the butter in a large skillet, add the sugar and stir over medium heat until the mixture caramelizes to a pale golden brown. Add the potatoes which have been cooked in their jackets and then peeled, or use canned potato balls which have been thoroughly drained. Stir the potatoes in the mixture until they are completely coated, heated and browned and the mixture has been pretty much used up. Serve immediately.

POTATO HERB CASSEROLE

Makes 6 cups

- 4 cups (2 No. 2 cans) potato balls
- 2 teaspoons salt
- 6 slices bacon
- ½ cup flour
- 4 cups rich milk
- 8 small raw white onions, peeled
- ⅛ teaspoon cayenne
- ½ teaspoon pepper
- ¾ cup chopped parsley
- ½ teaspoon rosemary
- ½ cup grated sharp Cheddar cheese

If canned potato balls are used, drain, reserving the liquid for later use in thinning soups. Chop the bacon and cook in a heavy skillet until crisp. Push the bacon aside and add the flour, salt and pepper to the fat. Stir until smooth, add the milk slowly stirring to make a smooth gravy. Add the remaining ingredients (except cheese), stir until mixed and turn into a buttered casserole. Top with grated cheese and bake in moderate oven (350°) until potatoes are tender, about 1 hour.

WHIPPED POTATOES WITH PIMIENTO

Makes 8 servings

- 8 medium-sized potatoes (3 pounds)
- Boiling water to cover
- 1 teaspoon salt
- ¼ cup butter or margarine
- 1 cup rich milk
- 2 tablespoons minced onion
- 1 (4 oz.) can pimiento, chopped

Boil potatoes until tender and cool enough to remove skins. Mash and beat (if with electric beater at low speed) until without lumps. Combine butter, salt and milk in a saucepan and heat before adding to the potato mixture. Pour the hot milk onto the potatoes, add the pimiento and onion and beat until well mixed. Beat the last couple of minutes at high speed to make the potatoes light and fluffy.

GOOD COUNTRY FRIED POTATOES

Makes 4 servings

- 3 tablespoons bacon drippings
- 1 tablespoon butter
- 4 cups sliced potatoes
- ½ cup slivered onions
- 2 teaspoons salt
- ¼ teaspoon freshly ground pepper

The best country fried potatoes are made from cold, boiled potatoes cooked in their jackets. Peel and slice them into the hot bacon drippings and butter which have been melted in a heavy iron skillet. Add the onion and sprinkle with salt and pepper. Watch carefully and stir just enough to keep them from sticking until the potatoes have been turned and browned on all sides. If using uncooked potatoes put the lid on the skillet for a few minutes to give the potatoes a chance to cook through while browning.

SWEET POTATO CECILIA

Makes 6 servings

3 pounds sweet potatoes	¼ teaspoon cinnamon
½ cup butter	Milk
½ cup sherry	Salt
¼ teaspoon nutmeg	Pepper

Boil potatoes in their jackets until soft, peel and put through ricer. Add butter, wine, nutmeg, cinnamon, salt and pepper to taste, and enough milk to moisten. Mix well. Put in buttered baking dish, dot top with butter and sprinkle with cinnamon. Bake in moderate oven (350-375°) until top is browned.

And do you know what my European friends want to eat at my house when they visit this country? This sweet potato dish, topped with marshmallows browned in the oven!

ASPARAGUS

Fresh asparagus is a springtime delight all over the world. In Europe, it is served with such joy and appreciation that its appearance in the market means it shows up on the daily table of everyone who can afford it. In this country we have a frozen and canned supply the year round, but here too it is a tender green delicacy of spring.

One pound of fresh asparagus makes two servings, but you may like to enjoy it as the main course—1 pound per person—when it is at its tender best. Cook it in your glass double-boiler base, stalks standing tips upright, in an inch of salted water. Cover and steam it until a fork will glide into the stalks with ease, about 20 minutes, but do not let tips become too soft.

Asparagus requires many washings to remove sand from the little scales, and the tough base should be cut off and used to enhance the soup pot.

Serving Ideas

Serve cooked asparagus on thin slices of ham on hot buttered toast. Spoon any sauce you like over the top. Hollandaise (*page 101*) is the usual accompaniment. A Cheese Sauce (*page 99*) is good, and ¼ cup sherry for each cup cheese sauce can be served over the asparagus.

Arrange asparagus tips in neat overlapping rows so that the tips of the asparagus can be seen. Sprinkle with grated Swiss or Gruyère cheese, then with butter which has been melted until lightly browned. Place under the broiler for 2 or 3 minutes to soften the cheese before serving.

Sprinkle the asparagus with browned melted butter and grate whole hard-cooked eggs over it so that both the white and yolk will add a decorative appearance. Or, cool and serve with your favorite French dressing. Garnish with strips of pimiento.

Sprinkle asparagus, arranged on a platter, with melted browned butter and crisp bacon bits.

Serve White Sauce (*page 99*) either plain or curried, over the asparagus.

ARTICHOKES

Makes 6 servings

6 tender fresh artichokes	1 clove garlic
Boiling water to cover	2 teaspoons salt

Prepare artichokes by washing in several waters or rinsing under running water. Add garlic and salt to boiling water and drop the artichokes into the water. Cover and cook until tender enough for a leaf to be easily pulled from stalk, about 20 minutes for small ones, twice that long for very large artichokes. Remove from water, drain, place upright on salad plates and serve with French Dressing (*page 192*). Or, serve small cups of melted butter for dipping each leaf into as it is removed to be eaten.

Variations

The French like to cool the artichokes, then press the leaves open to give a flowerlike appearance on the salad plate. Remove thistle-like center, exposing the delicious heart, and sprinkle with French Dressing (*page 192*).

Another idea that is strictly French is to leave a small fence of the leaves around the heart when trimming the heart for cooking. When they are tender and the choke removed, the center cavity is filled with minced cooked meat on mushrooms or chopped chicken livers moistened with Mayonnaise (*page 193*).

ARTICHOKES A LA MIREILLE:—Select 4 small artichokes. Remove hard outer leaves. Combine in a saucepan with 8 small peeled onions and 2 quartered tomatoes. Add ⅓ cup olive or salad oil and 1 cup chicken broth. Cover tightly, cook over medium heat 30 minutes. Cool and serve as they are with the sauce in the pan.

ARTICHOKE BASES:—Cook large artichokes, remove leaves and "choke," to secure large hearts. Serve these sprinkled with French Dressing (*page 192*) or stuff by piling mounds of any vegetables in White Sauce (*page 99*). Top with grated cheese and brown under broiler.

BROCCOLI ESPAGNOLE

Makes 4 servings

1½ pounds broccoli	12 ripe black olives, cut in swirls off the seeds
½ cup olive oil	
1 large clove garlic, cut in half	½ teaspoon salt
	¼ teaspoon freshly ground pepper
2 teaspoons lemon juice	

While cooking the broccoli combine the other ingredients. Cover and allow them to stand until the broccoli is tender. Place over low heat, stir until thoroughly hot, remove garlic and pour mixture over the broccoli after it is in a heated serving dish.

BRUSSELS SPROUTS WITH CHESTNUTS

Makes 4 servings

2 cups Brussels sprouts, cooked	3 tablespoons butter
	½ cup chicken stock
½ pound cooked chestnuts	Salt and pepper to taste

Cook Brussels sprouts by dropping into rapidly boiling water. Reduce heat and cook uncovered until tender, about 10 minutes. Drop the chestnuts while in their shells in another saucepan of boiling water and reduce heat and continue cooking for 15 minutes. This should enable you to remove them from their shells. Arrange alternate layers of drained Brussels sprouts and chestnuts in a buttered casserole. Dot with butter and moisten with the chicken broth. Bake uncovered in a moderate oven (375°) for 30 minutes.

BEETS SAUTERNE

Makes 6 servings

- ½ cup sugar
- 4 tablespoons lemon juice
- ½ tablespoon cornstarch
- 2 tablespoons salad oil or melted butter
- ¼ cup water or dry sauterne
- 2½ cups cooked beets (tiny, whole ones sliced or slivered)

Combine first five ingredients in a saucepan. Bring to a boil and cook for 5 minutes before stirring in the cooked beets. Stir until well mixed, reduce heat and cover, allowing to heat gently for 20 minutes.

BUTTERED BOILED BEETS

Makes 6 servings

- 3 bunches fresh beets
- Boiling salted water to cover
- 2 tablespoons butter or margarine
- 1 teaspoon lemon juice

Cut off all beet tops to within 3 inches of beets, leaving these on to prevent "bleeding" as they cook. Drop into the boiling salted water, cover, and continue cooking until tender, about 30 minutes for small beets. Drain, drench with cold water, slide skins off the beets. Melt butter in saucepan, return beets to pan for reheating and roll them around in the hot butter. Sprinkle with lemon juice and serve.

CABBAGE WITH CARAWAY SEEDS

Makes 6 servings

1 large firm head cabbage, coarsely shredded	1 tablespoon caraway seeds
Boiling water	3 tablespoons butter or margarine
1½ teaspoons salt	

Wash and shred the cabbage. Pour water into a large saucepan so that it is ½ inch deep in the pan. Add salt and bring to a boil. Add cabbage and cook uncovered over high heat, stirring once or twice, until barely tender, 5 to 8 minutes. Turn into serving dish, add butter and caraway seeds, toss lightly and serve quickly. Cabbage is so hopping full of such temperamental vitamins that it requires rapid handling if they are to be preserved.

CARROTS

Makes 6 servings

2 bunches carrots, sliced or shredded	Boiling water
1½ teaspoons salt	2 tablespoons butter or margarine

Prepare carrots by washing, removing tops, and slicing or shredding. Tiny new carrots can be left whole and, on the rare occasion when they are available, you would need 4 bunches instead of 2 of the regular size. Add salt to 1 inch of boiling water in large saucepan. Cover, cook until tender, 10 minutes for sliced or shredded, about 20 for whole. Remove, drain, reserving liquid for soup pot, add butter and serve.

Variations

Arrange cooked carrots which have been mixed

with White Sauce (*page 99*) either plain or curried, in a round dish making a well in the center. Fill center with cooked peas.

A carrot and pea arrangement is also beautiful when the two vegetables are cooked perfectly and minted by adding fresh chopped or dried mint just before serving the buttered unsauced vegetables.

VICHY CARROTS:—Are cooked in butter. Season, add a sprinkling of white or brown sugar during the cooking, and when ready to serve sprinkle generously with chopped parsley.

CORN PUDDING

Makes 6 servings

- 2 cups corn, cut off cob (or creamed, canned corn)
- 2 eggs, slightly beaten
- 2 tablespoons melted butter
- 1 teaspoon sugar
- 2 cups scalded milk
- 1 teaspoon salt
- ¼ teaspoon pepper

Combine all ingredients and mix thoroughly. Pour into a well greased casserole. Place in a pan of hot water and bake in a slow oven (325°) until firm or when a knife comes out clean when it pierces the center—about 45 minutes.

CORN FRITTERS

Makes 6 servings

- 1 cup corn, cut off cob (or canned corn kernels)
- 1 egg yolk, well beaten
- 10 tablespoons flour
- ½ teaspoon salt
- ½ teaspoon baking powder
- ¼ teaspoon paprika
- 1 egg white, stiffly beaten

Drain the corn, stir in the egg yolk. Combine dry ingredients, sift once and add to the corn mixture.

Beat the egg white until it holds stiff peaks, then fold gently into the batter. Drop by spoonfuls into hot fat which has been heated to 375° and fry until golden brown. Drain on paper towels.

BAKED EARS OF CORN IN HUSKS

Makes 6 servings

- 6 ears of tender corn, in their husks
- Water to cover
- ½ pound butter or margarine, melted

Loosen the ends of the husks on each ear of corn and remove silk. Cover with water, leave for 10 minutes, remove and drain. Place in roasting pan and bake at 400° 1 hour. Exceptionally large ears, not so tender, may take 5 additional minutes. Remove and serve with small bowls of melted butter.

Roast these over a bed of coals if you are barbecuing, allowing 20 minutes for small ears, 30 for large ones.

EGGPLANT PROVENÇALE

Makes 6 servings

- 1 eggplant, peeled and sliced
- ½ cup flour
- 4 tomatoes, sliced
- ¼ cup butter or margarine
- 1 teaspoon salt
- 1 clove garlic, slivered

Dip eggplant slices in flour and brown in a skillet in which some of the butter has been melted. Sauté tomato slices in another skillet. Sprinkle each vegetable with salt and with the garlic slivers. When slices are browned, combine in hot serving bowl and garnish with ½ cup coarsely chopped parsley.

CHILI STUFFED EGGPLANT

Makes 6 servings

- 1 (1½ pound) eggplant
- ¼ cup diced onion
- 1 tablespoon margarine or butter
- 1 pound cooked shrimp
- ¼ cup fine dry bread crumbs
- 1 raw egg yolk
- 1 teaspoon salt
- 2 teaspoons chili powder
- ¼ teaspoon ground black pepper
- 1 tablespoon dry parsley flakes
- ½ cup soft bread crumbs
- 1 tablespoon margarine or butter, melted

Cut eggplant in half, lengthwise. Parboil 15 minutes in 1 inch of boiling water. Remove from pan. Scoop out pulp to within ½ inch of the skin and chop fine. Sauté onion in margarine or butter. Mix with eggplant and shrimp, broken into pieces. Blend in bread crumbs, egg yolk and seasonings. Fill eggplant shells with this mixture, then sprinkle with soft bread crumbs mixed with the melted margarine or butter. Bake in preheated 400° oven until brown, 20 to 30 minutes.

MARINATED MUSHROOMS

Makes 3 cups

- 4 (3 oz.) cans broiled mushroom caps
- 2 cloves garlic, minced
- ½ cup olive or salad oil
- ¼ cup wine vinegar or sherry

Drain the mushroom cups being sure to store the broth for thinning canned soup. Combine all ingredients in a refrigerator dish which can be covered. Leave in refrigerator at least 24 hours and serve these as garnish around molded salads or as a tantalizer on a hors d'oeuvre tray.

Variations

FRESH MUSHROOM CAPS:—Remove stems and chop and sauté in butter and add to your scrambled breakfast eggs. Prepare the caps by simmering in water to cover, to which you have added a little lemon juice and salt. Cook for 5 minutes, drain and place caps in the marinade recommended for the canned mushrooms (see Marinated Mushrooms, *page 89*).

This recipe is easily cut in half or in fourths for smaller amounts but since it is a dish that will keep for several days the large quantity is recommended.

MUSHROOMS WITH THICK CREAM:—Select large mushrooms, wipe them with a damp cloth and remove stems. Place in a shallow, well greased baking dish stem sides up. Sprinkle with salt and pepper, dot with butter and pour enough white wine or milk into the baking dish to make ⅛ inch layer of liquid in the pan. Bake 10 minutes at 450°. Remove, place on dry toast and cover with thick cream which has been heated to the boiling point but not allowed to boil. Sprinkle with paprika.

STUFFED MUSHROOMS

Makes 8 mushroom caps

- 8 large mushrooms
- 2 tablespoons butter
- 1 tablespoon chopped onion
- ½ cup thick White Sauce (page 99)
- ¼ teaspoon nutmeg
- Chopped parsley
- Salt
- Pepper
- Cooked chicken livers, ham or sausage, finely chopped or ground
- Fine bread crumbs, buttered

Wipe the mushrooms; remove stems, and put caps aside. Combine the butter, onion and chopped stems in a small saucepan and sauté over medium heat 8 minutes. Add white sauce, nutmeg and season with salt and pepper to taste. Cool. Now add half as much cooked chopped chicken livers or finely ground ham or sausage as you have cream sauce mixture. Cook another 5 minutes to heat thoroughly and fill the cavities of the mushrooms. Sprinkle with the fine buttered bread crumbs and parsley and place in a greased baking dish. Bake in 425° oven for 15 minutes.

The mushroom caps can also be filled with uncooked sausage meat and then baked at 375° until the sausage is cooked, about 25 minutes.

ONIONS

Onions are probably used by more people all over the world than any other single vegetable. They are certainly the most popular of all seasonings used to enhance the flavor of almost any dish except desserts. Onions are delicious raw in salads or in sandwiches; they are delicate when cooked; they are out of this world when sliced, dipped in batter and crisped in deep hot fat; and they earn our admiration when limply sautéed in butter as part of many a good stew or fish concoction.

This is one vegetable you may want to buy already cooked in the can, if you want whole tiny cooked ones. Or nobly peel them and boil in salted water about 35 minutes, or pressure cook in 5 minutes.

FRENCH FRIED ONION RINGS

Makes 4 servings

- 1 egg, beaten
- 2 cups milk
- 1½ cups flour, sifted
- ¼ teaspoon salt
- ¼ teaspoon cayenne
- ⅔ cup milk or cream or evaporated milk
- ½ teaspoon baking powder
- ½ teaspoon marjoram
- 1 teaspoon MSG*
- 1 tablespoon sugar
- 3 sweet Bermuda onions
- 1¼ cups flour

Make batter by adding 2 cups milk to beaten egg. Combine salt, cayenne, baking powder, marjoram, MSG and sugar with flour and sift. Add to egg mixture and beat until smooth.

Peel onions, slice and separate into rings. Dip each ring in the milk or cream, then in extra flour, and drop into the batter. Repeat until all the rings are in the batter. Cover and chill until ready to fry, or crisp immediately. Pick up each ring with tongs and drop into the hot deep fat. Cook about ⅓ at a time until golden brown. Lift onto paper towel to drain. Sprinkle with salt. Keep warm in the oven until all the rings are browned. Serve hot. If using electric deep fryer, turn dial to 375°, remove basket, and fry for about 4 minutes.

ONIONS WITH CHOPPED PEANUTS

Makes 4 servings

- 1½ tablespoons butter or margarine
- 1½ tablespoons flour
- ½ teaspoon salt
- ¼ teaspoon freshly ground pepper
- 1½ cups rich milk
- 2 cups cooked whole onions, or canned, drained
- ¾ cup finely chopped peanuts
- ¼ cup fine buttered bread crumbs, toasted

* MSG is Monosodium glutamate, marketed under trade-names Accent and Enhance.

Melt the butter or margarine, blend in the flour and seasonings. Add milk and cook slowly until thickened, stirring constantly. Pour the cooked onions into a well-greased baking dish (bacon drippings are best for greasing). Pour sauce over the onions, sprinkle with the peanuts and the toasted buttered bread crumbs. Brown in a hot oven (400°) for about 20 minutes.

Variations

This is good without the browned top and a purely de luxe dish when thick cream has been spooned over the onions together with ¼ teaspoon dried marjoram. Cover and let stand for at least 15 minutes, return to heat and stir until thoroughly hot. Pour into hot serving dish and sprinkle the top with finely chopped or grated nuts which have been heated to insure their being crisp.

MARINATED ONIONS (RED)

Peel and slice red onions into a flat bowl. Cover with 2 parts Burgundy wine and 1 part vinegar, add as much olive or salad oil as you have liquid. For each 1½ cups of marinating juice this gives you add 1 tablespoon sugar, 1 teaspoon salt and 1 teaspoon dry mustard with 1 or 2 cloves of minced garlic. If you have an electric blender put marinade in the container and turn the machine on for ½ minute before pouring over the onions. Cover snugly and let stand overnight or all day.

You can also fill half the bowl with sliced fresh tomatoes for the marinating job and arrange them to be served together.

MARINATED BERMUDA SLICES

Make marinade as for Marinated Onions (Red) *page 93* using white dry wine, a good Chablis or similar white wine icy cold instead of the vinegar and Burgundy. Add ¼ teaspoon marjoram if you like. Use this for marinating thick slices of sweet Bermuda onion which have been peeled. Leave in marinade several hours. Drain and serve very cold.

ONIONS À LA ARABIAN NIGHTS

Makes 4 servings

- 1 pound small white onions, peeled
- 1½ cups sweet red peppers, seeded and thinly sliced
- ½ cup dry white wine
- ¼ cup olive or salad oil
- 1 teaspoon garlic salt
- Few grains cayenne pepper
- ¼ teaspoon freshly ground black pepper
- ¼ cup seedless raisins

Prepare the red pepper slices and place in a shallow buttered baking dish. Cover with the little white onions which have had a toothpick placed through them sidewise to keep them from falling apart. Combine oil, wine and seasonings and pour over the onions. If more liquid is needed to cover, add water. Cover tightly and bake in moderate oven (350°) 35 minutes. Remove onions and peppers to a hot serving dish. Pour the liquid into a saucepan, add raisins and boil until the liquid is reduced sufficiently for saucing the onions. Remove toothpicks, and serve onions hot or cool, or chill and serve icy cold. (The white wine can be replaced with lemon juice and water or with wine vinegar and water half and half.)

PEAS DE LUXE

Makes 8 servings

- 4 cups shelled green peas
- ⅓ cup butter
- 2 tablespoons chicken broth
- ½ teaspoon sugar
- 1 teaspoon salt
- ⅛ teaspoon cayenne
- 2 small heads lettuce, cut into 8 wedges
- 16 small white onions
- 1½ cups cream

This is the way the French prepare peas in Northern France, and the cooking resembles the Chinese insistence on little liquid.

Place everything except the cream in a large skillet which can be tightly covered. Place over moderate heat and cook until the peas are tender, about 15 minutes. Meanwhile, pour the cream into a small saucepan and bring it to a boil. Continue cooking until the cream is reduced to half the original amount. Arrange the lettuce quarters around the edge of a hot platter or large serving bowl with the little onions in between each serving of lettuce. Turn contents of skillet into the cream, stir over heat until blended. Make a mound of the peas-in-cream in the center of the bowl and serve.

FRIED TOMATOES

Makes 6 servings

- 6 firm tomatoes, ripe or green
- 1 egg
- 1 tablespoon cold water
- Finely sifted seasoned bread crumbs
- 4 tablespoons butter or bacon drippings
- 2 tablespoons flour
- 1½ cups sour cream
- 1 tablespoon chopped parsley

Wash the tomatoes, remove the thin slice from the stem end and slice the rest of the tomatoes about ½ inch thick. Beat the egg slightly, add the water. Dip the tomatoes in the egg mixture, roll in bread crumbs which have been seasoned to taste with salt and pepper. Allow the coated tomatoes to dry a little before frying in hot fat over medium heat. Brown on both sides. Lift onto hot platter, sprinkle the flour over the fat in the pan, mix well then add cream. Stir, cooking over low heat until thickened. Season if necessary, pour over tomatoes and sprinkle with parsley. Now I don't have to add, do I, "serve at once"!

TURNIPS or RUTABAGAS

Makes 6 servings

- 3 pounds turnips or rutabagas
- 1 cup boiling water
- 1½ teaspoons salt
- 3 tablespoons butter or margarine

Remove tops, cooking them separately as another vegetable. Scrub, peel and chop vegetable, dice or slice, cook in salted water, covered, until tender, about 15 minutes. Add butter and serve.

Variations

Cook 2 cups peeled diced turnips in salted water until tender. Remove turnips to hot serving dish. Season liquid remaining in the pan with 2 tablespoons butter and 1 tablespoon prepared mustard. Cook until blended, about 4 minutes, and pour over turnips stirring until each piece is coated.

Make seasoned mashed turnips by adding ½ teaspoon caraway seeds, crushed, and 1 tablespoon chopped onion for each cup of turnips. After the first 10 minutes of cooking when turnips are tender add butter or a little cream and mash until light and fluffy. Return to heat until thoroughly heated through and serve with crisp French Fried Onion Rings (*page 92*) for good company.

When serving yellow turnips with turkey for a holiday meal add ½ cup crushed pineapple, juice and fruit, for each 2 cups of mashed turnips. Mix thoroughly, return to heat and stir until you are sure it is piping hot for serving.

In France, turnips are pared into attractive oblong *noisettes* when vegetables are arranged around beef or veal or duck which is to be coated with clear aspic.

One of the most delicious additions to a tossed,

crisp, mixed salad are the coarsely grated or thinly sliced slivers of white raw turnip.

PURÉE OF TURNIP

Makes 6 servings

- 6 white turnips, medium size
- 1 teaspoon salt
- ½ teaspoon caraway seeds
- ¾ cup onions, thinly sliced (or coarsely chopped)
- ¼ cup butter
- ⅓ cup chopped parsley
- 1 teaspoon lemon juice
- 2 tablespoons cold butter

Place the turnips, unpeeled, in a large saucepan; cover with water and add the salt and caraway seeds. Cook for 15 minutes. Remove from heat, drain, peel, dice and return to saucepan. Add ¼ cup water, cover tightly and continue cooking over low heat for another 10 minutes stirring occasionally.

Melt the ¼ cup butter in a skillet and add the onions. Cook over low heat until the onions are translucent but not browned, then add the parsley and lemon juice. The turnips, by this time, should be tender. Mash or put in electric blender and run machine 1 minute. Pile turnips into a serving dish, dot with the cold butter and garnish with the sautéed onions. Serve hot with duck or a crown roast of lamb, as they do in England and in France.

Herb Flavoring for Vegetables

Use herbs sparingly, to emphasize the flavors of vegetables but not to overwhelm them. Begin by adding no more than ¼ teaspoon of the herb you want to the liquid in which the vegetable is cooking. Herbs become bitter if cooked too long, but if vegetables are properly cooked the herbs can be added along with the other seasonings of salt and pepper when put on to cook. You can also add herbs to the melted butter to be used for saucing the vegetable, but the herb flavor penetrates the vegetable best when cooked with it. Scatter seeds generously on the cooked vegetable if you want them crisp; cook vegetable with herbs or seeds if you want their flavor.

Season:

    Artichokes with tarragon

    Asparagus with savory or thyme

    Green snap beans with rosemary, sage, thyme, savory or nutmeg.

    Lima beans with savory, thyme, nutmeg or chopped mint

    Broccoli with oregano

    Cabbage with oregano, savory or caraway seeds

    Beets with tarragon, celery or poppy seeds

    Cauliflower by sprinkling with paprika after cooking

    Celery by sprinkling with paprika after cooking

    Carrots with thyme, chopped mint or dry mustard

    Eggplant with basil or marjoram

    Leeks with oregano, rosemary or savory, and paprika

    Onions with marjoram, oregano, sage or thyme

    Peas with marjoram, rosemary, tarragon, savory or chopped mint

    Potatoes with basil or rosemary, and paprika

    Rice with basil or through cooking with juices recommended with Rice recipes (*page* 47)

    Squash with basil or oregano

    Tomatoes with basil, oregano, sage or thyme

Sauces for Vegetables

Sauces can add to the appearance of vegetables, can be folded into the cooked vegetable, can be served separately or poured over the vegetable after cooking. Cheese sauces also provide a beautiful glazed top when browned under the broiler.

ALMOND BUTTER SAUCE

Makes 1 cup

> ½ cup butter or margarine
> ½ cup slivered blanched almonds
> 3 tablespoons lemon juice

Melt butter or margarine in a heavy pan and add the slivered almonds. Stir over medium heat until almond slivers are a golden brown. Add the lemon juice and pour over cooked broccoli, cauliflower, celery or green beans julienne.

CHEESE SAUCE

Makes 1 cup

> ½ pound processed American cheese
> ⅓ cup evaporated milk

Put cheese in top of double boiler, place over boiling water and stir until melted. Add the milk, continue to stir and pour over almost any fresh cooked vegetable.

WHITE SAUCE

This recipe for white sauce is given to use over vegetables which can be drained. The thick sauce is stirred into an equal amount of vegetable juice.

If you want your sauces thinner you can always thin them with chicken broth instead of vegetable juice or with dry white wine when you are being fancy, but always be sure the mixture is stirred over heat until thoroughly hot.

Makes 2½ cups

½ cup butter
1½ tablespoons minced onion
7 tablespoons flour
2 cups rich milk or undiluted evaporated milk
Salt and pepper to taste

Melt butter in saucepan, add onion and cook until tender. Add flour and stir until blended. Add milk gradually and cook over medium heat until mixture is thickened, stirring constantly. Season with salt and pepper.

Serve blended with equal amount of vegetable juice, over vegetables except strong-flavored ones such as broccoli, brussels sprouts, cauliflower and spinach. For these or other strong-flavored vegetables you will want a thinner white sauce made exactly the same except for doubling the amount of milk used.

SWISS CHEESE SAUCE

A delicate mild flavored sauce you can serve with many vegetable, egg and fish dishes. As a glaze for *au gratin* dishes, it will turn into a beautiful even golden brown.

Makes 2 cups

2 tablespoons butter
2 tablespoons flour
1½ cups milk
1 egg yolk
1 teaspoon salt
⅛ teaspoon cayenne pepper
½ cup (about 2 oz.) Swiss cheese, grated

Melt butter in saucepan, add flour and stir over low fire until well blended. Thin gradually with the milk and cook, while stirring, for about 10 minutes. Remove from fire and beat in egg yolk. Add seasoning and cheese and stir until cheese has been completely dissolved.

For *Mornay Sauce* add ¼ cup (about 1 oz.) cubed Swiss cheese.

If either sauce is used for glazing *au gratin* dishes, add 2 tablespoons heavy cream, whipped, before spreading over dish to be glazed.

DUTCH CRUMBS

Makes 1 cup

> ½ cup dry bread crumbs
> ½ cup butter or margarine

Melt butter or margarine in skillet, add crumbs. Heat together until lightly browned. Sprinkle over freshly cooked vegetables such as asparagus, green beans, broccoli and cauliflower.

HERBED CRUMBS

Make Dutch Crumbs (*page 101*) and stir in ¼ to ½ teaspoon of the herb you decide to use with the vegetable the crumbs are to be sprinkled on.

HOLLANDAISE SAUCE

Makes about ¾ cup

> ¼ pound butter or margarine
> 3 egg yolks, beaten
> 3 tablespoons fresh lemon juice

Cut butter or margarine in small pieces. Put in top of double boiler. Put the egg yolks in and lemon juice and let stand at room temperature for ½ hour.

Just before serving place over gently boiling water for 1½ minutes stirring briskly. Serve over freshly cooked asparagus, broccoli, carrots or artichokes.

LEMON BUTTER

Makes ¾ cup

> ½ cup butter or margarine, softened
> ⅓ cup lemon juice
> 1 teaspoon sweet paprika

Blend ingredients together. Serve over freshly cooked asparagus, broccoli, cabbage, cauliflower or artichokes.

WINE BUTTER SAUCE

Makes ½ cup

> ¼ cup butter or margarine
> ¼ cup dry red or white wine or sherry
> Salt to taste

Combine in a small saucepan. Stir until hot and blended and serve over any vegetables which you would serve buttered.

OLIVE CREAM SAUCE

Makes 1 cup

> 1 cup condensed cream of chicken soup
> 2 teaspoons lemon juice
> ⅛ teaspoon paprika
> ¼ teaspoon celery salt
> ½ teaspoon Worcestershire sauce
> 8 ripe or green stuffed olives, seeded and sliced

Combine all ingredients. Stir and serve hot with cooked fresh spinach.

HOT SOUR CREAM SAUCE

- 1 cup sour cream
- 1 tablespoon butter
- 1 tablespoon flour
- ¼ teaspoon salt
- ¼ to ½ teaspoon herb appropriate for the vegetable (optional)

Blend the butter and flour in a saucepan, add the cream and salt. Stir over low heat until thickened and heated through, stirring constantly, or cook in the top of a double boiler. Serve over asparagus, broccoli, cauliflower or potatoes. Finely chopped parsley, chives or red or green peppers may be added to vary the flavor and to give it an attractive appearance.

PEANUT BUTTER SAUCE

Makes 1 cup

- 1 tablespoon butter or margarine
- ¼ cup peanut butter
- 2 tablespoons flour
- ½ teaspoon salt
- ¼ teaspoon freshly ground pepper
- 1 cup rich milk or undiluted evaporated milk

Melt butter or margarine in the top of a double boiler over rapidly boiling water. Add peanut butter and stir until blended. Add flour and seasonings and stir until smooth, then add the milk slowly, continuing to stir. Cook until thickened to the consistency you like, stirring constantly. Serve on cooked cabbage, onions or cauliflower.

7

Fine Meat Dishes ... Beautifully Presented

Beef

BEEF IN ASPIC JELLY

French

In our country a rib roast of beef is considered the last word in fine food, unless there is a sirloin steak or perhaps a beautiful thick filet mignon. Whichever we enjoy, the meat is the thing. Roast potatoes and gravy is all anyone would ask for.

The French have different ideas. When they love a thing they plant a flower garden around it. And how they love *Boeuf en Gelée*, as tender a delight as anyone ever tasted. This is a tenderloin of beef, larded, simmered, surrounded by colorful vegetables prepared or cooked in uniform sizes, then the whole glazed with aspic which has been made from broth out of the stock pot. The stock is cleared by the use of 6 egg whites. Since the process is one which takes a whole morning—a pleasure no French man or woman would dream of making more brief—this recipe and its name are Americanized. But the beef is equally good, despite the speed-up system.

BEEF TENDERLOIN IN ASPIC

Makes 12 servings

- 6-pound beef tenderloin, larded and tied
- Water to cover
- Cracked beef bone and veal knuckle
- 2 or 3 onions
- 2 carrots
- ½ bunch parsley
- 1 cubed potato
- 1 tablespoon salt
- 1 tablespoon MSG*
- 1 teaspoon cracked pepper

Ask your meat man to wrap the tenderloin of beef in a thin layer of fat—or, do it yourself, tying it securely with a heavy string wrapped round and round the meat. Put the meat in a large pot, cover with water, add vegetables, add bones and seasonings. Bring to a boil, cover, reduce heat and simmer over very low heat until beef is tender (about 3 hours). Allow meat to cool in the broth. Remove beef, boil broth rapidly to reduce amount or add water to produce 3 cups strong broth. Strain through fine strainer lined with a double piece of cheese cloth.

ASPIC JELLY

- 1 envelope unflavored gelatin
- 1 cup cold water
- 3 cups seasoned broth
- 6 large black olives, seeded and sliced
- 2 hard-cooked eggs, sliced

Soften gelatin in cold water, add to hot broth and stir until dissolved. Pour ¼-inch layer of liquid into 9 x 5 x 3-inch loaf pan. Chill until consistency of unbeaten egg white. Alternate egg and olive slices down center of gelatin, pressing them into the aspic. Chill until set, then place beef, which has had string and fat wrapping removed, in the pan. Warm remaining gelatin mixture, if it has begun to congeal, and

* See footnote, page 92.

pour over meat until pan is full. If any aspic remains, pour into square pan and chill, at least 3 hours.

Presentation is important. Unmold the aspic loaf on a platter, surround it with colorful garnish molds, small whole tomatoes, or bunches of water cress or parsley flowerettes. Salad molds, relish molds, or attractive vegetables are appropriate. If extra aspic was left to chill in a pan, chop it as if it were a solid, with a knife on a chopping board, and spoon the amber sparklers into mounds at the base of the aspic.

Presenting Filet Mignon

Any aspic-glazed meat, fowl or fish is always painstakingly garnished by women all over Europe, for an occasion. But they do not entertain as much as we do. However, when friends or family do arrive to feast, they certainly find one.

Filet mignon is often served accompanied by small flutted pastry shells holding a vegetable or an artichoke heart topped with an attractive sauce. If no garnish appeared on top of the filet, it was probably seared on a ridged griddle on top of the stove, similar to our bacon griddles. Turn the filet so that browned lines will be made each way as the meat cooks. The result is most attractive.

TOURNEDOS

Like our Filet Mignon, Tournedos are remarkable in France, where the obeisance they receive is the only familiar thing about them. The French have done for filet mignon what the English did for beef in their roasts of beef and in their Steak and Kidney Pie *(page 108)*.

In the text book I used at the *Cordon Bleu* twenty "Tournedos" were listed, each presented with some distinguished style.

FINE MEAT DISHES ... BEAUTIFULLY PRESENTED

Cook Tournedos on top of the stove. You can cook them as the French do, in a copper saucepan on top of the stove, turning once. When blood shows it's ready to eat. Tournedos are nearly always served on shaped oblongs of bread fried in butter. After broiling or sautéeing in butter and placing on the hot fried bread, these are some of the variations you might use:

BÉARNAISE:—Edged with a ribbon of Béarnaise Sauce (*page 132*), and with fluffy mashed potatoes artistically arranged between each serving on the platter.

MONTMORENCY:—An artichoke heart or pastry shell filled with asparagus tips in butter is placed on top each filet mignon after it has been cooked and placed on its bread oblong. Madeira Sauce (*page 131*) is then poured over the Tournedos.

ROSSINI:—Filets are topped by a slice of *pâté de foie gras* and a slice of truffle (you could use a mushroom slice) and covered with a spoonful of a brown gravy sauce simmered in the pan with a little Madeira wine, after the filets are cooked. Garnish with water cress bunches which serve as a vegetable at the meal, along with potatoes.

MISTRAL:—The filets are served on a platter with Eggplant Provençale (*page 88*).

GABRIELLE:—The sautéed filets on the fried bread oblong appear on a platter, each one bearing a stuffed mushroom cap on top (*page 90*) and well moistened with Madeira Sauce (*page 131*). A half head of braised lettuce and a mound of crisp potato cakes (*page 77*), each about the size of a walnut, are between each "Tournedos."

BRISKET OF BEEF WITH HORSERADISH SAUCE

Makes 12 servings

6 pounds brisket, in one piece	Vegetable bunch, celery stalk and leaves, 2 quartered onions, carrot, parsley
Veal knuckle	
Beef bone, cracked	
1 tablespoon salt	
12 peppercorns	

Put bones in bottom of large kettle, place meat on top of them and cover with water. Place over high heat until it begins to boil. Reduce heat, cover, and simmer over very low heat 3 hours. Add seasonings and vegetable bunch, cover and continue cooking over low heat until tender, about 1 more hour. Remove beef to large bowl, and reduce broth by boiling over high heat until a rich, well-flavored broth is secured, about 20 minutes. Pour broth to cover meat, pouring through strainer. Remove bones and vegetables. Strain rest of broth to use for making a Steak and Kidney Pie (*page 108*).

Serve beef hot, with prepared horseradish slightly thinned with some of the broth or mixed with thick sour cream. Remainder of beef is excellent served cold, with the sauce. Or, thicken broth by softening 1 envelope unflavored gelatin in ½ cup of the cold broth. Heat 1½ cups of the broth, add softened gelatin to hot broth and stir until dissolved. Pour over beef in a loaf pan, cool and chill overnight. Slice and serve with the sauce.

STEAK AND KIDNEY PIE

Makes 8 servings

4 pounds top round beef, cut in 2-inch cubes	⅓ cup bacon drippings
1 pound beef kidneys	1 stick butter
½ cup flour	Rich beef broth
	2 teaspoons salt

FINE MEAT DISHES ... BEAUTIFULLY PRESENTED 109

½ teaspoon cracked pepper	1 tablespoon Bovril
¼ teaspoon cayenne	2 cups rich beef broth
4 tablespoons flour	2-cup recipe for biscuits

Cube the beef and cut the kidneys into pieces when removing all the white portion. Melt bacon fat and butter in large skillet. Put ½ cup flour in paper bag, add beef and kidney and shake until lightly coated. Brown in the hot fat, turning to brown evenly. Remove browned pieces to pressure cooker, add broth instead of the required water, cover, and cook at 15 pounds pressure 45 minutes. (Or brown beef and kidney slices in Dutch oven, add rich beef broth to depth of 1 inch, cover tightly and simmer over low heat on top of the range or bake in 325° oven until tender, about 3 hours. Proceed with finishing as directed following pressure cooker method.) When cool, remove meat to casserole. Add seasonings, 4 tablespoons flour and 2 cups beef broth to fat in cooker. Stir until blended. Add Bovril. Stir until smooth and slightly thickened. Pour over the meat.

Use prepared biscuit mix and undiluted evaporated milk to make drop biscuit dough. Follow package directions. Shape on aluminum foil to fit casserole, turn onto meat, remove foil. Pull dough to edge of casserole dish with fork and make rough marks on top. Pierce with a sharp knife in two or three places to make steam vents. Bake as directed, until biscuit topping is baked through and brown.

BEEF BURGUNDY CASSEROLE

Makes 6 servings

2½ pounds lean beef, chuck or round	3 tablespoons flour
2 tablespoons butter	2 teaspoons salt
2 tablespoons bacon drippings	½ teaspoon freshly ground pepper
	1 bay leaf

1 teaspoon thyme
1 clove garlic, minced
1 (No. 2) can small whole onions
1 (No. 303) can tiny whole potatoes
1 (No. 2) can whole carrots
Vegetable liquid plus water to make 2 cups
1 cup Burgundy or other dry red wine
2 tablespoons butter
1 tablespoon sugar
¾ cup Madeira wine
¼ cup brandy

Cut the meat into 2-inch cubes. They should be large because this is a superb company-type, wine-flavored stew. Combine butter and bacon drippings in a heavy skillet. Place over medium heat. Add meat cubes and stir until browned on all sides. Remove meat to a Dutch oven or a casserole. Add flour, seasonings and garlic to the fat in the skillet, stir until the flour is delicately browned and add the vegetable liquid. Stir until the mixture begins to thicken. Add the red wine and stir until blended. Pour this gravy over the meat in the casserole. Cover and simmer over low heat or bake in (350°) oven for 2 hours.

Melt 2 tablespoons butter in a skillet, add sugar and the drained vegetables, stir until lightly browned. Add to the casserole along with the Madeira wine. Cover and cook until the meat is tender, about another hour. Add brandy, stir and cover the casserole until ready to serve.

SWEDISH POT ROAST

Makes 8 servings

4 pounds pot roast, chuck, 4-inches thick
Tenderizer
1 tablespoon salt
½ teaspoon black pepper, freshly ground
2 medium-sized Spanish onions, sliced
1 clove garlic, minced
3 tablespoons shortening
1¼ cups thick sour cream
1 cup water
5 ounce package noodles, cooked

Put the beef on a platter and sprinkle on each side with Tenderizer. Allow it to stand 30 to 45 minutes before cooking. Sprinkle with the salt and pepper. Melt the shortening in a Dutch oven, or heavy pot with a snug fitting cover, and sauté onion slices in garlic until lightly browned. Push them to one side, and add the meat to the pot, turning to brown thoroughly on each side. Combine sour cream with water and pour over the meat. Top with the browned onions and cover, cooking over low heat for 2½ to 3 hours or until tender. The pot roast can also be baked in an oven (325°) for the same length of time.

When the roast is tender remove from the pan, make gravy from drippings and removing the sour cream and onion mixture from the top of the pot roast to stir into the gravy. Season to taste with salt, pepper and paprika. Pour gravy over the pot roast scraping every bit from the pan to serve over the meat and arrange the cooked noodles at one side of the platter.

Use 1 cup dry Burgundy or Claret in place of the 1 cup of water in this stew for a rich fruity flavor.
RIB ROAST OF BEEF:—That choice of all roasts of beef, is even more choice when basted with half Burgundy and half hot fat from the pan, while roasting.

BAVARIAN BEEF STEW

Makes 5 servings

- 2½ pounds round steak, cubed
- 3 medium-sized onions, sliced
- 3 tablespoons shortening
- 3 cups hot water (or 2 cups hot water and 1 cup dry red wine)
- 1 bay leaf
- 4 teaspoons salt
- 2 teaspoons caraway seed
- ¼ cup vinegar
- 1 medium-sized head red cabbage, cut in wedges
- ¾ cup crushed gingersnaps

Brown the beef and onions in hot fat in a Dutch oven or a heavy pot. Add the bay leaf, salt, caraway seeds and hot water; cover and cook slowly 1½ to 2 hours. Add vinegar, place the cabbage wedges on top, cover and cook 45 minutes to 1 hour. Remove the cabbage wedges and arrange on the edge of a hot serving platter. Pile the meat in the center. Add the crushed gingersnaps (which have been softened in a little warm water) to the liquid in the pan, stir until you have a smooth gravy and pour over the hot meat.

Variations

This is attractive served in a noodle ring made with spinach noodles.

This dish becomes more elegant as the cubes are larger: 1-inch cubes give the appearance of hash; 1½-inch cubes give the appearance of abundance and richness.

A good herb seasoning in this stew would be ⅛ teaspoon powdered thyme and 1 small bay leaf added after the meat has been browned.

SUPERB HAMBURGER

Makes 24 burgers

- 6 pounds round beef, ground twice
- 2 red onions, chopped
- 1 cup parsley, chopped
- 1 cup tomato (fresh chopped or drained canned)
- 1 tablespoon salt
- 1 teaspoon freshly ground pepper
- Fresh herbs or
- 1 teaspoon basil and
- ½ teaspoon marjoram
- 1½ cups cubed toast

Combine, mix lightly, divide evenly and form into 24 balls. Press to flatten. Broil for 5 minutes 4 inches from heat under moderately hot broiler. Turn and broil 1 minute on other side. Serve.

Veal

Veal steak is the favorite meat in much of Europe much as steak is in this country. One of the reasons is that veal is carefully fed and killed to produce it when most tender. It thus has a memorable flavor and is usually much better than veal bought in this country. For this reason use powdered Tenderizer to emulate fork-tender veal. Add MSG* to enhance its flavor and sauté in butter to avoid disturbing its delicacy.

SALTÉED VEAL STEAKS

Makes 4 servings

4 veal steaks, ¼ to ½ inch thick	1½ teaspoons salt
Tenderizer	1 egg, slightly beaten
MSG*	½ cup very fine bread crumbs
⅓ cup flour	3 tablespoons butter
½ teaspoon freshly ground pepper	

Sprinkle the veal with Tenderizer and MSG about 45 minutes before you are ready to cook them. Dip in flour to which seasonings have been added, then in the egg, then in the bread crumbs. As each piece is coated on both sides, place it in a large skillet in which the butter has been melted. Sauté over very low heat, covered, for about 8 minutes. Remove cover, turn the veal steaks and sauté without the cover, adding more butter if necessary to keep them from burning. Serve immediately.

You can also broil these veal steaks 5 inches from medium heat, turning after the first 5 minutes of cooking. They should be browned and tender in about 15 minutes. Or, broil them in a rotisserie turning to brown on both sides; use the time recommended by the equipment you are using.

* See page 92.

VEAL STROGANOFF

Makes 4 servings

- 1 pound boneless veal cutlet
- 1 teaspoon Kitchen Bouquet
- 1 teaspoon salt
- 1 teaspoon dry mustard
- 1/8 teaspoon pepper
- 1/8 teaspoon marjoram
- 3 tablespoons fat
- 1 cup sliced onion
- 1 (3 oz.) can sliced broiled mushrooms
- 1 tablespoon cornstarch
- 2 tablespoons cold water
- 1/2 cup sour cream
- 2 tablespoons catsup

Have butcher pound veal until 1/4-inch thick. Cut in 1-inch strips and place in bowl. Sprinkle with Kitchen Bouquet and seasonings, tossing lightly with fork to coat evenly. Melt fat in frying pan over moderate heat, add meat and brown lightly on both sides. Add onions and cook about 5 minutes, stirring frequently. Then add contents of can of mushrooms. Cover tightly and cook over low heat until meat is tender, about 45 minutes. Blend together the cornstarch and water, and add to meat, stirring until sauce thickens. Combine sour cream and catsup and stir into mixture. Heat slowly. Serve over hot cooked noodles (*page 55*).

VEAL ASPIC

Makes 4 servings

- 1 package lemon-flavored gelatin
- 1 1/3 cups boiling water
- 3 tablespoons vinegar
- 1/4 teaspoon salt
- Dash pepper
- 2 cups diced cooked veal
- 1 cup diced celery
- 1/2 cup Mayonnaise (page 193)

Place contents of package of gelatin in container of blender, add boiling water, cover container and run blender until gelatin is dissolved, about 3 seconds. Stop blender and add remaining ingredients in order given. Blend until mayonnaise is smoothly combined with gelatin and meat is finely cut, about 5 seconds. Chill until the thickness of egg white, then pour into a well-oiled 1-quart salad mold. Cover with aluminum foil or waxed paper and chill until firm.

VEAL BREAST STUFFED WITH SAUERKRAUT
Swiss

Makes 6 servings

- 4 pound breast of veal
- 3 cups sliced apples
- 1 cup sliced onions
- 3 tablespoons butter or margarine
- 1 (No. 2½) can sauerkraut
- 1 teaspoon salt
- ⅓ cup dark brown sugar
- 1½ teaspoons caraway seeds

When buying the breast of veal have a pocket for stuffing cut in the meat. Prepare the stuffing which is to go into it by combining the apples and onions and sautéing in the melted butter over low heat until a delicate brown. Add remaining ingredients to the skillet. Cover and continue cooking over low heat for 30 minutes, stirring occasionally. Remove cover, stir over high heat until the liquid is reduced and spoon the stuffing into the veal pocket. Close opening by sewing or with skewers secured by cord. Brush the whole roast with cooking oil and sprinkle with salt and pepper. Pour ½ to ¾ cup cooking oil in a large brown paper bag, large enough to completely cover the breast and twist tightly close at the end. Shake and turn until the whole bag is well oiled. Place the breast of veal inside, twist the end tightly shut and place it in a roasting pan. Slide in the oven (300°) and forget it until 3 hours later—45 minutes per pound. Remove from oven and you will find that it is tender and beautifully browned. Serve on hot platter. Makes 6 generous slices.

Or roast uncovered, in 325° oven, 45 minutes per pound.

Lamb

Following are some recipes showing a variety of ways to prepare lamb besides broiling lamb chops, which you undoubtedly already know how to do.

In France lamb is served rare, juicy pink as a choice roast of beef would be in our country. However, for American taste lamb is most often cooked well done. One of the nice things about it in addition to its delicate flavor is that almost every cut of lamb you can buy is tender. Nevertheless the same as for all meats, it should be cooked at low temperatures, whether being broiled, roasted or served in a curry.

Lamb and veal are, in the opinion of a good many curry addicts, the best meats served in curry sauce.

This meat is delicious almost any way you prepare it, but once a year or so you should serve a superb crown roast just to keep your hand in for an important occasion dinner.

CROWN ROAST OF LAMB

Makes 4 servings

- 8 rib crown roast of lamb
- 1 clove garlic, minced
- 1 teaspoon cracked peppercorns
- 2 teaspoons salt
- ¼ cup bacon drippings or salad oil

Arrange the crown roast (2 ribs per person) upside down in a roasting pan. Combine seasonings and oil, mix well and coat the surfaces of the crown inside and out with the seasoned oil. Roast in preheated, slow oven (300°) 35 minutes per pound for well done lamb. Do not cover or baste the lamb while roasting. Remove from oven, turn crown right side up on a hot serving platter. Cover the ends of the protruding bones with paper frills, with mushrooms or with black pitted olives. Fill the center with Purée of Turnip *(page 97)* or pile it full of buttered green peas to which a few small cooked onions have been added. This is most easily done by using tiny whole canned onions which can be stirred into the peas the last few minutes of cooking.

ROAST LEG OF LAMB:—To roast a leg of lamb rub the entire surface with ½ lemon until well moistened with the juice. Cut gashes in the meat in a few place and insert slivers of garlic. Dredge lightly with flour, sprinkle with coarse salt and cracked peppercorns and place fat side up in a roasting pan. Roast at 300° for 35 minutes per pound as you do for the crown roast. Do not cover or baste leg of lamb.

Serve either the crown or leg of lamb with unthickened juices from the pan (after fat has been skimmed off) with mint jelly, currant jelly or Danish Sour Cream Gravy *(page 296)*.

BENGAL CURRY LAMB

Makes 6 servings

- 2½ pounds lean lamb (shoulder or chuck, or use veal)
- 4 tablespoons butter
- ⅛ teaspoon black pepper
- 2 teaspoons salt
- 2 or 3 tablespoons curry powder
- ¼ teaspoon ground cloves
- ½ teaspoon crushed dried mint
- ⅔ cup finely chopped onions
- 3 tablespoons preserved or crystallized ginger, chopped
- ½ teaspoon granulated sugar
- 2 cups milk
- Milk from a fresh coconut (½ to 1 cup)
- ½ cup freshly grated coconut
- ½ cup freshly squeezed lime juice
- ½ cup heavy cream

Cut lamb into 1-inch cubes, removing bones and fat. Melt half the butter in a large skillet. Add onions and sauté until tender, about 5 minutes. Add remaining butter and brown lamb cubes. Add ginger, sugar, pepper, salt, curry powder, cloves, mint and milk. Mix well. Cover and cook over low heat 1 hour. Add coconut milk and freshly grated coconut. Cover and continue to cook 20 minutes, or until lamb is tender. About 15 minutes before serving, gradually stir in lime juice and cream, adding them separately and in the order given to prevent curdling. Serve on hot, fluffy rice with chutney, a green salad and cold beer. If fresh limes are not available, use canned lime juice or freshly squeezed lemon juice.

LAMB PIE WITH POPPY SEED CRUST

Makes 4 servings

- 3 pounds lamb shoulder
- ⅓ cup fat
- 1 teaspoon salt
- ⅛ teaspoon pepper
- ⅓ cup flour
- 3 cups lamb broth
- 1 teaspoon Kitchen Bouquet
- 2 cups cooked green peas
- 1 cup cooked small white onions
- 1 cup pastry mix
- 4 teaspoons poppy seeds
- 2 tablespoons water (approximately)

Cook lamb until tender with 2 cups water and 2 teaspoons salt, about 1½ hours. Cool slightly in broth. Remove meat from bones, cutting in 1-inch cubes. Melt fat in saucepan and stir in salt, pepper and flour. Pour fat from broth and add water to make 3 cups broth. Stir broth into flour mixture. Cook, stirring constantly until gravy thickens. Add Kitchen Bouquet, peas, onions and cubed lamb. Pour into shallow, greased 1½ quart baking dish.

Place pastry mix in bowl and stir in poppy seeds. Add water according to directions. Roll out to fit top of baking dish, cutting vents to allow escape of steam. Bake in hot oven (400°) until crust is done, about 25 minutes.

Pork

GINGER PORK WITH PEARS

Makes 6 servings

3 to 4 pound pork loin	1 teaspoon salt
1 tablespoon Kitchen Bouquet	2 teaspoons ginger
	1 sliced onion
1 tablespoon honey	3 firm pears

Have your butcher crack bones to make carving simpler. Blend together the Kitchen Bouquet, honey, salt and ginger, and brush this mixture over surface of the roast. Place pork fat side up in shallow roasting pan. Lay sliced onion over the top. Roast in slow oven (300°) about 1¾ hours, or until a meat thermometer registers 185° F. About half an hour before roast is done, quarter pears and remove cores. Arrange in pan around roast and baste with pan fat. When ready to serve, remove roast and pears to warm serving platter. Make gravy from drippings in pan using recipe for Swedish Pot Roast (*page 110*).

PORK SUKIYAKI

Japanese

Makes 4 servings

3 tablespoons oil	⅓ cup slivered onion
1 pound lean pork, thinly sliced	1 teaspoon Shoyu or Soya sauce
1 clove garlic, minced	1½ teaspoons salt

- ½ teaspoon ginger
- 2 tablespoons sugar
- ¼ cup bouillon
- 1 (3 oz.) can sliced broiled mushrooms, drained
- 1 cup bean sprouts, canned
- 1 cup celery, diagonally sliced
- 1½ cups thinly sliced turnips or white radishes
- Cooked long grain rice

Heat oil in a heavy skillet and add the paper thin slices of pork. Simmer about 5 minutes, moving the meat about to cook it thoroughly. Add the bouillon, seasonings and vegetables except celery and turnip or radish slices. Cover and simmer 10 minutes, then add celery and radishes. Stir well, cover and cook 3 minutes. Serve immediately over hot cooked rice.

Lean chicken or beef can replace the pork in this recipe, and like the pork should be sliced paper thin and across the grain.

SWEET AND SOUR PORK

Makes 4 servings

- 1 pound lean pork, cut in ½-inch cubes
- 2 tablespoons butter
- Salt
- Pepper
- 1 cup beef bouillon
- 1 cup green peppers, slivered
- ⅓ cup chopped onion
- ½ (No. 2) can pineapple chunks, drained
- ¼ cup sugar
- ¼ cup vinegar
- 3 tablespoons cornstarch
- 2 teaspoons Soya sauce
- ½ cup pineapple juice
- Rice

Melt the butter in a skillet, add the cubes of pork and cook, stirring constantly until the cubes are browned. Sprinkle generously with salt and pepper. Add the bouillon, cover and reduce heat. Continue cooking over low heat for 25 minutes. In all Chinese recipes the cutting of the meat and vegetables is very important. In slivering the peppers be sure that the strips are sliced into even slivers. Combine the sugar and cornstarch, add the vinegar, Soya sauce and pineapple juice. Add this mixture and the vegetables and pineapple to the skillet. Cover and cook another 10 minutes. Serve with fluffy rice.

VIGGO HANSEN'S FRIKADELLER

Viggo Hansen is the Scandinavian Airlines chef, who makes this remarkable Danish dish to perfection.

Makes 8 servings

- 1 pound pork
- 1 pound veal
- ½ cup chopped onions
- ¼ cup flour
- 4 whole eggs
- ½ cup light cream
- 1 cup milk
- 3 teaspoons salt
- 1 teaspoon white ground pepper

Put meat through meat grinder four times. Beat with large mixing spoon or slowly in electric mixer with salt and pepper. Add flour, mixing in well. Beat in eggs one at a time. Add cream and milk a little at a time. Add onions (simmered in a little butter for 5 minutes). Make meat balls, using a rounded tablespoon of the mixture for each one, and browning gently in a frying pan with a little butter for about 5 minutes on both sides. Then put in a hot oven (450°) and bake for 20 to 25 minutes. This oven baking makes the meat balls light and fluffy.

Serve this accompanied by green beans, after cold Cherry Soup (*page 28*), and finish up with English Trifle (*page 243*) for dessert.

BURGUNDY CHOPS

Makes 4 servings

- 4 pork chops
- ¼ cup flour
- ¾ teaspoon salt
- ⅛ teaspoon pepper
- 2 tablespoons fat
- 2 tablespoons rich prepared mustard
- 1 tablespoon brown sugar
- 1 tablespoon cornstarch
- 1 cup Burgundy wine
- 1 cup (8 oz. can) canned, crushed pineapple, undrained

Dredge chops with combined flour, salt and pepper. Melt fat in a large heavy skillet; add chops and slowly brown on both sides, then transfer to a casserole. Blend together mustard, brown sugar and cornstarch in a saucepan; stir in wine and pineapple. Cook, stirring constantly until mixture boils, then pour over chops. Cover casserole and bake in a moderate oven (350°) 1 hour, or until chops are tender.

SCRAPPLE
Electric Blender Method

Makes 12 servings

- 3 pounds pork shoulder
- 8 cups boiling water
- 2 cups fine corn meal
- 4 teaspoons salt
- 2 cups cold water
- 4 cups pork broth
- 6 tablespoons diced onion
- ½ teaspoon thyme
- 2 teaspoons powdered sage
- 1 teaspoon marjoram

Place pork and water in Dutch oven and cook, covered, until tender, about 1½ hours. Place corn meal, salt, cold water and 2 cups pork broth in top of 1½ quart double boiler, and bring to a boil. Meanwhile, put 2 cups pork broth and onion in container of electric blender and blend 5 seconds. Add herbs and cooked pork from which fat and bones have been removed, blend 15 seconds, and add to corn meal mixture. Place over boiling water and cook, covered, for 1 hour, stirring after 30 minutes. When done, pour into 2 loaf pans, 9 x 4 inches each. Chill until firm, then cut in ¼ inch slices. Roll lightly in flour and cook in hot fat until golden brown. Serve with syrup.

ROAST LOIN OF PORK
(In a Paper Bag)

Makes 8 servings

- 6 pound loin of pork
- 2 tablespoons butter or bacon drippings
- 1 teaspoon cracked peppercorns
- 1 teaspoon ground ginger
- 2 tablespoons salt
- ½ cup cooking oil
- Large brown paper bag

This is a method of roasting a loin of pork for you to try out when you have to be away from home several hours. Combine butter or bacon drippings with all the seasonings and brush the outside of the roast, coating it evenly with the seasoned mixture. Pour the ½ cup cooking oil in a large paper bag, large enough to cover the roast without touching it when the end is twisted shut. Shake the bag to coat all the paper with the oil. Put roast inside, fat side up, twist end of bag closed and tuck it under the roast to secure it, as you arrange it in a roasting pan. Do not cover. Place in 300° oven, and forget it until 4 hours later.

QUICK BARBECUED SPARERIBS

Men always appear to enjoy food that can be picked up and gnawed on. Just cut these spareribs before cooking into small pieces for eating "out of hand."

Makes 4 servings

- 2 pounds pork spareribs
- 1 onion
- ¼ cup catsup
- ½ cup water
- 1 teaspoon Worcestershire sauce
- ⅛ teaspoon chili powder

Cut ribs in pieces for serving. Place in baking dish. Slice onions over the top and add other ingredients. Cover and cook in a moderate oven (350°) about 2 hours.

Ham

COOKING A WHOLE OR HALF OF A HAM

A baked ham has many characteristics to recommend it. Its festive appearance, wonderful flavor and easy-to-carve qualities are outshone only by the fact that it's so easy to prepare successfully. Not the least of its attractions is that it will feed a lot of people. Or it will feed a few and provide ham for Ham in Vermouth Sauce *(page 38)* or the four recipes which follow this talk about baking and glazing hams.

Most of the hams on the market are the mild-cure type which do not require boiling. If you must boil it, you are still ahead. Save the wonderful juice to make Pumpkin Soup *(page 31)*. But it is a good idea to know what types you have to choose from, and what to do with them. The precooked, ready-to-eat variety only needs heating in the oven. You can glaze it in any number of ways. The easiest is to rub or coat the ham, top and sides, with brown sugar and then with crushed canned pineapple. Bake and you can't miss.

An uncooked ham must be baked longer, or boiled and then trimmed and glazed and baked. Your butcher will tell you which type you are buying if the tag on the ham fails to inform you. But this is an idea you won't find on a label—finishing your baked ham with a Colonial Beer Glaze *(page 127)*.

COOKING A WHOLE OR HALF A HAM

Place the ham on a rack in a shallow roasting pan. Do not add water. Do not cover. Place in preheated oven (325°) and allow 14 minutes per pound for a cooked, ready-to-eat ham. If uncooked, allow 25 minutes per pound.

Take ham from oven about half an hour before end of baking period, and remove rind. Cut the fat surface in shallow, criss-cross grooves about one inch apart, or cut small circles in the fat with a 1-inch cooky cutter. Stick in cloves to outline the cut portion, spread ham with a glaze and return to the oven for the remainder of the baking.

SPICY TENDERIZED HAM

Most of the hams you buy are wrapped with directions for cooking on the wrapper. In the event that your buy tenderized ham without directions, or ½ of a tenderized ham as so many people do, here is a standard recipe for its preparation.

1 10-pound tenderized ham
1 quart water
2 cups carrots, thickly sliced
8 small white onions, halved
1 whole bunch celery, stalks and leaves, cut in pieces
4 sprigs parsley
1 clove garlic
4 cups (1 quart) cider, beer, dry white wine or apple juice
Cloves
1 cup Madeira wine
¾ cup molasses or honey
Boiling water to cover

Unwrap the ham and have it ready to put in a pot which should be large enough to accommodate it and enough liquid to completely cover. Prepare liquid before putting ham in the pot. Combine 1 quart water, vegetables, garlic, parsley and the cider (or other liquor you decide to use) and place over medium heat until it begins to boil. Add the ham and enough boiling water to cover. When it begins to boil, reduce heat and simmer (do not boil), tightly covered 2½ hours. Remove ham from the liquor, trim off the skin and some of the fat, if the layer is thick. Score the fat in attractive squares and spike it with cloves in the center of each square, or, make circles in the fat with a round cutter and make a design with the cloves in circles over the ham. When the cloves are in place, drench ham with the Madeira, spread with molasses and place in a hot oven (400°) 8 to 10 minutes; baste 4 times while the glaze is being "set" by the heat.

Now is a good time to make Pumkpin Soup *(page 31)* or any lentil or split pea soup in which ham broth is so good. Boil liquor in the pot over high heat until reduced to rich, full-flavored broth. You have to taste it to decide this. Strain into a mixing bowl, and when cool chill. Skim fat from top and use the broth.

Mustard Glazes for Ham

Bake ham according to directions on wrapper. Remove from oven 45 minutes before done. Peel off rind and score fat. Spread with one of the following glazes, and return to oven for 45 minutes:

Combine 1 cup apple butter with ¼ cup rich prepared mustard. Spread on scored ham; decorate with whole cloves.

Combine 1 cup whole cranberry sauce with ¼ cup rich prepared mustard. Spread on scored ham.

Force enough canned apricot halves through a sieve to make 1 cup of purée. Combine with ¼ cup rich prepared mustard. Spread on scored ham; decorate with about 4 apricot halves interspersed with whole cloves.

Fruit and Wine Glazes for Ham

WINE GLAZE:—Use brandy, Madeira or Champagne to moisten the ¾ cup brown sugar for glazing.
COLONIAL BEER GLAZE:—This will remind you of mint julep days down South. Combine ½ cup brown sugar with 1 tablespoon dry mustard. Add enough beer or ale to moisten enough to spread easily. Coat the ham and continue to bake, basting occasionally with the drippings.
FRUIT JUICE GLAZE:—Use orange juice, pineapple juice or juice from canned sour pie cherries for moistening ¾ cup brown sugar to glaze whole ham. You can sprinkle ¼ cup wine over the ham before glazing with the juice and sugar.
DECORATE HAM by studding the circles or squares cut in the fat surface with cloves, or with whole cherries, cranberries or chunks of pineapple. The decoration should resemble the flavor of the glaze.

PAPRIKA HAM

Makes 4 servings

- 2 tablespoons fat
- 1 small onion, sliced
- 2 cups cubed, cooked ham
- 1 cup tomato sauce
- 2 tablespoons rich prepared mustard
- 1 teaspoon paprika
- 1 cup sour cream

Melt fat in skillet. Sauté onion until yellow and tender; add ham. Blend together tomato sauce, mustard and paprika. Stir into ham and simmer 30 minutes. Add sour cream and heat (do not boil). Serve over rice or noodles.

BAKED HAM IN WINE

Makes 6 servings

- 1 slice of ham, 2-inches thick
- ½ cup brown sugar
- 1 tablespoon cornstarch
- 1 tablespoon butter
- 1½ cups water
- ½ cup seedless raisins
- ½ cup dry white wine

Combine sugar and cornstarch, add butter and water, and cook 3 minutes stirring constantly. Remove from heat, add the raisins and wine. Stir until blended. Place ham in a greased baking dish, cover with the sauce, and put uncovered in a moderate oven (350°). Bake 1 hour and 15 minutes, or until tender.

HAWAIIAN HAM PIE

Makes 6 servings

- 2 cups sifted flour
- 2 teaspoons baking powder
- 1 teaspoon salt
- ⅔ cup shortening
- ½ cup canned crushed pineapple, drained
- ½ cup hot, canned pineapple syrup
- 1 egg yolk, unbeaten
- 2 cups hot medium White Sauce (page 99)
- 2 tablespoons rich prepared mustard
- 1½ cups cubed, cooked ham
- 1 cup cooked vegetables (peas, corn, carrots, etc.)

Sift together flour, baking powder and salt. Combine shortening, drained pineapple, pineapple syrup and egg yolk; blend into dry ingredients. Chill. Pat out ¾ of pastry as lining for a 1½ quart casserole. Combine white sauce, mustard, ham and vegetables. Pour into pastry lined casserole. Pat out remaining dough to fit top of casserole. Bake in a hot oven 425° about 30 minutes.

JELLIED MEAT LOAF

English

The nice thing about many of these delicious dishes of foreign origin is that they use left-overs in an admirable way to make a truly elegant party or family dish. This loaf would be a beauty on any cold buffet.

Makes 8 servings

- 2 cups beef bouillon, heated
- 1½ envelopes unflavored gelatin
- ½ cup cold water
- 2 cups ground cooked ham
- 4 hard-cooked eggs
- 2 cups ground cooked chicken, turkey, veal or pork

Pour the bouillon into a saucepan, place over medium heat and bring to boiling point while the gelatin is being softened in cold water. When bouillon comes to a boil pour it over the gelatin and stir until dissolved. Cool about 10 minutes, while removing shells from hard-cooked eggs which are going to be used in making this mold. Place the cold ground ham in the bottom of a greased loaf pan, and arrange the hard-cooked eggs lengthwise down the center of this layer so that they will be sliced through when the loaf is cut. Cover with cooked, well seasoned ground meat or fowl. Pour the gelatin mixture over the meat and let loaf chill in refrigerator until firmly set. . . . For company you could use ½ cup sherry for moistening the gelatin when making this loaf.

HAM ROLLS GLACÉ

Makes 6 servings

- 1 cup raw tart apples, grated
- ¼ teaspoon salt
- ⅛ teaspoon pepper

½ cup dry bread crumbs
1 teaspoon dry mustard
½ teaspoon ginger
1 teaspoon sugar
2 tablespoons melted butter or margarine
6 slices boiled ham, ⅛-inch thick

Combine apples with crumbs, seasonings and melted butter. Mix thoroughly. Spread each ham slice with a spoonful of apple mixture and roll as for jelly roll. Secure with toothpicks, if necessary. Arrange in shallow baking dish. Pour glaze (*see below*) over ham rolls. Bake in hot oven (400°) 30 minutes, basting frequently. Insert whole cloves in whole canned apricots and place around ham rolls about 5 minutes before removing from oven, baste with glaze.

GLAZE

Combine in saucepan ¾ cup Blue Label syrup, 3 tablespoons water, ¼ cup vinegar, 6 whole cloves and a 2-inch piece of stick cinnamon. Simmer 5 minutes. Add 1 teaspoon grated orange rind and 3 or 4 dashes Angostura Bitters.

Sauces for Meat and Fowl

RAISIN SAUCE
For Ham

Makes about 3 cups

2 tablespoons fat
¼ cup diced onion
⅓ cup concentrated frozen orange juice
1 small lemon, sliced and seeded
1 tablespoon cornstarch
1½ cups water
2 tablespoons brown sugar
⅛ teaspoon cinnamon
⅛ teaspoon cloves
¼ teaspoon dry mustard

FINE MEAT DISHES ... BEAUTIFULLY PRESENTED

½ teaspoon Kitchen Bouquet
½ cup seedless raisins
½ cup dark rum (optional)

Place fat, onion, orange juice and lemon in container of electric blender. Blend until lemon is finely cut, about 1 minute. Add remaining ingredients and blend until raisins are coarsely cut, about 30 seconds. Pour into saucepan and bring to boil, stirring constantly.

MINCEMEAT SAUCE

For Ham, Cold Fowl, Meat Loaves

Makes 2 cups

1½ cup mincemeat
1 cup water
2 tablespoons red wine or sherry
½ teaspoon dry mustard

Combine all ingredients in a saucepan. Place over medium heat and stir occasionally until it begins to boil. Reduce heat and cook 2 minutes longer. Serve separately to be spooned over ham steak, meat loaves or cold, sliced chicken or turkey.

Steak Sauces

MADEIRA SAUCE

For Steaks or Beef

Makes 1 cup

⅓ cup good Madeira wine
2 tablespoons Bovril
1 cup Brown Meat Gravy (freshly made or canned)
1 tablespoon tomato paste
3 tablespoons butter
Salt and pepper to taste

In searching for a way to make Madeira Sauce without the beginnings any self-respecting French woman has in her kitchen as the "beginning" for her sauces, I discovered something. Canned brown gravy, tomato paste, and Bovril replace the worthy efforts of the French cook remarkably well.

An important thing to be understood in making any wine sauce, is that wine must be cooked until it is reduced to contributing its "bouquet" rather than its volume. Hot wine has a bitter flavor. Cooked wine has a rich, fruity flavor. If you have an electric blender, put this sauce in it to blend a minute just before serving to make its texture pure velvet.

Combine wine and Bovril in small saucepan. Cook over medium heat, stirring until reduced to about half original amount. Add brown gravy, tomato paste, continue cooking until thoroughly blended, about 4 minutes, stirring constantly. Add butter, taste and adjust seasoning. Serve immediately or add to blender, run machine 1 minute, pour into gravy boat and serve.

You can make this sauce from cold gravy from yesterday's roast. Or you can make it with canned gravy to serve over broiled steaks. Best of all, thickened brown gravy can be made from the fragrant hot roast and quickly combined with the other ingredients for this Madeira flavored sauce or "gravy" as we would call it.

BÉARNAISE SAUCE

Makes about 1 cup

- 1 cup dry white wine
- ¼ cup tarragon vinegar
- 1 clove garlic, minced
- 2 tablespoons grated onion
- ¼ teaspoon chervil
- 3 cracked peppercorns
- ½ teaspoon salt
- Few grains cayenne pepper
- 3 egg yolks, beaten
- ½ cup butter, softened
- 2 teaspoons chopped fresh tarragon (optional)

| 2 teaspoons chopped fresh chervil (optional) | 1 tablespoon finely chopped parsley |

This sauce is highly regarded by the French—and by you if you try it—as garnish for filet mignon, and to serve with fish. A small wire whisk used for the beating, as this thickens in the top of a double boiler, is insurance against curdling sauce.

Line a wire strainer with cheesecloth and place over top pan of a double boiler. Combine first 8 ingredients in a saucepan, cook over medium heat until reduced to about 1/3 original amount. Pour through cheesecloth-lined strainer into the fresh pan. (You should have ½ cup—no more—should you want to measure it.) Beat yolks in separate pan, and place them and the butter which has been softened in room temperature, near you as the liquid is placed over boiling water. Stirring constantly with the whisk, add a little of the egg yolk and a little of the butter, alternating until yolks and butter have been added and the mixture thickens to consistency of slightly whipped cream. Remove from heat. Add freshly chopped fresh parsley, tarragon and chervil. Stir to blend, and serve immediately. Or keep hot over steaming (not boiling) water, tightly covered, for the 20 minutes you may need to broil your steaks and be ready to serve.

Meat Platter Garnishes

Dressing up your meals can be achieved with a twist of the wrist by being prepared for the inevitable —the company which comes unexpectedly and leaves you no time to prepare fancy fixins. A few relishes on the shelf will help as much with the meat or fowl you decide to serve, as those jars of sweet sauces do with desserts.

A table can look mighty pretty with no extra

trouble at all, if you arrange it with an eye to color contrasts and originality. An example is to make a gelatin salad of whatever flavor or mixture you select, chill it in individual molds to be unmolded around the cold or hot meat platter in a decorative wreath. Or mold two salads of different colors in the individual molds and arrange them on the meat platter. One for each person along with a helping of meat, makes the offering festive and the serving easy.

Grated vegetables can be placed the same way and held in crisp lettuce cups.

Doughnut size mincemeat or avocado or tomato aspic rings, unmolded on the meat platter, are pretty and very very good.

Water cress is the most ancient of green vegetables and one of the most beautiful. Use it in bunches to decorate a platter, providing a bunch for each person's salad.

And don't forget the usefulness, not to mention the vitamins, of parsley on meat, salad or sandwich platters.

Or when you are in the mood, try one of these garnishes to make the *presentation* of your main course live up to its delightful flavor. Once you start serving this way, there is no end to your own ingenuity in serving vegetables or salads as garnishes along with the meat.

BAKED WHOLE ORANGES

These are delicious and beautiful as a cold or hot garnish with baked ham, roast fowl, roast pork or roast lamb.

Makes 6 servings

- 6 whole unpeeled oranges
- Water
- 6 teaspoons butter
- 6 tablespoons sugar

Place the whole oranges in a large saucepan and cover with water. Allow the water to come to a boil, reduce heat, cover tightly and boil gently for 30 minutes. Remove cover and allow the oranges and liquid to cool. Cut a slice off the blossom end of each orange. Remove the core but not the fruit and fill the little hollow center with 1 teaspoon butter and 1 tablespoon sugar for each orange. Place in a covered baking dish (glass or earthenware is best). Pour in the water left from the boiling, add more if necessary to make the baking dish 2/3 full of water. Bake, closely covered, 1½ hours in a moderate oven (375°). The time will depend upon the size of the oranges. Serve these hot or cold with the following sauce:

SAUCE

Add 1 tablespoon cornstarch and ¼ cup orange juice to each ¾ cup of liquid remaining in the baking dish. Heat and stir until thickened.

ABBIE'S KUMQUATS

Stem fresh kumquats. Cover them with salted water (¼ cup for each 2 quarts of water) and let stand for 24 hours. Rinse, cover with boiling water and boil for 30 minutes. Drain, add fresh water and cook until the kumquats are tender.

Now add 2 cups corn syrup, 1 4-inch stick cinnamon, 1 cup vinegar and 1 tablespoon whole cloves for each 2 cups of kumquats. Place over medium heat and boil until the syrup is thick and the kumquats are thoroughly spiced, about 30 minutes. Remove spice bag, pour into a bowl, cool and serve.

Can these if you like, but this recipe is for you to serve with meats when kumquats are in season.

STUFFED BING CHERRIES

Remove seeds from 24 big black bing cherries, fresh or drained canned. Soften ½ cup peanut butter, and make into 24 balls to replace seeds. Chill and serve on meat platter.

SWEET POTATO ORANGE CUPS

Remove fruit from oranges which have been cut in half. Put freshly cooked or drained canned sweet potatoes through ricer or coarse sieve. Season with butter, salt and pepper and pile into the orange halves. Serve on meat platter, or top with a marshmallow if you like, and bake in a moderate preheated oven (350°) 15 minutes, or until browned on top.

LEMON BANANA MOLDS

Makes 12 cubes

1 can concentrated lemonade, canned or frozen	1 cup mashed ripe bananas 1½ cups milk

Combine ingredients, beat until blended and pour into an ice cube tray. Put the divider in place and freeze. Serve in small lettuce cups on a meat platter.

TROPICAL FREEZE

Makes 12 cubes

1⅔ cups (1 large can) undiluted evaporated milk	1 (6 oz.) can frozen orange juice, undiluted
¼ cup lemon juice	¼ cup sugar

Place evaporated milk in the refrigerator tray until crystals begin to form. Combine lemon juice and chilled milk in a chilled bowl and beat with rotary beater. When mixture holds peaks, fold in sugar and softened but undiluted orange juice and pour into a refrigerator tray. If to be used on a cold meat platter, put divider in place to freeze cubes. Serve cubes in small lettuce cups on platter with cold or hot roast beef or lamb.

If mixture is frozen without divider in refrigerator tray, slice and fold in with a variety of fruit to make a fruit salad to serve with hot roast beef or a roast of lamb.

JEWELED RINGS

Makes 6 individual molds

- 2 cups tomato juice
- 1 package lemon flavored gelatin
- 1 tablespoon horseradish
- 1 tablespoon lemon juice
- 1¼ cups cottage cheese
- ½ cup chopped walnuts
- 12 walnut halves

Heat tomato juice. Remove from heat, add gelatin and stir until dissolved. Add horseradish and lemon juice. Pour into 6 individual ring molds and chill until firm. Turn out on lettuce and arrange around large cold meat platter or serve separately on a bed of lettuce leaves. Combine chopped walnuts with cottage cheese and fill centers. Garnish with walnut halves.

If these small ring molds are to be served around cold meat or turkey fill the centers with Curry Mayonnaise *(page 195)*.

ORANGE STUFFING PATTIES

Makes 4 patties

- 2 teaspoons clear duck fat
- 1 cup orange bread stuffing (left over from roast duck)
- ½ cup diced left-over roast duck meat

2 teaspoons rich prepared mustard	1 egg, beaten
½ teaspoon salt	Toasted, dry bread crumbs

Melt the duck fat in a small skillet while combining the stuffing, diced duck, seasonings and beaten egg. Stir until thoroughly blended, adding enough toasted dry bread crumbs to bind the mixture enough for you to shape into four patties. Roll these in more fine crumbs and fry in the hot fat or bake in a moderate oven (350°) until brown. This takes about 30 minutes, and the patties should be turned once to brown evenly.

Of course these are crispest and quickest when browned in deep hot fat, at 375° until toast brown, about 4 minutes. Serve with any hot or cold game or fowl.

PICKLED CHERRIES

Makes 5 pints

2½ cups dark brown sugar, firmly packed	4 long sticks cinnamon, broken
2 cups cider vinegar	2 quarts sour red cherries, pitted
2 teaspoons whole cloves	

If you are using canned sour pie cherries for this drain well, and use 1 cup juice to replace 1 cup cider vinegar.

Cook brown sugar, spices and vinegar together allowing it to boil gently for 3 or 4 minutes. Add the washed, unpitted cherries and cook until heated through, about 5 minutes. Pour cherries and juice into 5 sterilized one pint jars, seal tightly. Serve with meat or fowl.

QUICK PINEAPPLE MARMALADE

Makes 1 cup

Add ¼ cup dark brown sugar to 1 cup canned crushed pineapple. Cook over medium heat, stirring constantly, until it thickens. Presto! You have a delicious marmalade. Pour into a serving bowl, cool and chill for tea time or for meat-company. Especially good with pork.

MARJORAM JELLY

Makes 4 cups

1 cup boiling water	⅛ cup lemon juice
2 tablespoons fresh marjoram leaves	3 cups sugar
	½ cup pectin (liquid)

Pour the water into a saucepan and bring to a boil. Add the marjoram, reduce heat, cover, and allow this to steep 30 minutes. Strain through double cheesecloth which has been rinsed in cold water and wrung dry. Return to heat, add lemon juice and sugar, stir until dissolved. Bring to a boil and add the bottled pectin, boiling about another 30 seconds. Remove from heat, skim, pour into sterilized jars and seal.

Something wonderful with egg or cheese soufflés or with any meat or fowl you serve.

WINE JELLY

Makes 2 cups

1 envelope unflavored gelatin	½ cup currant jelly
	⅔ cup claret
½ cup dry sherry	2 tablespoons brandy

Soften the gelatin in the sherry. Place the currant jelly in a small saucepan and melt over low heat only until it is dissolved. Add to the softened gelatin and stir until the gelatin is dissolved. Cool, add the claret and brandy and turn into an ornate mold, or a plain one if you don't care about making this fancy. Chill until set. Unmold when ready to serve and put this on the table along with lamb, hot or cold.

WATERMELON PRESERVES

Fills 3 pint jars

- 2½ pounds (about 8 cups) prepared melon rind
- 6 cups vinegar
- 1 cup water
- 2½ pounds (5 cups) sugar
- 12 thin slices lemon
- 9 to 12 drops of oil of cloves
- 1 4-inch stick cinnamon

Prepare the rind by removing the dark outer portion and most of the pink pulp. Cut into fancy shapes with small cutter, or use knife to cut into diamonds. Weigh or measure rind. Cover with salted water (½ cup salt to each 2 quarts water). Place over high heat, and when water begins to boil, reduce heat and simmer 30 minutes. Drain and cover with fresh water, cook 10 minutes, drain, cover with fresh water and cook another 10 minutes. Remove from heat and forget it overnight.

When ready to make the preserves, combine in a large kettle the vinegar, water, sugar, lemon slices and spices. Place over high heat. When it begins to boil reduce heat and simmer until the sugar has dissolved. Drain the prepared melon shapes, add to the hot liquid and cook over medium heat until the rind is clear and the syrup thick. Remove cinnamon stick. Pour into hot sterilized jars and seal. These preserves are a fine addition to any meat, fowl or curried main courses. And they are delightful garnishes of color and flavor for the Salad Plate Luncheon (*page 275*).

(Cantaloupe or citron melon rinds can also be preserved this way.)

8

Chicken, Turkey, Duck and Game on Your Table

All poultry should be roasted at a steady low temperature of 325° F. to secure the greatest tenderness and to insure the meat's being juicy and evenly cooked.

Always roast poultry uncovered resting on a rack in a shallow baking pan. It is done when the leg joint moves freely when grasped firmly and moved away from the breast of the bird.

Prepare turkeys and chickens for roasting by skewering the wings into place after the tip has been slipped to the back of the bird. Skewer the legs or truss them when lacing string across the skewers which are used to close the cavity. To close the cavity of a stuffed fowl by use of skewers place 2 or 3 skewers through the skin on one side and run the skewer through the skin on the other until these form a ladder down the opening. With a piece of heavy string form a lattice by winding it around the skewers and then around the end of the legs, if you haven't skewered them, and tie the string firmly.

Stuffing is not necessary before roasting a chicken. If you like, however, you can fill the cavity of a bird, before roasting, with small whole onions or with white seedless grapes. Place a tangerine in the cavity of the fowl to close it. An unstuffed chicken, turkey or duck requires a few minutes less per pound to roast.

Chicken

ROAST CHICKEN
(Paper Bag Method)

Makes 4 servings

1 (5-pound) roasting chicken, dressed	½ teaspoon freshly ground pepper
1 lemon, halved	Paprika
¼ cup butter, softened *not melted*	½ cup cooking oil (not butter)
1½ teaspoons salt	Brown paper bag

Rinse and dry chicken. Rub inside and out with lemon half. Combine butter with salt and pepper. Mix thoroughly and coat chicken well, covering back very lightly. Sprinkle with paprika. Chill in refrigerator while preparing stuffing. Fill chicken with Gourmet Stuffing *(page 143)*, but do not pack tightly. Close cavity with 2 skewers, lace closed with string.

Pour cooking oil into bag which is large enough to cover chicken without touching breast. Shake until oiled. Put in roasting pan and insert the chicken breast side up. Twist end of bag shut and turn it under so that it will stay closed.

Put this in the 325° oven and forget it for 4 hours.

Don't open the bag during the cooking. If you cook it a little longer, it won't be ruined.

The paper bag cooking is not new, for cooking in parchment is one way to produce anything from vegetables to fish or roasts so that eating the contents is pure ecstasy. However, a paper bag is something everyone has. So use it. It will reward laziness or absence, since no basting or watching is required.

CHINESE ROAST CHICKEN: — After rubbing chicken inside and out with lemon, use pastry brush to brush inside and out with Soy sauce. Stuff with one-half amount of Gourmet Stuffing *(page 143)* recipe, and close cavity with whole tangerine. Then glaze chicken. Add ½ cup honey to softened butter, beat until blended and coat chicken, thickly on top, thinly on back. Chill 30 minutes to "set" the thick breast coating. Roast in paper bag.

GOURMET STUFFING
Makes about 4½ cups

- 3 cups butter cooked brown rice
- 1 cup chicken livers
- 2 tablespoons bacon drippings
- 1 (8 oz.) can tiny whole onions
- 1 (6 oz.) can whole mushrooms, drained
- ½ cup coarsely chopped parsley
- ½ teaspoon pepper
- 1½ teaspoons salt

Prepare brown rice by sautéing ½ cup dry rice in ¼ cup (1 stick) butter over low flame, stirring occasionally until butter is absorbed. Add 1 cup chicken broth. Cover and cook over medium heat 10 minutes. Sauté chicken livers in bacon fat until browned. Combine in a mixing bowl all ingredients (except 8 of the mushrooms reserved for garnish) and toss until mixed.

Cooked left-over rice can be used in this dressing. Melt the butter in a skillet and add 3 cups cooked rice. Stir with a fork to spread evenly. Cover tighly, allowing it to "steam" in the butter over low heat 5 minutes.

TARRAGON CHICKEN

Makes 4 servings

- 1 large frying chicken, about 3½ pounds, disjointed
- ½ teaspoon freshly ground black pepper
- ¼ cup melted butter or margarine
- ½ cup dry white wine
- ⅓ cup brandy, heated
- 4 butter balls
- 1 cup flour
- 1½ teaspoons salt
- 1 (8 oz.) can tiny whole onions
- 1 (6 oz.) can sliced broiled mushrooms, drained
- 1 teaspoon tarragon (or about 1 cup fresh tarragon)

When chicken has been cut up, rinsed and dried, combine flour, salt and pepper in a paper bag. Shake until blended, then add the chicken pieces to coat with the flour. Melt butter in a large heavy skillet, add floured pieces of chicken. Cook over medium heat until the chicken is lightly browned, turning to make it golden on all sides. Remove from heat, add the hot brandy and ignite it with a long match or a lighted candle. Add onions, drained mushrooms, wine and tarragon. Cover tightly. Place over low heat and cook until tender, about 45 minutes. Be sure not to lift the lid during the first 30 minutes of cooking.

Serve on a hot platter. Pour juice from the pan over the chicken; be sure to get every crusty bit from the skillet. Top with a few butter balls which are icy cold and allow them to melt as the chicken is presented at the table.

BAKED CHICKEN IN CREAM:—And when you are in a hurry, or going to church, and want something delicious the minute you reach home coat the chicken, either a frying chicken or an old one, in the seasoned flour. Brown lightly in half butter and half bacon drippings on top of the stove and pour in enough cream to cover the chicken. Sprinkle with paprika, cover, or seal with aluminum foil. Put in a 325° oven and leave it there to simmer in its juice and be steamy done and ready to eat when you reach home 2 hours later.

HAWAIIAN CHICKEN:—Add 1 cup drained pineapple chunks, for each 4 servings of chicken, to 1 cup cream of mushroom soup which has been thinned with 1 cup chicken broth. Combine in a saucepan, stir over medium heat until thoroughly hot. Pour over the chicken when it is in the serving dish ready to be put on the table, and sprinkle with toasted coconut.

This is a handy way to prepare chicken for an impressive dish because the canned pineapple, mushroom soup, chicken broth and coconut can all come out of cans on the shelf.

COQ AU VIN
French

"It is a mistake to think that only an old chicken is good to put in the pot for *coq au vin*," says my French recipe. Originally old fowl were used to secure greatest flavor.

Makes 6 servings

- 2 young chickens
- 1 teaspoon salt
- 1 teaspoon vinegar
- Soft butter
- Flour
- 20 small onions
- 6 slices bacon, chopped
- * Herbs for bouquet
- 1 clove garlic, minced
- ½ cup brandy
- 1 bottle red wine
- ½ pound mushrooms
- 1 lemon
- Seasoning
- Fried bread crusts for garnish
- 20 (½-inch) cubes salt pork or squares of bacon

* A bouquet of fresh herbs includes thyme, a bay leaf, and some parsley for added flavor. Or add ½ teaspoon thyme, 1 bay leaf and 2 tablespoons chopped parsley.

Take 2 young meaty chickens freshly killed. Drain off the blood into a bowl, adding a pinch of salt and a teaspoon of vinegar so that the blood does not coagulate. Pluck the chickens, clean and singe off the pinfeathers over a flame. Then cut them up into pieces. Season and flour the pieces of chicken and coat with butter. Sauté chicken in a large heavy frying pan with about twenty small onions and the chopped bacon, until golden browned. Drain off and reserve the grease and lightly powder the chicken with flour. Add a piece of chopped garlic and the brandy and return to medium heat. Cook about 1 minute.

Then cover the chicken with the red wine, add salt and pepper and allow to cook over low heat, covered, 30 minutes. Put in the mushrooms which have been cleaned and dipped in lemon juice, saving the most beautiful caps for decoration. Continue cooking, covered, until chicken is tender, about 15 minutes. Remove chicken to hot deep-serving platter and keep hot while making the gravy. Sauté bread triangles in butter and arrange around chicken along with parsley flowerettes.

Now add ½ cup of the grease to the chicken blood and pour it into the skillet. Reduce heat. With a regular movement move the pan around so that the blood incorporates itself well with the gravy, bringing it just to the boiling point. The gravy will thicken as in a stew or ragout.

ABBIE'S CHICKEN CURRY

Makes 4 servings

- 2 full-breasted pullets, dressed
- 6 cups water
- 1 vegetable bunch (celery, onion, carrot, potato)
- 4 peppercorns
- 1 teaspoon salt
- 4 cups Sauce Supreme (page 147)
- 1 teaspoon (or more) curry powder

This is not a true Bengal Curry, but a superb delicate creamy curry. Abbie is the lady you have read about in *Successful Entertaining at Home* who does not like to cook but who—when turned loose in her kitchen—cannot avoid turning out tantalizing things to eat.

If you want to duplicate her masterpiece of curried chicken, shop for two tender, full-breasted pullets. Once you have them, put them in a pot, cover with water and add the seasonings and vegetables (2 celery stalks, 3 medium onions, springs of parsley, 2 carrots—or whatever you have on hand). Cover tightly, place over high heat until the water begins to boil, reduce heat immediately and simmer slowly until chickens are tender, about 1 hour. Allow pullets to cool in the broth. Remove them. Strain broth and throw those vegetables away, for you've had the best of them. Boil the remaining broth uncovered until reduced to 2 cups. Use it to make 4 cups Supreme Sauce. Add curry powder to suit your taste.

Slice breast meat, so that it comes off in round pieces 2 or 3 inches across and about ¼-inch thick. Add these to the Sauce, stir until heated through and serve accompanied by Curry Condiments *(page 148)*.

Remove rest of the meat from bones to make Chicken Ring Mold *(page 180)* or use it to double this recipe, also doubling amount of sauce. The white meat slices, however, are what make this curry look so beautiful.

SAUCE SUPREME

Makes 5 cups

- 1 stick (¼) pound butter
- ¼ cup flour
- 2 cups rich seasoned chicken broth, heated
- 2 cups heavy cream
- 3 egg yolks, beaten
- ¼ cup cold chicken broth or milk
- ¼ teaspoon paprika
- salt to taste

Melt the butter in a large saucepan. Add flour and stir until blended, but not browned. Slowly add the hot chicken broth, then the heavy cream, continuing to cook over low heat and stirring constantly until thoroughly blended and heated through. Add cold broth or milk to beaten yolks, stir to thin mixture, pour slowly into the creamed sauce, and cook 5 minutes stirring constantly. Add paprika and salt to taste. For this curried dish, you will now add the curry, tasting to discover when the flavoring suits you, adding more than the recipe designates if you like it hot. Remove from heat, add the chicken, cover until ready to reheat for serving.

Use half cream and half undiluted evaporated milk for this sauce if you like. Serve with bowls of condiments.

Note: Pour any leftover curried chicken into shallow baking dish. Sprinkle with grated cheese and heat in 350° oven until top is brown, about 30 minutes. This is still a "company dish."

CONDIMENTS TO SERVE WITH CURRIED DISHES

The flower-garden arrangement of small bowls filled with condiments, makes the presentation of a curried dish an alluring display.

The one you must have is chutney. True, the East Indians serve only the first 4 condiments on this list, but there is nothing to prevent your going into the Ten-boy curry category with ten bowls of condiments on the table. Here is a list of possibilities:

Chutney
Chopped candied orange peel
Grated coconut
Chopped parsley
Chopped hard-cooked egg whites
Chopped peanuts
Coarsely ground coffee
Crumbled crisped bacon

Grated hard-cooked egg yolks
Mushrooms, hot, sliced
Sliced scallions, all of them

SUB-GUM-GAI-PEN

Chicken and Celery

Makes 6 to 8 servings

- 2½ cups diced uncooked chicken
- 3 tablespoons chopped green pepper
- 2½ cups sliced celery
- 2½ cups sliced celery-cabbage (chinese cabbage)
- ¾ cup seasoned chicken broth, fresh or canned
- 2½ teaspoons salt
- 2 tablespoons oil or shortening
- 3 fresh tomatoes
- 4 teaspoons Soy sauce
- 2½ tablespoons cornstarch
- ¼ cup cold chicken broth
- 3 to 4 cups fluffy cooked rice

There is a trick to making a Chinese dish Chinese fashion. One is to make portions of meat exactly the same size and to cut vegetables into small slivers so that they cook quickly. To make them prettier, the Chinese devised diagonal slicing for vegetables, and if you make this dish you should slice the celery and celery-cabbage on the diagonal making 1/8-inch thick slices.

Combine chicken and salt. Heat oil or shortening in a 9- or 10-inch skillet. Add chicken and cook over moderate heat until tender. Add green pepper, celery, cabbage and chicken broth. Cover. Cook about 10 minutes. Cut each tomato into eighths and add along with Soy sauce. Blend cornstarch with cold chicken broth and stir into the mixture, being careful not to break up tomatoes. Cook until the juice thickens, then serve over rice.

CHINESE WALNUT CHICKEN:—Omit tomatoes. Add 1½ cups walnuts, blanched and toasted (*page 299*), and crisp bits of ham made by chopping 3 slices boiled ham and cooking in butter. Stir these crisps into the dish just before serving.

CHICKEN BURGUNDY

Makes 4 servings

- 2 plump pullets, cut into pieces
- 4 strips bacon
- 2 tablespoons butter
- 1½ teaspoons MSG*
- ½ teaspoon freshly ground black pepper
- 2 teaspoons salt
- 1 teaspoon sweet paprika
- ½ cup coarsely chopped onion
- 1 teaspoon dried tarragon
- 1 cup flour
- 4 cups red burgundy
- 16 prunes
- 8 dates, seeded and chopped
- 1 cup seedless white grapes
- ¼ cup seedless raisins

Prepare the chicken and dry the pieces with a paper towel. Put bacon strips in skillet and sauté slowly until bacon is cooked. Remove and drain. Add butter, onions and tarragon to the skillet and sauté slowly. Combine flour and seasonings in a brown paper bag and shake to mix thoroughly. Add chicken pieces and shake until coated. Add these to the skillet, sauté, turning to brown on all sides. Remove to casserole (3-quart size or larger), pour fat from the skillet over the chicken, scraping the skillet to remove all the brown bits, sprinkle with the drained bacon and cover with the burgundy. Add remaining ingredients. Cover and bake in 350° oven for 45 minutes. Remove cover and continue baking until the chicken is tender.

The browned chicken can be combined with the wine and fruit and cooked in an electric controlled dial deep-fat fryer, instead of baking in the oven. Set control dial at 300° and when the liquid begins to boil turn control dial of cooker down to 175°. Cook until chicken is tender, about 1 hour. Reduce heat and serve from the fryer.

* See footnote, page 92.

CHICKEN BONNE FEMME

Makes 4 servings

- 1 (3-pound) plump pullet, disjointed
- ½ cup flour
- 2 teaspoons salt
- ½ cup chopped ripe olives, pits removed
- 1 cup heavy cream, scalded
- ½ teaspoon pepper
- ¼ cup butter
- 2 cups fresh mushrooms sliced or quartered
- 2 egg yolks, beaten
- ¼ cup dry sherry

Put the flour in a paper bag, add the salt and pepper, shake until blended and add the chicken pieces. Shake again, lift out each well coated piece, and brown in the butter which has been melted in a large skillet. When the chicken is brown add the mushrooms. Turn into a well greased casserole, cover. Bake in a moderate oven (350°), until tender, about 45 minutes. Remove and keep hot (covered) after pouring off all but about ¼ cup of the fat into the skillet in which the chicken was browned. Add the cream, beaten egg yolks and chopped olives to fat, and stir over medium heat until thickened. Add sherry, taste for seasoning and adjust if necessary, then pour over the chicken and it is ready to serve.

The nice thing about this dish is that it can be baked while you are sipping cocktails or enjoying conversation. The gravy can be made in a few minutes and poured over the chicken and then you are ready to dine.

SURREY FOWL WITH CREAM SAUCE

Makes 4 servings   *In pressure cooker*

- 1 roasting hen, dressed but left whole
- Salt
- Pepper
- 1 cup water
- 8 whole baby carrots
- 1 cup thick cream
- 1 tablespoon grated lemon peel

½ cup chopped onion	2 tablespoons butter or margarine
4 sprigs parsley	
Celery stalk	2 tablespoons flour

Leave the hen whole (or divide it into pieces if it won't fit into the pressure cooker). Place it on the rack, add the seasonings, water and giblets. Close the cooker, bring to 15 pound pressure and cook 7 minutes for each pound of fowl or 8 minutes per pound if it is a stewing chicken. Allow the pot to cool, remove chicken from the cooker and add the carrots to the broth. Return to heat and cook under pressure 4 minutes. Remove the carrots to a hot dish and strain the broth into a saucepan. Add cream and grated lemon peel. Stir the mixture over low heat until thoroughly blended and hot. Remove from heat. Melt the butter in top of double boiler over direct heat, add the flour and stir until blended, cooking over low heat for about 5 minutes, but do not brown. Add the broth and cream mixture and cook over boiling water for another 15 minutes, until thickened. Taste, add more salt and pepper if necessary, and if you like ⅛ teaspoon mace.

Peel the skin off chicken and remove the chicken from the bones, keeping the meat in as large pieces as possible. Arrange the white meat in the center of a big platter, the dark meat around the edge. Pour the sauce over the chicken so that it is evenly covered, then place in the refrigerator to get very cold. Just before serving garnish with the whole carrots, crisp hot curls of bacon and bunches of parsley.

CHICKEN MEXICAINE
Casa Minasso's

Makes 6 servings

3 or 4 pound roasting chicken, dressed	1 small carrot, scraped
	2 tablespoons olive oil

2 stalks celery	½ green pepper, chopped
1 tablespoon salt	2 tablespoons butter
1 teaspoon thyme	3 medium-sized onions, sliced
1 sweet pimiento, cut in strips	2 bay leaves
½ cup sliced fresh mushrooms	2 tablespoons chopped parsley
1 (No. 2) can whole tomatoes	Rice

Cut chicken into serving pieces. Place in large kettle, add salt, celery, carrot and enough water to almost cover (about ¾ cup per pound). Cover and simmer until chicken is tender, 1½ to 2 hours. Let chicken cool in stock. In heavy skillet, heat olive oil and butter. Add onions, green pepper and mushrooms; sauté until tender. Add tomatoes, bay leaves and thyme. Remove chicken from bones, cutting into bite-size pieces. Add to sauce with enough skimmed chicken stock to cover. Cover and simmer 30 minutes. Add pimiento and continue to cook until heated. Sprinkle chopped parsley over chicken mixture and serve with fluffy rice.

CURRIED BAKED CHICKEN BREASTS

Makes 4 servings

4 chicken breasts	1 teaspoon curry powder
½ lemon	2 cans chicken broth
⅓ cup fat	1 cup cream or undiluted evaporated milk
¼ cup minced onion	
¼ cup flour	1 teaspoon Kitchen Bouquet
1 teaspoon salt	

Wash chicken breasts thoroughly and dry carefully. Rub with lemon. Melt fat in large frying pan over moderate heat. Add chicken breasts and brown lightly on all sides. Remove browned chicken to 2-quart baking dish. Place onion in frying pan and cook 1 minute. Stir in flour, salt and curry powder. Add chicken broth, milk and Kitchen Bouquet. Cook, stirring constantly, until sauce thickens and boils. Pour sauce over chicken and cover casserole. Bake in moderate oven (350°) until chicken is tender, about 45 minutes. Serve immediately.

CRISP COUNTRY FRIED CHICKEN

Makes 4 servings

- 1 frying chicken (3 pounds or larger) fresh or frozen, disjointed
- ½ cup flour
- 1½ teaspoons paprika (optional)
- 1½ teaspoons salt
- ½ teaspoon freshly ground black pepper
- ½ cup bacon drippings
- ½ cup butter or margarine

If using a fresh chicken rinse in cold water and pat dry with paper towels. If using frozen chicken thaw at room temperature before beginning to fry the chicken.

Combine flour and seasonings in a paper bag. Toss until they are thoroughly mixed, add chicken pieces and shake until well coated. Combine bacon drippings and butter or margarine in a large heavy skillet. Remove the floured pieces of chicken from the bag and place in the hot fat. Cook over medium heat, cooking the largest pieces first and turning to brown them evenly. To fry chicken perfectly you can't crowd it. Use 2 skillets if necessary. If the large pieces are browned first and the very small ones added for browning later, a large skillet is sufficient. When browned, cover snugly and reduce heat, continuing to cook over medium heat for at least another 30 minutes. Uncover during the last 10 minutes of cooking so that the chicken will be crisp. The complete process of cooking, browning over low heat and crisping requires 1 to 1¼ hours.

To tell when fried chicken is done pierce the thickest part of the drumstick with a sharp knife. If the meat cuts easily and is brown, not pink, the chicken is ready to serve.

GUINEA HEN FRICASSEE

Makes 4 servings

6 slices bacon, diced	¼ cup chopped onions
1 (3½ to 4 pound) guinea hen, disjointed	1 cup dry red wine
	1 cup boiling water
2 tablespoons flour	Salt
Giblets, chopped	Paprika

Fry bacon until crisp, then remove from pan. Dredge guinea hen pieces with flour and brown in bacon fat. Add giblets, onion, wine and water and season. Be very liberal with the paprika. One level tablespoon of the common mild kind will not be too much. Cover and simmer gently for 2 to 2½ hours or until fowl is very tender. Serve with white or wild rice.

Turkey

DO YOU HAVE A TURKEY BUT NO CARVER?

Instead of serving the beautiful bird brown and fragrant with paper frills where its feet should be, the turkey can be carved in the kitchen. With a sharp knife it is a quick and easy job to remove both sides of the breast meat in a single slice, pressing the knife against the bone. Place these on a chopping board. Lift the leg and thigh off the turkey and make one deep gash down each turkey leg and remove the bone. Place this boneless meat on the chopping board. Now slice the boneless dark meat with the grain and arrange it on one side of a platter.

Slice the two big pieces of breast meat into even slices without disturbing the contour and arrange the two mounds on the other side of the platter. Now present the hot platter with its mounds of already sliced white and dark meat on the holiday table. This may remove the pleasure of seeing the bird, but it is a relief and a delight to most hosts.

Or proceed in the French fashion and present the bird garnished and with paper frills for all the guests to see, then remove it to the kitchen to do the carving and bring it back ready to serve as just suggested.

And did you ever season a turkey this way before roasting it? Rub the skin with a nipped clove of garlic, then with half butter and half bacon fat, then sprinkle with salt and paprika. Stuff it with any dressing you like and chill overnight. The next day cover the turkey with paper thin slices of onion and leave them there while the turkey roasts, removing them the last half hour for final browning of the skin.

Another idea: When you begin to carve a turkey remove the drumsticks for separate carving. Then make a deep cut the length of the thigh cutting clear to the bone. Ease the bone loose from the joint and pull it away leaving the dark boneless meat to be carved very easily. Unless someone begs the drumsticks they may be left for another meal another day.

BUFFET TURKEY

Makes 8 servings

- 1 turkey (about 7 pounds) ready-to-cook
- ½ cup fat
- 2 teaspoons Kitchen Bouquet
- 2 tablespoons honey
- 1 tablespoon water
- 2 tablespoons brown sugar
- 1 teaspoon salt
- ½ teaspoon ginger

Prepare turkey for roasting. Place a slice or two of bread in the neck cavity to hold skin in firm position. Tuck wing tips back to hold flap of neck skin in place. Truss legs in position and place turkey on rack in shallow roasting pan, breast side up. Bring fat, Kitchen Bouquet, honey, water, sugar, salt and ginger to boil in small saucepan. Brush about 1/3 of this mixture over turkey and roast in slow oven (325°) until turkey is tender, about 2½ hours. After 1 hour, brush turkey with ½ remaining glaze, and repeat again after the second hour. When turkey is done, cool at room temperature for 1 hour, then place in refrigerator until cold.

TURKEY MOUSSE

Makes about 8 cups

- 1 envelope unflavored gelatin
- ¼ cup cold water
- 1 cup turkey broth
- 1½ teaspoons salt
- ¼ teaspoon pepper
- ¼ teaspoon dry mustard
- ¼ teaspoon marjoram
- 3 egg yolks
- 2 tablespoons lemon juice
- 3 cups diced cooked turkey
- 1 cup heavy cream
- 1 bunch water cress

Soften gelatin in cold water, then dissolve over low heat. Place in container of electric blender. Add turkey broth, salt, pepper, mustard, marjoram, egg yolks, lemon juice and turkey. Cover container and turn on blender. Run until smooth, about 2 minutes, stopping to stir down every 30 seconds. Whip cream with rotary egg beater. Fold blended ingredients gently into whipped cream. Pour into large loaf pan, 9 x 5 inches. Cover with aluminum foil or waxed paper. Chill until firm. Serve on cold platter liberally garnished with water cress.

Stuffings for Chicken or Turkey

You can combine cooked rice with slightly cooked

and coarsely chopped chicken livers, tiny whole onions from a can and a few nuts, either pecans or chopped walnuts. Always stir stuffing lightly and fill the cavity but do not pack it or the dressing will be too dry.

Generous butter added to the stuffing helps baste the bird as it roasts.

APPLE STUFFING

Makes 8 cups

- 2 cups tart apples, sliced or chopped
- 5 cups crisp bread crumbs
- ½ cup seedless raisins
- ½ cup chopped cooked prunes
- 4 tablespoons butter or margarine, melted
- ¼ cup brown sugar
- 2 teaspoons grated lemon peel
- ½ teaspoon sweet paprika
- ½ teaspoon cinnamon
- ¾ teaspoon salt
- ¼ cup apple juice

Rub the cavity of the bird with ½ a lemon, squeezing to coat it well. Then combine all ingredients for the stuffing in a large mixing bowl, stir lightly with a fork and use to stuff chicken, turkey or loin of pork or duck.

Scoop up some of this dressing after it is well blended. Mold in a rounded oval with a tablespoon. Sprinkle lightly with flour and deep-fat fry it until crisp brown. Serve around the roasted chicken or turkey, when you are serving it either hot or cold without stuffing.

WILD RICE AND SAUSAGE STUFFING

Enough for 6 squabs or 1 roast chicken
Double recipe for turkey

- 1 cup wild rice, uncooked
- ½ pound sausage pork links
- 1 tablespoon poultry seasoning

1 tablespoon chopped pars- ½ teaspoon pepper
ley   1 teaspoon salt
1 tablespoon chopped onion

Cook 1 cup wild rice, after washing in several cold waters, by dropping it into boiling salted water and cooking until tender. Rinse with boiling water and drain. Add remaining ingredients to rice, except sausages. Cut sausages into bits and cook in small amount of fat. When crispy brown, drain and add with 2 tablespoons of the sausage drippings to the rice.

Duck

TO ROAST DUCK

Ducks usually run from 4 to 4½ pounds when they are dressed and ready to cook. Whether roasted whole or split in half, they should be rubbed outside and inside with salt. Arrange on a rack in an open roasting pan and roast in a slow oven (325°) about 2½ hours until tender, crisp and brown. Drain off the fat every half hour or so and baste the duck each time with whatever glaze is going to be used. This can be done by rubbing the bird with half an orange, squeezing the juice over the bird and rubbing the skin with the softened half, and each time leaving the orange skins in the pan while the duck is cooking, to add their flavor to both the duck and the gravy.

Three oranges are required for basting if orange is used.

DUCK GRAVY

Drain the juices from the pan, and all but 1 tablespoon of fat. Add 1 cup of water to the drippings and scrape all the brown stickings to the pan. Add 1 cup concentrated orange juice to which 2 tablespoons of cornstarch have been blended. Cook over low heat, stirring constantly until thick.

ROASTED DUCK WITH ORIENTAL PLUM SAUCE

Makes 4 servings

- 1 duckling (4 to 5 pounds) ready-to-cook weight
- 2 tablespoons honey
- 1 teaspoon Kitchen Bouquet

Quarter duckling, remove wing tips and backbone. Arrange the pieces, skin side up, on rack in a large, shallow roasting pan. Roast in slow oven (325°) until duckling is tender, about 1½ to 2 hours. About 30 minutes before duckling is done brush all over with a mixture of the honey and Kitchen Bouquet. Return to oven and allow to finish roasting. If a crisp skin is desired, after duckling is done run under moderate broiler for about 10 minutes. Serve immediately with Oriental Plum Sauce.

ORIENTAL PLUM SAUCE

Makes 1¼ cups

- 1 cup plum jam
- 2 tablespoons vinegar
- 1 tablespoon orange juice
- ½ teaspoon Kitchen Bouquet
- ¼ teaspoon allspice
- ½ teaspoon dry mustard

Combine all ingredients and blend together until smooth, about 15 seconds. Serve with roast duckling or pork.

BONELESS DUCK WITH MUSHROOMS

Makes 6 servings

- 1 Long Island duckling (4 to 5 pounds) ready-to-cook weight
- 2 cups water
- 1 teaspoon salt
- 3 stalks celery

POULTRY AND GAME ON YOUR TABLE

1 carrot	mushrooms
2 bay leaves	3 tablespoons cornstarch
1 cup dry white table wine	½ teaspoon Kitchen Bouquet
1 (3 oz.) can sliced broiled	Cooked rice

Quarter duckling and place in Dutch oven. Add water, salt, celery, carrot and bay leaves. Bring to boil, cover, lower heat and allow to simmer until duckling is tender, about 45 minutes. Remove from heat, strain broth into pint measuring cup and allow fat to rise. Meanwhile remove skin from duckling and cut meat into julienne strips. Skim off fat from broth and pour out all but 1 cup broth. Place broth and wine in a saucepan and bring to boil. Combine drained mushroom broth with cornstarch and Kitchen Bouquet and add to boiling mixture, stirring constantly until thick and clear. Stir in mushrooms and duck meat. Allow to heat again but not boil. Serve immediately with hot cooked rice.

DUCK BIGARDE

Makes 4 servings

1 duckling	1 teaspoon lemon juice
Rinds of 1 orange and 1 lemon	2 tablespoons cornstarch
	½ teaspoon salt
1½ cups orange juice	½ teaspoon ginger
1 teaspoon coarsely diced onion	½ teaspoon Kitchen Bouquet

Quarter duckling and roast uncovered for 1 hour in a slow oven (325°). Transfer to baking dish. Meanwhile place remaining ingredients in container of electric blender, or combine in mason jar and shake until blended. Blend 1 minute. Pour into saucepan. Bring to boil, stirring constantly. Pour over duckling in baking dish. Cover and continue baking until tender, about 30 minutes more.

Cooking Game . . . or When Your Husband Bags a Bird

If you have a husband who is a hunter by all means encourage him and admire the birds or bird he brings home. Cook it, serve it, make a party out of it for a few friends whose tastes are well enough known to you to be sure your feast will be appreciated.

Serve turnips, green peas and wild rice with wild duck and don't forget the currant jelly.

Try fried hominy and potato chips with quail. Currant jelly with this, too.

When he brings home partridge serve a helping of sauerkraut and a partridge to each guest.

With pheasant remember wild rice or brown rice cooked in chicken broth, and have plenty of tart jelly.

Notes on Game Birds

Pheasant

Cooking pheasant is decided by age. If the spur at the back of the foot is pliable and the end is rounded you have a young bird appropriate for roasting. Older birds had better be cooked in the pressure cooker or pot roast fashion.

Braised celery, wild rice or the delicious brown variety of rice along with cranberry jelly and all tart jellies are good company for pheasant.

Refrigerate pheasant with a few stalks of celery inside each bird for 2 days before cooking.

One pheasant serves 2 to 4.

Pheasant is regarded as royal family among game birds. It is expensive, it is rare, and the bird is very, very dry. It should be well "larded" to produce a moist delicious roast bird. Here are two ways you can achieve this: one is conventional and time consuming; the other is effective and requires no watching at all.

To prepare pheasant for roasting, in case the hunter didn't do it: Allow pheasant to develop slight aroma, usually about 4 or 5 days after it is killed, and the breast begins to change color. Only then must the bird be plucked and cleaned for cooking, much as you would a chicken. Fill the cavity lightly with a stuffing with lots of butter in it or put a whole quartered orange inside.

ROAST PHEASANT AU VIN BLANC

Makes 2 servings

A brace of pheasants (2 birds) prepared for roasting
¼ pound butter softened
½ cup bacon drippings, softened
2 cups dry white wine
1 teaspoon salt
½ teaspoon freshly ground pepper

Soften the butter and bacon drippings by allowing them to stand at room temperature. Mix together and use them to coat the birds so that they have a thick, even layer of the fat. Place in an open roasting pan and bake in a slow oven (325°) until tender, 1 to 1¼ hours. Baste frequently with a wine mixture which is made by combining the salt and pepper with the white wine.

PHEASANT ROASTED IN PAPER BAG:—Proceed exactly as you would for roasting the pheasant in the oven with this one exception. Prepare the wine sauce, dunk 2 slices of dry bread in it until they absorb the wine, then place one inside each bird. Oil two brown paper bags, large enough to completely cover the bird and be twisted shut at the end, by pouring about 1/3 to 1/2 cup cooking oil into the bag and shaking and turning it until it is well coated. Put the birds one inside each bag, twist the ends shut tightly, place in a roasting pan and bake in a very slow oven (300°) 2 hours without opening the bags.

PHEASANT IN PRESSURE COOKER:—One woman I know copes with the dryness of pheasant by disjointing the plucked and cleaned birds, placing them in a pressure cooker, adding a can of cream of mushroom soup thinned with about 1/2 cup dry sherry and 1/4 cup cream. She then cooks them till moist tenderness, about 30 minutes after pressure has reached 15 pounds. Large birds require 45 minutes.

Wild Duck

Wild duck is a great favorite with gourmets and although there are several types of wild ducks, mallards are especially favored. Opinions differ on how long ducks should be aged after they have been plucked, drawn and cleaned with every pinfeather carefully removed. Usually refrigerate them 2 or 3 days before cooking; serve 1/2 duck for each person.

Gourmets like their duck rare with blood red juice oozing from each gamy flavored bite. You may prefer it medium well done, and if so cook it a little longer.

Grouse

Grouse is considered a relation of quail and of partridge or prairie chicken.

BROILED GROUSE

Makes 4 servings

4 grouse	1 teaspoon salt
Water to cover	1/8 teaspoon freshly ground
1 large onion, halved	pepper
4 stalks celery	1/2 cup olive oil or salad oil

Split the cleaned grouse down the back. Arrange them in a Dutch oven or any heavy pot, cover with water. Add the onion, celery and seasonings. Cover and simmer for 30 minutes. Remove the grouse, drain and brush them with the oil. Place skin side down on a piece of aluminum foil or directly on the broiling rack and broil under medium heat 15 to 20 minutes, or until brown, turning once and basting frequently with the oil.

Partridge

Partridge are at their best early in the hunting season. When the breastbone gives easily under pressure, the meat is almost sure to be tender. To produce the superb flavor of partridge at its best refrigerate them for 2 or 3 days, after they are drawn and cleaned, before cooking them. As with most game the fat must be supplied to produce a juicy bird when cooked. Game birds live on grain, and don't grow their own fat, but it is easy enough to supply with a layer of butter and bacon drippings or by almost wrapping the bird in thin slices of salt pork.

Serve half a bird for each person, and remember that sauerkraut goes well with partridge.

PARTRIDGES HUNTER STYLE

Makes 3 servings

3 partridges, disjointed	1 teaspoon parsley,
3 tablespoons butter	chopped
1 carrot, chopped fine	3 tablespoons flour

1 medium-sized onion, chopped fine	½ cup sherry
1 teaspoon thyme, chopped	2 cups chopped mushrooms
1½ cups consommé	Salt and pepper

Brown pieces of partridge well in butter, add chopped onion, carrot, thyme and parsley and brown lightly. Stir in flour and gradually stir in consommé, wine and chopped mushrooms. Season and simmer, covered, until partridge is tender, 15 to 30 minutes. Serve with croutons.

Woodcock

The dark meat of woodcock is a great delicacy. These birds are best during the months when there is a frost. Refrigerate 2 or 3 days before cooking, after they have been plucked, drawn and cleaned as soon as possible after they were bagged. Wrap the birds with salt pork or bacon slices and baste with a dry red wine. Stir a few dry juniper berries into the brown gravy you serve with woodcock, one bird for each person.

Quail

Refrigerate these delightful birds for 2 or 3 days before cooking (let's hope they were plucked, drawn and cleaned soon after they were bagged). Quail are small, serve 1 or more for each person. Lard quail as you do the other birds, or baste them with salad oil or butter. Serve fried hominy and cranberry jelly with quail.

Wild Goose

ROAST CANADIAN GOOSE WITH CRANBERRY STUFFING

1 wild goose (10 to 12 pounds)	½ cup chopped celery
	1½ cups fresh cranberries,

- 8 thin slices salt pork or 10 slices bacon
- ¼ cup butter
- 2 cups uncooked brown rice
- ½ cup chopped onions
- ground coarsely
- 2 cups chicken broth
- ½ cup chopped parsley
- 1 teaspoon salt
- ½ teaspoon freshly ground pepper
- ½ teaspoon thyme

When the goose is cleaned cover with the strips of salt pork or bacon so that it will be basted while roasting. Melt the butter in a large skillet, add onions, celery, rice and cook over medium heat stirring constantly until the rice is deep brown. Add the ground or chopped cranberries and the remaining ingredients. Stir thoroughly, cover and continue cooking over low heat for 15 or 20 minutes, until rice is tender. Add water if more liquid is needed before the rice is done. Cool mixture.

When the rice stuffing is lukewarm or cool, spoon into the cavity of the goose. Place skewers across the opening and lace tightly closed with cord. Place in roasting pan with the breast side up, and bake in a 325° oven for 5 to 6 hours (25 minutes per pound), basting occasionally.

Venison

ROAST LEG OF VENISON WITH SOUR CREAM

Makes 10 to 14 servings

- 4 medium-sized onions, sliced
- 4 medium-sized carrots, sliced
- 6 stalks celery, sliced
- 6 bay leaves
- 1 cup water
- 1 (6 to 7 pound) leg of venison
- ½ pound fat salt pork, sliced
- Salt and pepper
- ½ cup butter
- 1 cup flour
- 3 cups sour cream
- 1½ cups dry red wine
- 1½ cups currant jelly

Put vegetables and bay leaves in baking pan and add water. Put in meat, skin side up. Place in very hot oven (450 to 500°) until browned, 20 to 30 minutes. Turn and cover with strips of salt pork and season. Reduce oven temperature to moderate (350 to 375°) and roast, approximately 30 minutes to the pound or until meat thermometer shows 180°. Remove meat, strain liquid and skim. Melt butter, add flour, then add to strained liquid. Gradually add sour cream, jelly and wine and simmer until thick. Pour over venison and serve.

VENISON LOAF

Makes 6 servings

- 2 tablespoons butter
- 2 cups mashed potatoes (or 1 package frozen mashed potatoes)
- 1 pound venison, ground
- ½ pound bulk sausage
- 1 teaspoon salt
- ½ teaspoon freshly ground pepper
- 1½ cups coarsely chopped onions
- 1 egg
- ¼ cup dry red wine
- 2 tablespoons catsup

In a large skillet melt the butter and add onions. Sauté until they begin to brown. In a mixing bowl combine all other ingredients, and mix thoroughly. Add the onion mixture, mix again and place in a well greased oblong loaf pan or in a 2-quart ovenware glass casserole. Bake in slow oven (350°) for 1½ hours.

9

Salad Secrets

Everybody likes salads, likes the *look* of them. Ah! There is the catch. How can they be beautifully arranged? How can it be done quickly and effectively?

These pages are devoted to Salad Know-How, which should enable you to select the salad which will contribute the most to the appearance of your table as well as be tops in flavor and texture for the meal it enhances.

What There Is to Choose From

GREEN SALADS:—How to select the greens and how to "toss."
MIXED VEGETABLE SALADS:—How to make Picture Salad Bowls and "bouquet" arrangements before tossing.
RING MOLDED SALADS:—As useful as your coffee cups; as handy as an extra bowl; as decorative as a nosegay.
SOUFFLÉ SALADS:—In which the mayonnaise is molded with the seafood, meat, vegetables or fruit.
FRUIT SALADS:—Beautiful plate arrangements and some foreign fixings.

SALADS WITH AN INTERNATIONAL REPUTATION
FROZEN SALADS

Do You Serve Salads in All These Ways?

As company for the main course, on salad plates or in one big bowl?
As garnish on the meat platter, in small molds or piled into lettuce cups?
As a quick, beautiful and delicious way to serve the vegetables at a buffet?
As a main dish, accompanied by soup or sandwiches to complete the meal?
As a dessert to the family or at a party?
As the colorful but edible centerpiece decoration on a party table?

Green Salads

The green most often used for green salads is iceberg lettuce. But it's nice to use a deeper shade of green with it. There are lots of greens to choose from during the year, for in the markets you will also find bibb, Boston and leaf lettuce, water cress, romaine, chicory, chinese cabbage, escarole and several others. The tender dark green leaves of fresh spinach are excellent salad greens, and so are the chopped tops of scallions.

Fresh crisp greens are absolute "musts" in successfully making a fine salad. Select the best quality available and clean and refrigerate them as soon as possible. It is a good idea to clean greens the minute they reach your kitchen. Remove any wilted parts, wash the greens well in lukewarm water. No, it won't wilt them and it will clean them more thoroughly than cold water. Drain them in a wire salad rack or on paper towels. Greens should be stored without a drop of moisture except their own, but they should be stored so that not a drop of their own moisture is lost.

Store the cleaned dry greens in the refrigerator vegetable crisper or in plastic bags to chill and crisp. Water cress, parsley and mint keep well in glass jars with lids screwed on firmly to hold their flavor inside.

How to Make a "Tossed" Green Salad

Chop these greens when you use them: chives, parsley, scallion tops or water cress stems.

Cut chinese cabbage into ½-inch slices when adding them to your salad.

All other greens should be broken or pulled into bite-size pieces. Never cut head lettuce unless making wedges or removing hearts to make lettuce cups.

Grated onion, minced garlic and onion slices are good in all mixed salads and green salads.

Select the greens you intend to combine in your salad and the dressing you intend to use over it, or the oil and vinegar and seasonings to add as you "toss."

Assemble the greens, break or chop—as is suitable for the greens used—and put into the salad bowl. If your seasoning is added in the dressing, shake the dressing and pour over the salad in circular motion. With a large fork and spoon pick up and turn the greens until the leaves are coated and glossy. You only want enough dressing to coat the leaves. When this is achieved, tossing is over.

To add the seasonings as you assemble the salad proceed as follows: Assemble the greens in your bowl. If you are fond of garlic, nip the end of a clove and rub the inside of the bowl before adding the greens. If you use herbs—and if not, why not? —sprinkle a pinch of basil (about ½ teaspoon for a quart of greens) gently over the greens. Follow with ½ teaspoon of tarragon, 1 teaspoon salt and then freshly ground pepper to your liking. Almost any herbs can be used, of course, but this one is good in salad. Now pour oil in a fine thin stream making a circle and a cross over the top of the greens. Pour vinegar making only a cross. This is because you want much more oil than vinegar and having a pattern in mind insures your getting it. Pick up the greens with fork and spoon and toss until leaves are glossy. Taste, and adjust seasoning if you think necessary.

Basil, marjoram and tarragon are good in almost any salad. Use discreet sprinkling of oregano in seafood; add rosemary or chopped mint to fruit or meat or green salads. Try a single herb or use several in combination.

Good Green Salads

Combine any greens you like, or try one of these:

Velvety spinach leaves, lettuce chunks and leaves, chicory or endive. Tear into bite-size pieces, mix 2 parts French Dressing (*page 192*) and 1 part finely chopped water cress, pour over salad and toss until greens are coated. Use just enough to coat the vegetables, with no extra dressing in the bowl.

Combine any greens from the refrigerator, add part or all of a package of frozen julienne string beans (unthawed). Add French Dressing (*page 192*) and toss.

Combine raw broccoli flowerettes, carefully cut from tender stalks, with garden lettuce leaves. Add a pinch of ginger to the dressing you select.

Add heavy sprinkling of chopped parsley to pale endive; serve with French Dressing (*page 192*).

For all the shades of green in the woods combine escarole, water cress, romaine and chicory with bite-size pieces of head lettuce. Toss with Chiffonade Dressing *(page 193)*.

Combine the dark green leaves of escarole with the pale green of chinese cabbage, coat by tossing with the dressing you like best.

Frost wedges of head lettuce, chilled and crunchy, with Mayonnaise *(page 193)*.

Sprinkle lightly with chopped fresh mint another time, before adding the sour cream coat.

Add slices or cubes of ripe avocado to any of the green combinations for wonderful texture contrast.

Mixed Vegetable Tossed Salads

The minute you add tomatoes or radish slices to greens, or any of the other colorful crisp raw or cooked vegetables so good in tossed salads, it is no longer a "green" salad. But it sure is a good one and a beautiful one.

The mixed green salad arranges itself with the natural grace and color contrast of the pine woods in the country. With colorful vegetables added, you can have "premeditated" beauty in picture salad bowls.

Picture Salad Bowls

For Bouquet Arrangements, begin with a chilled salad bowl:

Make a mound of water cress in center of the bowl, surround with small whole or sliced radishes, or ripe tomato slices, encircle with broken romaine and lettuce pieces, compose a border of endive and carrot curls. Add dressing after everyone has seen it! Then toss.

Arrange crisp greens in shades of light to dark around the edge of a cold salad bowl. Fill the center with a mound of water cress or thinly sliced unpeeled cucumber. Outline the center portion by a ring of overlapping slices of red radish or with hard-cooked egg slices. Sprinkle with herbs. Cover and keep cold in refrigerator until serving time. Serve the dressing separately to be added after it has been admired by everyone. Add dressing, toss and serve.

Pile any combination of greens you have or like into the center of the bowl. Surround with circles of vegetables in contrasting colors. It could be slices of cucumber and onion for a white circle, tomato slices forming a red circle next to it, radishes either sliced or left whole for the next. Add your favorite dressing and toss when ready to serve.

When arranging salad for a big party fill a tray with bowls or lettuce cups holding either individual or bountiful servings of a variety of salads. A guacamole dip made for a meat garnish would be a good bowl to have on this tray, too. If you have a variety of olives don't put the black ones in one bowl and the stuffed ones in another and the jumbo in another, but combine an assortment of each in each.

COCONUT PINEAPPLE SLAW

Makes 6 servings

- 3 cups cabbage, finely grated
- 1 cup coconut, chopped
- 1 cup crushed pineapple, drained
- ½ cup pineapple juice
- 3 tablespoons lemon juice
- 1 teaspoon salt
- 1 teaspoon MSG*

Measure the cabbage into a mixing bowl. It packs down after liquid is added, so that the quantity fools you. Combine all other ingredients, mix well and pour over the cabbage. Toss lightly. Chill in covered bowl.

* See footnote, page 92.

RED CABBAGE SLAW

Makes 4 cups

- 2½ cups shredded red cabbage (or half red and half white cabbage)
- ½ cup evaporated milk, undiluted
- 1 teaspoon salt
- ½ teaspoon salt
- ⅓ cup herb flavored or wine vinegar
- ½ cup sugar
- 1 teaspoon celery seed

Shred crisp cabbage as fine or coarse as you like it. Combine all other ingredients in a bottle, shake well and pour over the slaw. Cover and chill until ready to serve.

Ring Molded Salads

Remember what I said about salads in ring molds being used as often as your coffee cups? They are that useful: so pretty and appetizing; offer such variety in color and in flavors. They can be made in advance, with almost anything you have on hand and will look as expensive as all get out. The filled ring mold definitely puts your best food forward when serving time arrives.

The recipes for the salads suggested here are for large ring molds. You can, of course, shape them in any mold. And what nicer way to serve luncheon portions than in individual ring molds? Which reminds me . . . most of these recipes are Jim Dandies for filling small molds to unmold on a meat platter, forming a ring of Salad Garnishes *(page 137)* around the meat.

However, about ring molded beauties. Fill the mold you use with water, measure carefully to see how many cups it will hold, then adjust these recipes to fill it completely. This makes it prettier, insures its unmolding without breaking.

How to Mold Salads

TO MAKE SALADS MOLD QUICKLY:—Use ice and water or partially frozen fruit juice for the cup of cold liquid in the recipe.

Place bowl of liquid gelatin in bowl of ice and water to chill to the "slightly thickened" stage. Stir occasionally.

Set mold of salad in pan of ice and water; then place in refrigerator. Salad will be ready to unmold in 1 hour.

Molded salads become firm faster in metal molds or pans.

NO FANCY MOLDS NEEDED:—For basic 4-cup recipes use 6 individual molds or a 1-quart mold. Molds for salads need not be fancy. Just look in your kitchen cabinet and see what you have.

For individual molds, choose individual metal molds of any shape, custard cups or ordinary coffee cups.

For a large single mold use loaf pan, square cake pan or a bowl. Or, if available, use ring molds or other shaped pans, even if they are not especially designed for gelatin dishes.

To measure your mold, use a standard measuring cup and count the number of cups of water required to fill the mold. A 1-quart mold holds 4 cups.

HOW TO UNMOLD AND SERVE:—When the salad is firm, dip a small pointed knife in warm water; use it to loosen the salad around the top rim of the mold. Then quickly dip the mold just to the top in lukewarm water. (If water is too hot, it will melt the salad.) Shake mold slightly to loosen the salad. Then cover with a plate and turn mold and plate over together. Lift mold off the salad.

There's a trick to centering a large mold of salad upon the plate. Slightly moisten the top of the salad while in the mold and moisten the serving plate, too. Then unmold as directed and slip the salad into the center.

Small molds of salad may be unmolded onto the salad greens. For a large mold it is easier to unmold the salad onto the serving plate first. Then arrange crisp greens around the salad close to the base of the mold.

MUSHROOM RING MOLD

Makes 5 cups

- 2 (6 oz.) cans mushrooms, whole or sliced
- 2 envelopes unflavored gelatin
- 1 cup hot, well seasoned chicken broth
- 3 tablespoons chopped onion
- 2 tablespoons chopped chives
- ½ cup parsley flowerettes
- ¼ teaspoon ground cloves
- ½ teaspoon freshly ground black pepper
- 2 cups dry sauterne
- Salt to taste

Drain mushrooms, reserving liquid in bowl. Add gelatin and let stand 5 minutes until softened. Add hot chicken broth and stir until dissolved. Add seasonings, except salt, then mushrooms, cover and cool at room temperature for about 30 minutes. This allows the seasonings to "steep." Add wine, taste for seasoning and add salt if necessary. Pour into 5-cup ring mold. Chill until set and unmold. Fill center with chicken or turkey salad or with whole crisp red radishes with part of their green stems left on. Garnish with pale greens.

To make this extra pretty, cut diamond or coin-size dots from pimiento slices and arrange on top of the mold as it is served.

MINCEMEAT SALAD RING

Fills 6-cup ring mold

- 2 packages lemon flavored gelatin
- 1½ cups hot water
- 2 cups orange juice
- 2 cups mincemeat
- ½ cup chopped nuts

Dissolve gelatin in hot water. Add orange juice and chill mixture until slightly thickened. Stir in remaining ingredients and pour into an 8-inch ring mold (6 cup) and chill until firm.

    Fill center with chilled thick sour cream to serve as a rich salad.

    Fill center with cubed smoked turkey and surround with thin slices of buttered ice-box rye bread or with very thin bread and butter sandwiches, for a sandwich and salad luncheon plate. Garnish with drained whole fruit.

    Pile crisp water cress in center to accompany roast chicken or roast turkey for a holiday or company buffet.

CRANBERRY RING

Fills 8-cup mold

- 1 quart cranberries
- 1½ cups granulated sugar
- 2 envelopes unflavored gelatin
- ½ cup orange juice
- 2 cups diced unpeeled apples
- 1 cup chopped walnuts

Grind the cranberries in a food chopper using the fine blade. Add sugar, mix, and let stand for 15 minutes, stirring occasionally. Soften gelatin in the orange juice for 5 minutes, then stir over hot water until dissolved. Mix gelatin mixture with cranberries, apples and chopped walnuts. Pour into mold, chill in the refrigerator until set. Unmold and garnish with crisp lettuce; serve plain or with a dressing of Mayonnaise *(page 193)*.

CLEAR ASPIC JELLY
For Savory Salad Base

Makes 2 cups

- 1 envelope unflavored gelatin
- ½ cup cold water
- 1¼ cups boiling water
- ½ cup dry white wine or sherry
- 1 tablespoon concentrated frozen lemon juice
- 1 cup well seasoned condensed chicken broth or beef bouillon
- 1 tablespoon grated onion
- 1 teaspoon Worcestershire sauce
- ⅛ teaspoon cayenne

This is the aspic "jewel case" for greens, seafood, chicken or an endless variety of chopped ingredients.

Sprinkle gelatin over cold water. When it is softened, add hot broth and stir until dissolved. Add all other ingredients, stir and cool to consistency of unbeaten egg white. Then make these combinations in ring molds or individual molds or in any shapes desired.

CUCUMBER MOLD:—Add 1½ cups chopped cucumber with ¾ cup sour cream, a few drops of green vegetable coloring and 2 tablespoons lemon juice.

DEVILED EGGS RING MOLD:—Fill fold with 1/3 of the aspic, chill until set. Prepare deviled eggs and make a cross with strips of pimiento on top the congealed gelatin where the deviled eggs will be placed, one on top of each cross upside down. Cover the eggs with the remaining gelatin and chill until set.

CRAB AND AVOCADO RING:—Combine 1 cup crabmeat, from which the cartilage has been carefully removed, with 1 cup diced avocado, 2 tablespoons lemon juice and 1 teaspoon dry mustard. Stir into the gelatin mixture when it has congealed to the consistency of unbeaten egg white. Chill until set. Unmold and serve with the dressing you prefer piled into the center.

CHICKEN RING MOLD:—Add 2 cups chopped chicken, 1/3 cup seeded ripe olives, 1 cup diced celery, 1 tablespoon tarragon vinegar or ½ teaspoon dried tarragon, 1 cup seedless white grapes, fresh or canned. Combine all ingredients and stir into the aspic and chill until set. Serve with Mayonnaise (*page 193*) in the center.

HAM RING MOLD:—Combine 1 cup chopped, cooked ham with ½ cup dark red cherries drained and ½ cup chopped celery. Stir into the aspic and chill. For the ham you can replace the dry sherry with ¼ cup Madeira wine.

VEGETABLE RING MOLD:—Combine vegetables which will show off with color contrast. Coarsely shredded cabbage looks well with a little green pepper, thin slices of carrots, sliced radishes, a few peas and whatever else you want to put into it. The vegetables can be either cooked or raw. Omit sherry when making the aspic and replace with ¼ cup lemon juice. You can use a total of 1½ to 2 cups of vegetables in making this ring mold.

APPLE JELLY SALAD

Fills 1½ quart mold

- 2¾ cups apple juice, heated
- 2 packages lemon flavored gelatin
- 2 tablespoons lemon juice
- ¼ cup mayonnaise
- 1 cup grated carrots
- ½ cup sliced celery
- ½ cup grated cucumber
- ¼ teaspoon salt

Dissolve the gelatin in hot apple juice and allow it to cool to consistency of unbeaten egg white before combining with the remaining ingredients. Stir until blended and pour into melon shaped mold or into ring mold. Chill until firm.

Serve with roast pork or with roast chicken.

SAUERKRAUT MOLD

Fills 1-quart mold

- 1 (3 oz.) package lemon flavored gelatin
- ½ cup boiling water
- 1 cup cold water
- 2 tablespoons finely chopped onion
- ¼ cup thick sour cream
- 1½ cups canned sauerkraut, drained and chopped
- ⅓ cup chopped raw apple
- ½ cup chopped or coarsely grated cucumber

Add the gelatin to the boiling water, remove from heat and stir until dissolved. Add the cold water, sour cream and stir until thoroughly mixed. Chill in refrigerator until consistency of unbeaten egg white. Fold in the remaining ingredients and fill a 1-quart mold. Chill in refrigerator until firm, and garnish with red apple wedges and cucumber slices and with small lettuce cups filled with sour cream.

SOUFFLÉ SALADS

Again a practical beauty. The soufflé salad combines anything you have or like with the mayonnaise you ordinarily serve separately. Anything goes into it, from lobster to cole slaw to a medley of fruits. Use these soufflés to aid your color scheme, your flavor scheme—as an appetizer, an entree, an accompanying dish or a dessert.

One reason they are so practical is that they are ready to serve in about an hour. This is much faster than the usual molded salad, in case you care. You may want it to wait all day. It will do that, too.

SOUFFLÉ SALAD

Makes 4 to 6 cups

1 package lemon or lime flavored gelatin	¼ teaspoon salt Dash of pepper (omit for fruit salads)
1 cup hot water	
½ cup cold water	1 to 2½ cups vegetables, fruit, meat, poultry, fish, cheese or hard-cooked eggs
1 to 2 tablespoons vinegar or lemon juice	
½ cup mayonnaise	

Dissolve gelatin in hot water. Add cold water, vinegar, mayonnaise, salt and pepper. Blend well with rotary beater. Pour into refrigerator freezing tray. Quick-chill in freezing unit (without changing control) 15 to 20 minutes, or until firm about 1 inch from edge but soft in center. Turn mixture into bowl and whip with rotary beater until fluffy. Fold in vegetables, fruit, meat, poultry, fish, cheese or eggs. Pour into 1-quart mold or individual molds. Chill until firm in refrigerator (not freezing unit) 30 to 60 minutes. Unmold and garnish with salad greens. Serve with additional mayonnaise, if desired.

(When making vegetable and meat salads, add ½ to 1 tablespoon finely chopped onion.)

Flavoring Soufflé Salads

Try using Garlic Mayonnaise (*page 195*), Curry Mayonnaise (*page 195*) or Plain Mayonnaise (*page 193*) made with lemon for seafood, fowl, lamb or veal.

Or serve an additional helping of another dressing in a separate sauceboat with the salad. Spoon blobs of seasoned dressing around the base of salads you made with regular mayonnaise. The dressing can be spooned around the base after a garnish of salad greens is arranged. You can also put it around in expert design with a pastry tube.

Decorate in the fashion just suggested, using Fruit Salad Dressing (*page 196*) to garnish a soufflé salad made with fruit.

Mold any combination soufflé salad in small molds to put on the meat platter.

Double the soufflé recipe, and make half into small molds to use the next day.

Fruit Salads

A fruit salad is popular with almost everybody at any time but it is usually the choice for a Dessert (*page 252*). And no wonder, for fruits "go together" as gracefully as an assortment of greens.

And have you ever served fruit salads at breakfast? When fruit is so abundant in the market you can't get enough of it, try the salad idea for early family or late Sunday Party Breakfasts. Preparing the fruit is easy; but as with everything else in the world there are some tricks to it.

Tips on Fixing Fruit for Salad

Apples in a salad may look prettier if left unpeeled when you core and slice or dice them.

Bananas should be fully ripe, have yellow peel flecked with brown. Slices keep their color if sprinkled with lemon, orange or grapefruit juice or when submerged in fruit juices of a fruit mixture. When you intend to use banana slices, run a fork down the length of the peeled banana, making ridges lengthwise. Then slice. See? . . . you made scallops.

Banana Logs are made by snipping off the ends of peeled banana (you can eat those or put the pieces in a fruit mix) and cutting banana into 2- or 3-inch lengths. Now roll them in orange or lemon juice, then in chopped coconut. Try Nutmeg Coconut (*page 184*) on these, or Toasted Coconut (*page 184*).

Grapefruit or Oranges can be peeled spiral fashion,

or, more quickly by slicing off peel at top and bottom, then cutting peel off the sides with downward strokes. Wedges are made by cutting on each side of the membrane and removing clear wedge of fruit.

In slicing fruit, make even slices for a pretty salad.

Make cups from orange or grapefruit shells by cutting the whole fruit in a sawtooth zigzag pattern around the center. Scoop out the fruit and use halves as containers for meat or fruit mixture or for sherbet or cranberry sauce.

Lemons show up on any well-dressed salad or seafood platter, and on the sides of iced tea and punch glasses. Lemons do not go into the fruit salad but their juice picks up the flavor of fruit or vegetable salad in a remarkable way. Lemons show up everywhere, even in a dried fruit compote, and floating (in slices) atop a cup of soup.

Lemon wedges can be made by cutting large lemons in eighths or small lemons into sixths. Or slice evenly and nip edges with scissors to make decorative shapes.

Coconut is pretty on top of salads or puddings, cakes or pies. To make Nutmeg Coconut sprinkle ¼ teaspoon nutmeg over 1 cup shredded moist coconut. Toss lightly to distribute the flavoring.

Tint coconut by sprinkling few drops of vegetable coloring over the amount you want to use. Then toss.

Toasted Coconut is made in the oven; stir to brown evenly.

Grapes used in salads should be seedless, or seeded, except for decorative bunches of grapes which should be left untouched or frosted.

Frost grapes, peaches, plums or cherries by setting fruit in freezer compartment a few hours. When you bring it into the air, don't touch it but allow the frost to form. Or, frost grapes by rolling in lemon juice or white wine and then in finest granulated sugar.

MELON GINGERALE SALAD

Makes 6 servings

- 3 chilled cantaloupes, halved and seeded
- 3 cups melon balls
- 1 cup blueberries
- 12 to 18 whole ripe strawberries
- 1 quart chilled gingerale
- Sprigs of fresh mint

Fill melon cavities with mixture of melon balls and blueberries. Fill with gingerale and garnish with strawberries and springs of mint. Serve on green plates, blue plates or large green leaves arranged on white plates.

DREAM BOAT FRUIT PLATTER

Makes 6 servings

- 1 lime-flavored gelatin ring mold
- Salad greens
- 1½ cups mayonnaise or other creamy dressing
- 1 cup raspberries
- 6 slices pineapple, fresh or canned
- 2 large bunches grapes, white or purple
- 6 peaches, peeled and halved
- ½ cup lemon juice

Unmold lime ring onto center of oblong platter. Arrange salad greens sparingly around edge of platter and to cover platter around ring. Circle the gelatin ring with red raspberries and fill center of ring mold with the dressing. Cut pineapple slices in halves or thirds and place along each side of platter. Place grapes at each end and fill in remaining space with peach halves. Sprinkle with lemon juice and serve.

WALDORF JEWEL SALAD

Makes 12 large servings

- 4 cups diced apples (unpeeled or peeled)
- 2 tablespoons lemon juice
- 1 tablespoon sugar
- 2 cups diced celery
- 2 cups orange chunks

1 teaspoon salt	1 cup fresh cranberries
½ teaspoon nutmeg	¾ cup mayonnaise

Sprinkle apples with lemon juice and seasonings. Combine all ingredients, toss until mixed and serve on greens.

CRANBERRY CRABMEAT MOUSSE SALAD

Makes 8 to 12 salads

1 envelope unflavored gelatin	sauce
¼ cup cold water	½ teaspoon salt
1 can condensed cream of mushroom soup	1 (6½ oz.) can crabmeat
1 package cream cheese	1 cup chopped celery
1 small onion, grated	2 tablespoons lemon juice
1 tablespoon Worcestershire	2 (1 pound) cans jellied cranberry sauce, chilled

Soften gelatin in cold water. Heat ¼ can soup; add gelatin and stir until dissolved. Soften cream cheese with fork or electric mixer. Beat in remaining soup, add heated soup mixture. Fold in remaining ingredients except cranberry sauce. Pour into 8 x 8-inch pan and chill until firm.

To serve: Slice each can of cranberry sauce into 6 plump slices. Put each slice on mound of lettuce. Cut jellied crabmeat salad into squares and place atop each cranberry round. Top with cranberry cut-out or with ripe or stuffed olives.

Salads with an International Reputation

Make an English Trifle Salad by combining any fresh or drained canned fruit you like with an equal amount of country style cottage cheese. The more varieties of fruit the merrier. Mix lightly with a fork, pile into a bowl and garnish with fruit wedges. Serve with any creamy dressing or with mayonnaise. How easy to make this for a crowd.

SALADE NIÇOISE

The French call this *Salade Niçoise,* and it is the prettiest, tastiest, most filling thing you ever saw.

Combine drained tuna fish with tomato wedges and a few cold cooked green beans. Sprinkle with French Dressing *(page 192)* and arrange on lettuce leaves on glass salad plates or in a clear glass salad bowl. Garnish with black ripe olives which were dipped in the dressing to make them new-born shiny. Serve with Garlic Mayonnaise *(page 195).*

SHRIMP AND AVOCADO SALAD

To make a delicious but quick Shrimp and Avocado Salad, combine cooked shrimp and cubes of avocado, about half and half. Sprinkle liberally with lemon, stir in sour cream, enough to hold it together. If you like curry, here is a good place to add a sprinkling.

CHEF SALAD

Make your Chef Salad by rubbing the bowl with a cut clove of garlic. Add an assortment of greens. Arrange cold cooked ham, chicken, turkey—any cold meats cut into cubes or match-stick size pieces—along with slivers of Swiss cheese. Don't mix this until company has admired it. Then add French Dressing *(page 192)* and toss. Serve immediately, of course.

SHEPHERD'S HOUR

This in France is called the Shepherd's Hour but is exactly the salad you will want for a New Year's party.

Mold any gelatin salad you like in a round layer-cake pan, filling the pan to the top. Chill, unmold on a platter, coat with mayonnaise and arrange the face of a clock on top the mayonnaise. Make Roman numbers on the clock with 35 strips of cold cooked tongue cut in strips about 1-inch long. It is a good idea to space these on a piece of paper first; make the top figure and the bottom one before filling in the others.

The hands can be made with shaped strips of avocado or with longer pieces of tongue. Make the button in the center, which holds the clock's hands together, with a ripe olive. Surround a savory salad with half slices of red tomato. If it is a fruit salad surround it with fruit garnish.

DE LUXE COLE SLAW PLATE

A Canadian spring salad plate can be as attractive as dogwood in bloom. This one is beautiful Coconut Pineapple Slaw (*page 174*) served in a large lettuce cup. Accompanying it were prunes stuffed with cream cheese which had been tinted pink, a single white grape was perched on top. There were also deviled eggs beautifully filled from a pastry tube and radish roses and carrot curls. It might have come from the Ritz.

LOUISIANA SALAD BOWL

Make a Louisiana Salad Bowl by combining a few green asparagus tips and chopped celery with cooked shrimp. Toss with a Curried Mayonnaise (*page 195*). Serve in a big lettuce cup on a plate with deviled eggs lounging on a bed of water cress and garnished with ripe olives.

HOT POTATO SALAD
Danish

Makes 6 to 8 servings

- 6 slices bacon, crisped and crumbled
- ¼ cup chopped onion
- ½ cup vinegar
- ½ cup water
- 2 tablespoons sugar
- 1½ teaspoons salt
- ⅛ teaspoon pepper
- 5 cups sliced cooked potatoes
- ¼ cup chopped parsley
- 2 tablespoons chopped green pepper
- 3 hard-cooked eggs, shelled and sliced

Sauté the bacon until crisp, drain on paper towels and crumble. Add the chopped onion to the bacon fat, cook over low heat for a moment, add vinegar, water, sugar, salt and pepper. Cook stirring constantly for about 2 minutes This is the sauce to go over the sliced potatoes and these should be prepared by boiling the red variety of potatoes in their jackets until tender. Cool the potatoes enough to remove skins. Slice very fine. Add all remaining ingredients to the potatoes, drench with the hot liquid and toss together. Serve while warm in a very hot bowl.

HONGKONG CRABMEAT SALAD

Makes 6 to 8 servings

- 2 cups crabmeat
- 2 cups sliced celery
- 2 cups bean sprouts
- 1½ teaspoons salt
- ¼ teaspoon ground black pepper
- 1 tablespoon lemon juice
- 1½ teaspoons Soy sauce
- ¼ cup mayonnaise
- Lettuce
- Paprika and fresh parsley for garnish

Remove cartilage from crabmeat. Place all ingredients except lettuce in a bowl. Toss lightly. Serve on lettuce. Garnish with a dash of paprika and fresh parsley.

CHICKEN SALAD

How do you make Chicken Salad? Try these ways: Combine diced cooked chicken—cut in generous squares if you want to do something special—with half the amount of fresh white seedless grapes, or chopped pineapple. Add a tablespoon or two of orange juice and fold together with enough mayonnaise to hold it but not to cover it. You want this to show. Your cooked chicken was flavored, but you may need more salt and a smidgen of paprika over this. Pile into a chilled bowl lined with salad greens. Garnish with seeded ripe olives and tomato wedges.

Or pile individual portions of this salad on top of jellied cranberry slices—you can get 6 slices from a can—top with Cream Cheese Dressing (*page 195*).

CUCUMBERS IN SOUR CREAM

Abbie makes the best Cucumbers in Sour Cream you ever ate. She chills peeled, sliced cucumbers which have been heavily sprinkled with salt and "rested" for an hour or two in the refrigerator. This extracts some of the unwelcome juice, so drain it off and press the slices with a paper towel to remove extra liquid. Try to keep the sliced cucumber slices together so that the whole pale sliced cucumber is served on a plate coated and surrounded by sour cream, seasoned with 3 tablespoons tarragon vinegar for each cup of thick cream. Sprinkle with black pepper or paprika.

MARINATED WHOLE ONIONS

Marinated Whole Onions are good in a little bowl on the salad tray. Or, at cocktail time, they can be made by selecting onions of uniform size, and then sticking a toothpick through them cross-wise before putting them in water to cook until tender but not soft. Cool, marinate in French dressing and serve in a bowl by themselves sprinkled with ¼ teaspoon rosemary and ½ teaspoon basil for each 2 cups of onions. Tiny whole canned onions, already cooked, can be drained and marinated the same way.

When combining sliced and diced fruit or vegetables remember to alternate colors. For example, line a bowl with salad greens, arrange alternate circles around the edge with avocado and tomato wedges, fill the center with diced vegetables or avocado. Use half an avocado to serve chicken or tuna salad and put the avocado half on greens.

Frozen Salads

The flavor and texture of frozen salads will be best if they are allowed to stand at room temperature for a few minutes just before serving.

FROZEN CHEESE AND DATE SALAD

Fills 1 refrigerator tray

- ¼ cup evaporated milk
- 2 tablespoons lemon juice
- 1 (3 oz.) package cream cheese
- ¼ cup mayonnaise
- ¼ cup sliced dates
- ¼ cup diced ripe olives
- ¼ cup pitted black cherries, chopped
- ¼ cup chopped pecans
- ¼ cup crushed pineapple

Chill milk in refrigerator tray until ice crystals are formed. Remove to a chilled bowl and beat until smooth. Add lemon juice and continue beating until very stiff. Combine cheese with mayonnaise and blend until smooth. Fold thoroughly but lightly into whipped milk, then add dates, olives, cherries, nuts and pineapple. Turn into waxed, paper-lined refrigerator tray. Freeze until firm, at least 4 hours. Cut in slices or squares and serve plain on lettuce or top with Fruit Salad Dressing (*page 196*).

FROZEN PEANUT BUTTER SALAD

Fills 1 refrigerator tray

- 1 (3 oz.) package cream cheese
- ½ cup chopped green pepper
- ½ teaspoon salt
- 2 tablespoons lime juice
- ¼ cup pimiento, chopped
- ½ cup peanut butter
- ¾ cup chopped celery
- ¼ cup mayonnaise
- ¼ cup heavy cream, whipped

Blend all ingredients and fold in whipped cream. Pour mixture into refrigerator tray and chill until firm.

Salad Dressings

A good salad dressing depends upon hard beating and complete blending of the ingredients to make it its best. These recipes are given for use in an electric blender but they can also be made in a deep salad bowl beating with a rotary beater. Or, combine ingredients in a bottle and shake well.

FRENCH DRESSING

Makes 1¼ cups

- ¼ cup finest vinegar
- 1 cup best olive oil
- ¾ teaspoon salt
- 1 teaspoon dry mustard
- ¼ teaspoon ground white pepper
- ½ teaspoon paprika
- 1 tablespoon white onion, chopped

Place all ingredients in container of blender. Cover and turn on blender. Run until smoothly blended, about 30 seconds.

Variations

GARLIC FRENCH DRESSING:—Chop 2 cloves garlic and let these stand in the vinegar to be used for the salad dressing 3 or 4 days before the dressing is made. Remove garlic and follow recipe for French Dressing (*page 192*).

ANCHOVY DRESSING:—Make French Dressing (*page 192*) using lemon juice in place of vinegar and add a small can of anchovy filets, drained. Blend until smooth as directed.

CHIFFONADE DRESSING:—To French Dressing (*page 192*) recipe add 1 tablespoon coarsely diced green pepper. After blending add 1 hard-cooked egg (in quarters) and blend only until the egg is chopped medium fine, about 1 second.

ROQUEFORT DRESSING:—Follow French Dressing (*page 192*) recipe, crumbling 3 ounces of Roquefort or Blue cheese into the container with the other ingredients. Blend as directed.

FRUIT SALAD DRESSING:—Add 2 tablespoons chopped chives to French Dressing (*page 192*) recipe. Blend 30 seconds. Stir in 2/3 cup sour cream.

QUICK FRENCH DRESSING:—Use one of the Salad Dressing Mix packets, prepared in envelopes, offering different seasonings and cruet which is an instruction bottle for concocting perfect dressing.

MAYONNAISE

This creamy dressing is extremely adaptable. Use it as it is, add seasonings, thin it with cream, or combine it with whipped cream or cottage cheese to become a thick, velvet-textured dressing on fruit or vegetable salads.

Mayonnaise is not difficult to make, but you can't hurry it. Should you, and it rebels by curdling, all is not lost. By the way, make a big supply of mayonnaise when eggs yolks are left from angel cake or meringues.

How to uncurdle dressing. Beat an egg yolk or a whole egg with a rotary beater. Add to the curdled mixture as slowly as you added the oil, beating constantly. It will be smooth and creamy. Use lemon juice or juice of a lime instead of vinegar if you like.

BASIC RECIPE

Makes 1 cup

- 1 egg yolk, beaten
- ¼ teaspoon salt
- ⅛ teaspoon white pepper or cayenne
- ¼ teaspoon dry mustard
- ½ teaspoon vinegar
- ½ cup olive oil or salad oil
- ½ teaspoon vinegar

Add seasonings and first ½ teaspoon vinegar to beaten egg yolk, and beat with rotary beater until blended. Begin adding olive oil, few drops at a time, beating constantly. When about a fourth has been blended, add next ½ teaspoon vinegar. Pour oil into mixture a little at a time, continuing to beat. When all the oil is added, add last portion of vinegar, beat a few seconds, seal and store.

BLENDER MAYONNAISE

Basic in Electric Blender

Makes 1¼ cups

- 2 egg yolks
- 2 tablespoons vinegar or lemon juice
- ½ teaspoon dry mustard
- 1 teaspoon salt
- 1 cup olive or salad oil

Place egg yolks, vinegar, mustard and salt in blender container. Add ¼ cup oil. Cover and turn on blender, running about 5 seconds. Without stopping machine, remove cover and pour remaining oil in in a fine thin stream. Stop blender when last of oil is added.

I have no shame about continually, and repeatedly, bringing up this subject of a blender. This mayonnaise is as good an example as anyone would want of the time saved and of the use of food you might otherwise not utilize. It is one thing to use those extra egg yolks when less than 5 minutes is necessary for the dressing; it is another when from 20 minutes to a half hour is necessary if blending is done by hand.

Variations

GARLIC MAYONNAISE:—Add 2 plump minced cloves of garlic to one cup of mayonnaise. If the cloves are small, mince 3 of them to stir into the dressing. You will like this on hot vegetables or with cold or hot meat platters.

CURRY MAYONNAISE:—Stir in ½ teaspoon curry powder and 1 tablespoon chili sauce for each cup of mayonnaise. Serve on seafood or on chicken salads. Stir into the yolks of hard-cooked eggs when deviling them. Very good on bread for sandwiches, too.

CREAM CHEESE DRESSING FOR TART FRUIT SALADS

Makes about 1½ cups

- 2 (3 oz.) packages cream cheese
- ¼ cup mayonnaise
- ½ teaspoon onion juice
- Salt—maybe?

Let cheese stand at room temperature until softened. Combine with other ingredients, beat until blended. Add salt if you like.

PEANUT BUTTER SALAD DRESSING

Makes 1½ cups

- 1 egg, beaten
- 2 tablespoons brown sugar
- 2 tablespoons red table wine, or wine vinegar
- 1 tablespoon butter or margarine
- ¼ cup peanut butter
- 6 tablespoons cream
- ¼ teaspoon salt

Combine in a saucepan the egg, sugar, wine or vinegar and the butter. Cook over low heat until thick and smooth, stirring constantly. Add peanut butter to the cream. Add salt and stir until blended. Add to the cooked mixture and blend well. Chill before using over vegetable or fruit salads.

FRUIT SALAD DRESSING

Makes 1⅔ cups

- ½ cup mayonnaise
- 1 tablespoon frozen orange juice concentrate, undiluted
- 1 teaspoon lemon juice
- ½ teaspoon Angostura Bitters
- ½ cup heavy cream, whipped

Combine all ingredients except cream, and stir until blended. Whip cream until it holds soft peaks. Fold in the mayonnaise mixture. Serve immediately on fruit salad or cover and chill until serving time.

10

Party Pies

Pie Crusts, Shells and Meringues

FLAKY PIE CRUST

Handle the crust gently.
Mix the dough with a delicate touch.
Use as little flour on the board as possible.
Press lightly in quick, hard strokes with the rolling pin.

Makes 2-crust (10-inch) pie:

2½ cups sifted flour	6 to 8 tablespoons cold water
1¼ teaspoons salt	
¾ cup shortening	

Sift the flour and salt together into a mixing bowl. Cut in the shortening until the mixture has the appearance of coarse meal. Sprinkle the cold water, a tablespoon at a time, and mix gently with a fork after each addition. Use only enough water to make the dough stick together, the less water the better and the less handling the better. Press the dough into a ball and divide in 2 parts, one slightly larger than the other.

BOTTOM CRUST:—Flatten the larger ball of dough on a lightly floured board or pastry cloth and press into a circle about ⅛-inch thick and about 1-inch longer than your inverted pie pan. When the bottom crust has been rolled out fold the circle in half and place in pie pan. Unfold it and fit it into the plate but do not stretch the dough. Trim the dough with scissors, leaving ½-inch edge extending beyond the pie pan. Add the filling and prepare.

TOP CRUST:—Roll out the smaller ball of dough into a circle exactly as you rolled the bottom crust, making it just a little thinner than the bottom crust. Fold the dough in half, cut slits or a fancy design in the center so that the steam can escape while the pie is baking. Place over the pie filling and unfold to cover. The crust can be trimmed to extend about ½-inch beyond the edge of the pie pan. Tuck the edge of the top crust under the bottom crust edge and seal by pressing together and forming a fancy edge, either by scalloping it with the pressure of thumb and finger or by pressing it with the tongs of a fork.

Bake according to directions for the pie you are making.

Variations

LATTICE-TOP:—To make a lattice-top roll out the ball of dough for the top crust to no more than ⅛-inch thickness. Cut into strips with a pastry wheel. Lay half the strips over the filling then cross with the other strips to form a lattice top. Fasten the ends of the strips by folding them under the bottom crust and pinching them together when forming the pattern around the edge of the pie.

ORANGE-FLAVORED GINGER CRUST:—Use orange juice instead of water when making the pastry. Then roll it out on a board which has been lightly powdered with ginger. Use this crust for a chicken pie or steak or pork pie filling.

STIR AND ROLL PASTRY

Makes 2 (9-inch) crusts or 8 (3-inch) tart shells

- 2 cups sifted all-purpose flour
- 1½ teaspoons salt
- ½ cup salad oil
- ¼ cup cold milk

Sift flour into large mixing bowl, and add other ingredients quickly. Stir lightly with a fork until blended sufficiently to form into a ball. Divide in half, place each ball between sheets of waxed paper and roll out to ½-inch thickness. Place bottom crust on pan, wax paper side up and remove paper. Shape edges and bake according to directions for pie being made. For baked pie shell, to be filled after baking and cooling, bake in hot oven (475°) 10 to 12 minutes.

CHEESE PIE CRUST

Makes pastry for 2-crust (9-inch) pie

- 4 ounces grated Cheddar cheese (about 1 cup)
- 2 cups sifted flour
- 1 teaspoon salt
- ⅔ cup homogenized shortening
- 5 to 6 tablespoons cold water

Grate the cheese and set it aside while the flour and salt are being sifted together in a mixing bowl. Cut in the shortening, then add a tablespoon of cold water at a time, mixing lightly with a fork after each addition. When the pastry will hold together divide in half and form in 2 balls, being careful not to overhandle as these are flattened and rolled out in the design you prefer.

This is especially good for an apple or pumpkin pie. You would need only ½ the recipe for an uncovered pumpkin pie.

QUICK LEMON CRUST

Makes 2 (8-inch) pie shells or 1 double crust for 1 (8-inch) pie

- 2 cups sifted all-purpose flour
- 1½ teaspoons salt
- ½ cup salad oil
- 2 tablespoons canned or frozen lemon juice
- 2 tablespoons cold water (or increase canned or frozen lemon juice to 4 tablespoons)

Sift flour in bowl with the salt. Add oil and lemon juice all at once. Stir these ingredients lightly with a fork until well blended. Form into ball. Divide dough in 2 parts and roll between sheets of waxed paper. For a single crust pie, be sure to pierce bottom and sides of the crust with a fork. Bake in a hot oven (425°) for 10 minutes or until browned.

CRUMB PIE SHELLS

Makes 1 (9-inch) pie shell or 4 (3-inch) tart shells

- 1½ cups crushed crumbs of vanilla wafers, gingersnaps, graham crackers, zwiebach, or low calorie artichoke rusks
- ¼ cup granulated sugar
- ¼ cup soft butter or margarine

Combine the crumbs and sugar and mix until blended. Add the softened butter and stir thoroughly. Press the crumbs against the sides and bottom of a 9-inch pie pan. If you want to make this easier to remove, first line the pan with aluminum foil. Bake in (350°) oven for 10 to 15 minutes. Cool before filling.

Make Nut Crumb shells by stirring ½ cup chopped pecans into the sugar when mixing the crust.

To make the crumb shell fancy when using either vanilla wafers or gingersnaps reduce crumbs to 1 cup. After the bottom of the pie pan has been lined with the crumb mixture, cut whole wafers in half and arrange scalloped edge.

These can also be used without baking for cream or gelatin fillings.

Crumb Crusts

GRAHAM CRACKER CRUST
With Electric Blender

Makes 1 cup crumbs or thin 9-inch pie shell

Crumble 14 graham cracker squares into container of electric blender. Blend until all crackers are crumbled. Sift through coarse sieve. Blend remaining coarse particles again.

To make bottom for Cheese Cake, combine 1 cup crumbs with ¼ cup melted butter and 2 tablespoons sugar. Pat evenly over bottom of pan.

To make crust for chiffon or cream pie, pat evenly over bottom and sides of 9-inch pie pan. Chill thoroughly before filling.

CORNFLAKE CRUMB CRUST

Makes 1 (9-inch) shell

4 cups cornflakes, crushed until fine	4 tablespoons melted butter or margarine
2 tablespoons sugar	

The cornflakes are easy to crush if you put them in

a clean tea towel, roll it up tightly and crush with the hands until you have enough crumbs to make the required amount. Add the sugar and melted butter or margarine and mix thoroughly. Press into a 9-inch glass or tin pie pan, reserving 3 tablespoons of crumbs to sprinkle over whatever cream filling you are going to put in the shell. Chill thoroughly.

CHOCOLATE COCONUT CRUST

Makes 9-inch pie shell

2 squares unsweetened chocolate	water
2 tablespoons butter	⅔ cup confectioner's sugar
2 tablespoons hot milk or	1½ cups coconut, cut (toasted or plain)

Combine chocolate and butter in the top of a double boiler and cook over boiling water, stirring until melted. Add the hot milk or water to the sugar and mix thoroughly. Add to the chocolate mixture and stir until blended. Add the cut coconut and mix well. Spread on bottom and sides of well greased 9-inch pie pan. Refrigerate and chill until firm. Fill with any cream filling. Chill again before serving.

Or fill with ice cream and serve immediately. Let stand at room temperature about 10 minutes before cutting.

COCONUT CRUST

Makes 9-inch pie crust

⅓ cup soft butter	1 cup sifted flour
3 tablespoons sugar	1 cup chopped coconut
1 egg yolk	

Cream butter and sugar together, add egg yolk

and mix thoroughly. Add flour. Blend well. Stir in coconut. Press mixture into greased 9-inch pie pan. Chill 30 minutes. Bake in 350° oven until browned, about 25 minutes.

MERINGUE SHELLS

Makes 1 (9-inch) pie shell or 4 (3-inch) tart shells

4 egg whites	¼ teaspoon cream of tartar
½ teaspoon salt	1 cup sugar

Egg whites beat to greater volume if at room temperature, so take them out of the refrigerator a few minutes before you go to work. If you beat them with a big French-type wire beater you will get a lighter and drier meringue for meringue shells than you can get with an electric or rotary beater. Anyhow, this is the way you make them:

Beat the egg whites until they are foamy. Add the salt and cream of tartar and continue beating until they are stiff but not dry. Begin adding the sugar by spoonfuls, continuing to beat until the meringue is stiff and dry.

Now arrange the meringue in a large 9-inch circle, smoothing it with a spatula to ¼- to ¾-inch thick. If the meringue is spread on unglazed paper or several folds of wax paper it will be easier to manage. Place the paper on the baking sheet. Build up the sides of the circle with the remaining meringue, with spoonfuls so that the edge is about 1½ inches above the inside of the meringue shell. Bake in a very slow oven (250°) until the meringue shell is dry and ever so lightly browned, about 2 hours. Cool before filling.

MERINGUE

A high, light meringue on top your pie is a thing to wish for but is not always achieved. A few of the experts in one of those big companies where pies are made day in and day out, many of them topped with high, light meringue, have worked out these rules for success when topping your pie with meringue.

Makes meringue to cover 1 (9-inch) pie

3 egg whites	½ teaspoon vanilla or 1 teaspoon lemon juice
6 tablespoons sugar	

Beat egg whites until dry and stiff. (Better volume is obtained if whites are not too cold.) Add sugar gradually—1 tablespoon at a time, beating well after each addition. Continue beating until stiff peaks form when egg beater is lifted. Add flavoring. Spread meringue lightly over cooled filling in pie shell, making sure it touches pastry rim all around (this helps prevent shrinkage). Make graceful swirls or peaks in the meringue with back of tablespoon or spatula. Bake in slow oven (325°) 25 to 30 minutes, or until meringue is firm and delicately browned. Cool pie on rack away from drafts.

Parfait Liqueur Pies

COINTREAU PARFAIT PIE

Makes 8-inch pie

1 package lemon- or orange-flavored gelatin	1 pint vanilla ice cream
1 cup hot water	1 baked 8-inch pie shell, cooled
⅓ cup Cointreau	

Dissolve gelatin in *hot* water in 2-quart saucepan. Add Cointreau. Add ice cream by spoonfuls, stirring until melted. Then chill until thickened, but not set (15 to 25 minutes). Turn into pie shell. Chill until firm (15 to 25 minutes). Garnish with whipped cream and shaved chocolate, toasted almonds or coconut.

CHERRY JUBILEE PARFAIT PIE

Makes 9-inch pie

- ⅓ cup brandy
- 1 cup drained pitted dark sweet cherries (fresh or canned)
- 1 package raspberry-flavored gelatin
- Hot cherry juice plus water to make 1 cup
- 1 pint vanilla ice cream
- 1 baked 9-inch pie shell, cooled

Pour brandy over drained cherries and let stand several hours or over night. Drain, reserving liquid. Dissolve gelatin in *hot* cherry juice and water in a 2-quart saucepan. Add brandy, then add ice cream by spoonfuls, stirring until melted. Chill until thickened but not set (15 to 25 minutes). Fold in drained brandied cherries. Turn into pie shell. Chill until firm (25 to 35 minutes). Garnish with whipped cream and additional cherries.

EGGNOG PARFAIT PIE

Makes 9-inch pie

- 1 package lemon-flavored gelatin
- 2 tablespoons sugar
- 1 cup hot water
- 1 pint vanilla ice cream
- 1 teaspoon vanilla
- 1 teaspoon rum flavoring
- 2 eggs
- 1 baked 9-inch pie shell, cooled

Dissolve gelatin and sugar in *hot* water in 2-quart saucepan. Add ice cream by spoonfuls, stirring until melted. Add vanilla and rum flavoring, stirring to blend. Then chill until thickened but not set (10 to 20 minutes). Beat whole eggs until thick and fluffy.

Blend into gelatin mixture. Turn into pie shell. Chill until firm (30 to 40 minutes). Sprinkle with nutmeg. Garnish with whipped cream and shaved chocolate.

Colorful Pies

CRANBERRY PIE

This pie is a real beauty, requires no baking once the pastry shell has been made and won a prize at the Cranberry Festival in Massachusetts, where cranberries grow. It is a pie which will be prized by you or by anyone who tastes it. This is the way you make it.

Makes 9-inch pie

- 9-inch pastry shell, baked
- 1 (1 pound) can whole cranberry sauce, lightly crushed
- 1 tablespoon cornstarch
- ½ cup granulated sugar
- ⅓ cup water
- 1 envelope unflavored gelatin
- ¼ cup cold water
- 2 egg whites, stiffly beaten
- ⅛ teaspoon salt
- 2 teaspoons lemon juice
- 1 teaspoon almond extract
- 1 cup heavy cream, whipped

Combine cranberry sauce and cornstarch in saucepan and cook over medium heat, stirring constantly until thickened. Let this cool while you are putting on the next act.

Combine the sugar and water and cook until a drop in cold water will form a soft ball. Add the gelatin which has been softened in ¼ cup cold water and stir until the gelatin is dissolved. Pour this syrup very slowly over the beaten egg whites, continuing to beat constantly. Add salt, lemon juice and almond extract and continue beating until the mixture is blended and cool.

Beat the cream and fold into the egg white mixture and pour into pie shell. Chill and spread the cranberry sauce over the top. Place in refrigerator until serving time.

CHOCOLATE RAINBOW PIE

Makes 9-inch pie

- 1 9-inch Chocolate Coconut pie shell (page 202)
- ½ pint vanilla ice cream
- 1 pint raspberry sherbet
- ½ pint lemon sherbet
- 1 square of bitter chocolate

Soften the ice cream and sherbets just enough to handle. Press the vanilla ice cream into a thin layer over the bottom of the coconut shell, spread a thicker layer of raspberry sherbet over that and top with the lemon sherbet. Garnish with coarsely grated bitter chocolate and chill again before serving.

PINEAPPLE MERINGUE PIE

Makes 8-inch pie

- ¼ cup cornstarch
- ¾ cup sugar
- ½ teaspoon salt
- 3 eggs, separated
- 1 (No. 2) can unsweetened pineapple juice
- 1 tablespoon butter
- 1 8-inch baked pie shell
- 6 tablespoons sugar
- Dash of salt

Mix together cornstarch, sugar and salt in a saucepan. Add egg yolks and blend thoroughly. Gradually stir in pineapple juice. Cook over low heat, stirring constantly, until mixture thickens. Add butter. Cool. Turn into baked pastry shell. Top with a meringue (*page 293*) spooned into wreath around edge of pie, leaving center open. Bake in a moderately hot oven (400°) until meringue browns, about 6 minutes.

LIME MERINGUE PIE IN COCONUT SHELL

Makes 9-inch pie

- 1 cup sugar
- 5 tablespoons cornstarch
- 1/8 teaspoon salt
- 2 cups water
- 3 egg yolks, beaten
- 3 tablespoons butter
- 1/3 cup lime juice
- 1 teaspoon grated lemon peel
- 1 teaspoon grated lime peel
- 1 coconut pie shell (page 202)

This lime meringue pie is intended for a coconut shell but it is delicious in a baked pastry shell as well. Combine in the top of a double boiler the sugar, cornstarch, salt and water and stir until blended. Cook over low heat stirring until the mixture thickens. Place over boiling water, covered, and cook for another 10 minutes to secure a pleasant thickness without any of the taste of starch. Add the beaten egg yolks and stir, allowing the mixture to cook for another 3 or 4 minutes. Remove from heat and add the butter, juice and grated peel. Cool the custard, pour into the cold pie shell and cover with meringue (*page 203*), being careful to make attractive peaks and to spread the meringue clear to the inner edge of the pie shell. Brown in a slow oven (325°) for 15 minutes or until delicately brown. Cool before serving.

SOUR CREAM APPLE PIE

Makes 9-inch pie

- 1/2 cup sour cream
- 6 tart apples
- Pastry for 9-inch double crust
- 3/4 cup sugar
- 1/4 teaspoon cinnamon
- 1/4 teaspoon cloves
- 1/4 teaspoon salt

Core, pare and slice the apples. Line a deep pie pan with the pastry, spread a layer of apples over the bottom, sprinkle with a mixture of sugar, cinnamon, cloves and salt and repeat until all is used. Pour the cream over the top, moisten the rim of the pastry, and add the top sheet of dough making 2 or 3 slits in the top to allow steam to escape. Press the top to the lower crust. Bake in a moderately hot (425°) preheated oven 40 to 45 minutes, until the apples are tender or until the crust is golden brown.

Make Cheese Pastry (*page 199*) for your apple pies sometimes.

PUMPKIN PIE

Makes 9-inch pie

- ¾ cup sugar
- 1 tablespoon cornstarch
- 1 teaspoon ginger
- 1 teaspoon cinnamon
- ¼ teaspoon cloves
- ½ teaspoon salt
- 3 eggs, slightly beaten
- 1½ cups cooked fresh or canned pumpkin or Hubbard squash, or 1 package frozen squash
- 1½ cups rich milk
- 1 tablespoon butter or margarine
- 1 9-inch flaky pie shell, unbaked

This makes a plump, spicy, fragrant pie as American as the United States flag. Mix sugar, cornstarch, spices, salt and slightly beaten eggs in bowl. Add remaining ingredients; blend well. Pour into unbaked pie shell. Bake in hot oven (450°) 1 hour or until silver knife inserted in center of filling comes out clean.

Variations

Flavor whipped cream with a little cinnamon, sweeten lightly and serve on top of Pumpkin Pie.

Serve whipped cream flavored with several tablespoons of dark rum over Pumpkin Pie. Arrange this as you would completely cover for a meringue pie, put through a pastry tube around the edge to form a design, or make a crisscross as though it were a crisscross pastry top pie.

Serve finely chopped peanuts, black walnuts or Brazil nuts over the top of Pumpkin Pie.

Slices of sharp Cheddar cheese are good with spicy Pumpkin Pie. As is always true with cheese, it is creamier and more full-flavored if served in a napkin wrapped wheel for each person to cut off his own portion.

Use half granulated sugar and half tightly packed dark brown sugar for your Pumpkin Pie sometime.

Cool baked Pumpkin Pie, cover with meringue and brown before serving.

When making Pumpkin Pie try brushing the bottom of the unbaked crust with melted butter and sprinkle with coarsely chopped pecans. Dot with 2 tablespoons of any tart jelly (plum, currant or grape) then fill with the pumpkin mixture and bake. If you decide to use a meringue topping for this you can garnish it with pecan halves.

PINEAPPLE PUMPKIN PIE

Make your favorite pumpkin filling, using evaporated milk for extra richness; bake as usual, but take pie from oven 10 minutes before it is done and spoon 1 cup well drained crushed pineapple over the center of the filling to within 2 inches of the crust. Return to the oven and bake 10 minutes more. Garnish with whipped cream. Isn't that some pumpkin!

ALOHA CHIFFON PIE

Makes 9-inch pie

- 1 tablespoon plain, unflavored gelatin
- ¼ cup cold water
- 3 eggs, separated
- ¾ cup granulated sugar
- 1 cup crushed pineapple, not drained (a flat or buffet-size can)
- 1 teaspoon grated lemon peel
- 3 tablespoons strained lemon juice
- ¼ teaspoon salt
- 1 9-inch baked coconut pie shell (page 202)

Add gelatin to cold water; let stand while you combine in the top part of a double boiler the egg yolks, ¼ cup of the sugar, the pineapple, lemon peel and juice. Cook over hot water, stirring frequently until smoothly thickened (10 to 15 minutes). Add softened gelatin and stir until dissolved. Remove from heat and let cool slightly. Add salt to egg whites and beat stiff. Gradually beat in the remaining ½ cup sugar. Fold the slightly cooled pineapple mixture into the meringue. Heap mixture in cooled coconut crust. Chill until firm—2 to 3 hours. Garnish with whipped cream.

DEEP DISH PEACH PIE

Fills 2-quart baking dish

- 9 tablespoons Minute tapioca
- ¼ teaspoon mace
- 1⅓ cups sugar (all white, or part white and part brown)
- ½ teaspoon salt
- 8 cups (4 No. 2½ cans) drained sliced peaches
- 2½ cups peach juice
- ¼ cup lemon juice
- 2 tablespoons butter
- ¼ to ½ cup light rum
- Pastry for 1 crust pie

Combine tapioca, sugar, salt, mace, peaches and juices. Stir lightly and turn into a 2-quart baking dish. Dot with the butter and cover with the pastry which has been rolled to fit the top of the baking dish. Cut slits in an attractive pattern so that the steam can escape and make a little round hole about the size of a pencil in the center. Press the pastry to the rim of the dish making an attractive fluted edge and bake in hot oven (425°) 30 minutes. Remove and use a little funnel to add the rum. Place a piece of aluminum foil over the opening (there are others through which the steam can escape) and return to oven for baking another 15 minutes. You serve this warm usually, but to tell you the truth it is good hot or cold.

For fresh peach pie, half the size of this big one, use 1½ tablespoons tapioca, ¼ cup granulated sugar with ¼ cup brown sugar, ⅛ teaspoon mace, 4 cups sliced fresh peaches, 2 tablespoons lemon juice, 1 tablespoon rum and 1 tablespoon butter.

The rum is optional in any dish you make, and if you don't care for it in fruit pie omit it and use 1 tablespoon less tapioca in the large pie. For the small pie omission of the rum requires no further adjustment.

LEMON CREAM PIE

For 1 (8-inch) pie   *For 3 pies for a party*

1 Quick Lemon Crust (page 200) (8-inch)	3 pie shells
1 can frozen lemon concentrate	3 cans
Water to make 1½ cups liquid	4½ cups
1 envelope unflavored gelatin	3 envelopes
¼ cup granulated sugar	¾ cup
⅔ cup heavy cream, whipped	2 cups

Add water to concentrate for lemonade to make 1½ cups liquid. Soften the gelatin in ½ cup of the lemonade and water mixture, and dissolve over hot water. Combine remaining lemonade and water with sugar and dissolve gelatin, stirring well. Chill until mixture is partially set. Whip gelatin mixture, then add whipped cream. Pour into baked pie shell and chill until filling is set. Garnish with whipped cream and green or red maraschino cherries.

To make 3 pies for a party, use ingredient list on the right. Follow directions given for 1 pie.

BANANA BUTTERSCOTCH PIE

Fills 9-inch pastry shell

- 1½ cups milk, scalded
- ½ cup sugar
- ¾ cup brown sugar, firmly packed
- ¼ cup, sifted, enriched flour
- ½ teaspoon salt
- ½ cup cold milk
- 3 egg yolks
- 1 tablespoon soft butter or margarine
- 3 tablespoons peanut butter
- 1 large banana, ripe
- Meringue to cover
- 1 9-inch baked pie shell, cooled

The chef at a Trout Club in Canada surprised everyone so successfully with this combination that he was immediately bombarded for the recipe.

Put the cold milk on to heat and combine in the top of a double boiler the white and brown sugar, flour, salt, milk and egg yolks and the softened butter. Stir until thoroughly blended. Add the hot milk and place over boiling water to cook until thickened, stirring occasionally. Remove from heat, add the peanut butter and stir until blended. Cover and allow the filling to cool while baking the pie shell which should be cool before it is filled. Arrange banana slices on bottom of pie shell, add the filling, top with meringue (*page 203*) being careful to cover the top clear to the crusty edge. Place in 350° oven until meringue is brown. Cool before serving, or serve while lukewarm.

COFFEE VELVET CREAM PIE

CRUST

Makes 9-inch pie

- 1¾ cups finely crumbled vanilla wafers
- ⅛ teaspoon salt
- ½ teaspoon cinnamon
- ¼ cup butter

Combine all ingredients and mix until thoroughly blended. Reserve ¼ cup of the crumb mixture and press the remainder onto the sides and bottom (not rim) of 9-inch pie pan. Bake in 350° oven 10 minutes. Allow to cool before filling.

COFFEE VELVET CREAM PIE FILLING

- ¼ cup cold water
- 1 envelope unflavored gelatin
- 4 teaspoons instant coffee
- ¼ cup hot water
- 4 egg yolks beaten
- ¼ teaspoon salt
- ¼ cup sugar
- 4 egg whites
- ½ cup sugar
- ½ teaspoon almond extract
- 1 cup heavy cream, whipped

Soften gelatin in cold water. Add the coffee powder to the hot water, let these stand while adding the salt to the egg yolks and beating until they are thick and light colored. Gradually add the ¼ cup sugar to the egg yolks. Add hot coffee mixture and cook in top of a double boiler for 3 minutes, stirring constantly. Remove from heat and add the softened gelatin. Stir until completely dissolved. Chill until the mixture begins to set.

Beat the egg whites until stiff but not dry. Add the almond extract and gradually add the ½ cup sugar continuing beating the egg whites until stiff and satiny. Fold the coffee mixture into the egg whites and fold in the whipped cream. When blended pour into the pie shell. Sprinkle the ¼ cup crumb mixture (which was reserved for this purpose) over the top for decoration. Chill for several hours before serving.

To Freeze Pies

The miracle has come true of making pies weeks ahead, freezing them in a home freezer or the freezer section of a freezer-refrigerator, and enjoying them fresh from the oven when convenient! Favorites for freezing are double-crust pies: apple, cherry, peach, mincemeat or deep-dish fruit and berry pies.

Pies can be frozen unbaked or baked. If frozen unbaked, do not cut steam vents in top crust; wrap in moisture-vaporproof material and seal; label, date and freeze.

To thaw, remove wrappings and cut small steam vents in top crust. Bake in (425°) oven for 65 to 70 minutes.

If pie is frozen baked, let pie cool thoroughly at room temperature, then wrap in moisture-vaporproof material and seal; label, date and freeze. *To thaw,* remove wrappings from frozen pie and heat in (400°) oven for 25 to 35 minutes.

Pie shells can be frozen unbaked or baked and kept on hand for use as needed. Freezing unbaked always turns out a fresher baked pie for me. If pie shell is frozen unbaked, it is easier to freeze it before wrapping, then wrap immediately in moisture-vaporproof material and store in freezer.

To thaw, unwrap shell and bake in (450°) oven 5

minutes; reprick shell and bake about 10 minutes longer.

If pie shell is frozen baked, let the baked shell cool thoroughly at room temperature, then wrap in moisture-vaporproof material and seal; label, date and freeze.

To thaw, leave shell wrapped and let stand at room temperature or unwrap and heat in (400°) oven 5 minutes.

11

Cakes from Many Lands

Cakes

LEMON CAKE
Spanish

In much of Europe, but especially in Spain, oranges, lemons and dates have been great delicacies for hundreds of years. Although an oven capable of baking a cake as we know it is a rare thing in Spain, their cake, *tarta*, resemble puddings more often than cake as we know it. This is a cake which would delight the heart of any Spanish cook. It uses the ingredients, so beloved by her, in an American oven.

Makes 2 8-inch round layers

- 2½ cups sifted enriched flour
- 2 teaspoons baking powder
- ½ teaspoon soda
- 1 medium-sized lemon, use pulp and grated peel
- 1 cup of dates

½ cup butter or margarine	2 eggs, slightly beaten
½ cup white sugar	1 cup buttermilk or sour milk
½ cup brown sugar, firmly packed	

Combine sifted flour, baking powder and soda and sift together once. Grind in a food grinder or blender or chop by hand the whole lemon (from which you have carefully removed seeds) and the seeded dates. Add ½ cup of the dry, sifted ingredients to this and mix lightly with a fork. Combine butter and white and brown sugar in a large mixing bowl and cream together thoroughly. Add the beaten eggs and mix or beat with an electric beater for 1 minute. Fold in the fruit until thoroughly mixed. Begin adding dry ingredients and milk, alternating until all has been blended with the creamed mixture. Blend thoroughly after each addition. If electric mixer is used beat at low speed. Pour into 2 well greased and lightly floured 8-inch layer pans. Bake in moderate oven (350°) 30 to 35 minutes.

Cool and frost with Lemon Butter Cream Frosting (*page 239*) or with Caramel Sour Cream Frosting (*page 235*).

EXOTIC CAKE
French

Makes two oblong layers 9 x 12

2¾ cups sifted cake flour	¾ cup milk
1¾ cups sugar	1 teaspoon almond extract
2 teaspoons double-acting baking powder	1 teaspoon orange extract
1½ teaspoons salt	3 eggs, unbeaten
1 cup homogenized shortening	1 egg yolk, unbeaten
	1 cup shredded coconut, finely chopped

Combine cake flour with sugar, baking powder

and salt and sift into mixing bowl. Add the shortening, milk, flavorings and one of the eggs. Beat 200 strokes by hand or 2 minutes by mixer at low speed. Scrape the bowl and spoon or beater with a spatula. Add the 2 remaining eggs and the yolk and beat another 200 strokes. Stir in the finely chopped coconut and pour the batter into 2 9 x 12 oblong pans which have been well greased. This cake can also be baked in 3 9-inch well greased round cake pans. Bake in moderately hot oven (375°) until the cake is done, about 25 minutes.

Cool and remove from pans onto a cooling rack. Cool thoroughly before putting the layers together and frosting with Rum Butter Frosting (*page 239*). Sprinkle the top of the oblong cake very thickly with more of the finely chopped coconut. Decorate the sides with diamonds of glazed orange peel and small rounds of angelica.

BABA AU RHUM

French

Fills 1 (8-inch) tube pan

- ½ cup vegetable shortening (at room temperature)
- 1 teaspoon grated lemon peel
- 2 cups sifted cake flour
- 2 teaspoons double acting baking powder
- ¾ teaspoon salt
- 1¼ cups sugar
- ¾ cup milk
- 1 teaspoon vanilla
- 2 eggs
- ½ cup currants

Babas are the most French of all cakes, and until this simple recipe was devised making a Baba involved yeast batter which is prepared very much as sweetened yeast bread. Rum syrup was then heated to exactly the right temperature and poured over the Baba a little at a time. The cake absorbed the syrup until it swelled to about twice its size. A beguiling performance, but one which was often frightening to those of us unfamiliar with Babas; unable to keep the hot syrup at an even temperature. This recipe, however, is easy to make and is absolutely delicious.

Combine the soft shortening with the grated lemon peel in a large mixing bowl. Stir to blend and soften shortening. Combine the sifted cake flour, baking powder, salt and sugar in a large sifter and sift over the shortening. Add the vanilla to the milk and pour into the bowl, mixing until all the flour is dampened. Then beat 2 minutes at low speed in an electric mixer or 300 vigorous strokes by hand. Add eggs, beat 1 minute with electric mixer or 150 vigorous strokes by hand.

Pour batter into well greased and floured 8-inch tube pan or ring mold, sprinkle with currants and bake in preheated 350° oven 55 minutes, until cake springs back when touched. Cool cake 10 minutes and remove from pan to finish cooling on a rack.

Make the sauce and pour half the boiling hot sauce into the tube pan. Return the cake to the pan and pour the rest of the hot syrup over it. When it has cooled, cover and allow to chill and marinate over night. Serve with very cold, lightly sweetened whipped cream in the center to be spooned up with each serving of rum cake.

Individual Babas can be made in custard cups, being sure to fill them no more than ½ full. Sauce in the same way as the large Baba.

RHUM SAUCE

½ cup sugar
¾ cup apricot nectar
1 teaspoon lemon juice
½ cup rum

Combine all ingredients in a saucepan and stir over low heat until the sugar is melted and the syrup begins to boil. Remove from heat immediately and sauce the cake.

BRAZILIAN CHOCOLATE CHIFFON CAKE

For 10-inch tube pan

- 2¼ cups sifted cake flour
- 1⅔ cups sugar
- 3 teaspoons baking powder
- 2 teaspoons powdered instant coffee
- 1 teaspoon salt
- ¼ teaspoon cinnamon
- ½ cup salad oil
- 6 egg yolks
- ¾ cup water
- 2 teaspoons vanilla
- 2 to 3 squares unsweetened chocolate, melted
- ½ teaspoon cream of tartar
- 6 egg whites

Mix and sift first six ingredients. Make a well and add, in order, salad oil, egg yolks, water and vanilla. Beat with spoon until smooth. Add melted chocolate; blend well. Add cream of tartar to egg whites. Beat until egg whites form *very stiff peaks*. Gently fold first mixture into egg whites until well blended. Fold, do *not* stir. Turn batter into ungreased 10-inch tube pan. Bake in slow oven (325°) 70 to 75 minutes or until cake springs back when touched lightly with finger. Immediately invert pan over funnel or bottle to cool. Let stand until cold. To remove from pan loosen side of cake with spatula.

PETITE LAYER CAKE

- 2 9-inch layers, white cake
- 2 cups heavy cream
- 1 tablespoon 100% instant coffee
- ½ cup brown sugar, firmly packed
- ¼ teaspoon almond extract
- 1 teaspoon vanilla
- ⅛ teaspoon salt

Split the cake layers into thirds so that there will be six layers of white cake. Prepare the filling and frosting for these by combining the powdered coffee, brown sugar and flavorings with the heavy cream and beating it until the cream stands in soft peaks. Spread the mixture on all except 1 layer of the cake. Put all the cakes together, placing unfrosted layer on top. Frost the sides and top with the remaining cream. Chill several hours or over night before serving.

SNOW BERRY CAKE

Makes 2 (8-inch) round layers

- 2½ cups sifted enriched flour
- 3 teaspoons baking powder
- 1 teaspoon salt
- ⅔ cup homogenized shortening
- 1 cup sugar
- 1 teaspoon grated lemon peel
- ¾ cup milk
- 4 egg whites, beaten stiffly
- ½ cup sugar
- 1 cup jellied cranberry sauce, cubed or
- 1 cup fresh or frozen raspberries

Combine the sifted flour, baking powder and salt and sift these together. Combine the shortening, sugar and lemon peel and cream together well. When thoroughly blended begin adding the dry ingredients and milk, a little at a time alternately, and beating after each addition to blend thoroughly. If an electric mixer is used beat at low speed. Beat the egg whites until they hold soft peaks, then begin adding the sugar a little at a time until the meringue holds peaks which are shiny but not dry. Fold gently into the batter and fold in the cranberry sauce or raspberries. Pour into 2 well-greased and lightly floured round layer pans. Bake in moderate oven (375°) 30 to 35 minutes. Cool and frost.

Variations

If you used cranberry sauce a good frosting for putting between the layers and covering the top would be a Seven Minute Frosting (*page 237*) which has been tinted pink with red vegetable coloring and flavored with vanilla.

If raspberries were used in the cake put the layers together and frost with tinted Whipped Cream Frosting (*page 233*) or with pure white whipped cream frosting and garnish with some of the whole berries.

Christmas is a good time to serve this cake with cranberries inside and with cut-outs of small Christmas trees made from slices of canned cranberry jelly decorating the top.

Serve this cake the year round with raspberries inside and with more raspberries heaped in a circle around the cake to be served with each slice.

HAZELNUT TORTE

Makes 4 to 6 servings

2 egg yolks	½ cup sifted flour
½ cup sugar	½ teaspoon salt
⅓ cup salad oil	2 egg whites
2 tablespoons milk	1 cup heavy cream,
½ teaspoon vanilla	whipped
¾ cup ground hazelnuts	Sugar

This is very good as you'll find out. And you can double the recipe easily enough to serve more people.

Beat egg yolks slightly; gradually beat in ¼ cup of the sugar, then the salad oil. Add milk, vanilla, and nuts. Fold in mixed and sifted dry ingredients. Beat egg whites until stiff but not dry; gradually beat in the remaining ¼ cup sugar. Fold into batter.

Bake in greased and floured deep 8-inch layer cake pan in moderate oven (300°) 50 minutes. Cool. Split layer in half. Put together with half of the whipped cream, sweetened with sugar to taste. Spread remaining cream over top and garnish with chopped nuts.

If you want to, use ground pecans, walnuts, or blanched and toasted almonds in place of hazelnuts.

MERINGUE LOAF

Makes 4 servings

12 saltines, crushed	1 cup sugar
⅓ teaspoon baking powder	1 teaspoon vanilla
3 egg whites, beaten stiffly	12 maraschino cherries, chopped
¼ teaspoon salt	
1 teaspoon lemon juice	½ cup chopped nuts

Grease a spring form mold with butter, and set aside. Crush saltines to fine texture, and separate eggs which have been allowed to lose chill of refrigerator sufficient to be about room temperature. Add salt to egg whites and beat until frothy. Add lemon juice and begin adding sugar, a tablespoon at a time, beating at high speed until all the sugar has been added. Add the baking powder and vanilla and continue beating another five minutes, until all sugar is melted and the meringue stands in stiff dry peaks when beater is lifted. Fold in the saltines, cherries and nuts. Turn into the buttered pan and bake in preheated oven (350°) for 35 minutes. Open oven door and allow to cool ten minutes before removing from oven. Allow to cool in pan, loosen edge with spatula and turn loaf onto platter. Slice and serve plain or with a bowl of warm custard or crushed berries to spoon over the meringue.

CANADIAN CUP CAKES

Makes 1½ dozen

- 2 cups sifted enriched flour
- 1 teaspoon baking powder
- ½ cup butter or margarine
- 1 cup sugar
- 2 eggs, beaten
- ⅔ cup buttermilk or sour milk
- ½ teaspoon soda
- ¼ teaspoon salt
- 1 teaspoon vanilla
- ½ teaspoon almond extract
- 1 recipe Chocolate Filling
- 1 cup chopped coconut

Combine sifted flour, baking powder, soda and salt and sift together once. Cream the butter and sugar together in a large mixing bowl and add the eggs and beat well for 1 minute. Add the vanilla and almond extract to the milk and begin adding alternately with the dry ingredients to the cream mixture in the bowl, beginning and ending with dry ingredients. Blend thoroughly after each addition using low speed for electric mixer. Spoon batter into well greased muffin tins or in tins which have been lined with fluted paper cups. Be sure that each is filled equally. Bake in moderate oven (375°) 20 to 25 minutes. Cool and cut a cone shaped portion from the center of each cup cake. Fill with a chocolate filling and sprinkle with chopped coconut.

CHOCOLATE FILLING

Heat 3 tablespoons sugar, 3 tablespoons water and 2 squares (2 ounces) unsweetened chocolate until the chocolate is melted. Add 3 egg yolks, one at a time, and beat thoroughly after each addition. Blend in 1 teaspoon vanilla. Beat 3 egg whites until soft mounds are formed and add 3 tablespoons sugar gradually. Continue beating until stiff peaks form when beater is raised. Fold in the chocolate mixture, handling the batter gently until thoroughly blended.

These cakes can also be filled with Butter Cream Frosting (*page 238*) in any of the flavors you like.

CARAWAY RING CAKE
Danish

All through Germany and the Scandinavian countries caraway seeds add to the delightful cheeses and breads encountered. At tea time anyone from that part of the world might serve you cake made very much like this.

Fills 9-inch tube pan

- 2 cups sifted enriched flour
- 2 teaspoons baking powder
- 2 teaspoons cinnamon
- 1 cup butter
- 1½ cups sugar
- 3 teaspoons caraway seeds
- 5 egg yolks, beaten
- ⅓ cup milk
- 5 egg whites, stiffly beaten

Combine sifted flour, baking powder and cinnamon and sift together once. Cream the butter, sugar and caraway seeds together until thoroughly blended. Beat the egg yolks until thick and lemon colored and add them to the creamed mixture; stir until thoroughly mixed. Begin adding the dry ingredients and milk, a little at a time, alternating and beating after each addition until thoroughly blended before adding another. If electric mixer is used beat at low speed. Beat the egg whites until they form stiff peaks, and fold gently into this batter. Pour into a 9-inch tube pan which has been well greased and lightly floured *on the bottom only*. Bake in a moderate oven (375°) 45 to 50 minutes. Cool and glaze.

CINNAMON GLAZE

This spicy glaze is exactly right for topping off this tea cake. Sift 2 cups confectioners sugar, add 1 teaspoon cinnamon and sift once more to blend. Add 4 or 5 tablespoons of cream which has been heated in a tiny saucepan. Blend until the mixture is the right spreading consistency. Spread this over the cake after it has cooled. Garnish with a very light border of caraway seeds if you like.

MOCHA REFRIGERATOR CAKE

Makes 6 to 8 servings

1 package (1 cup) semi-sweet chocolate morsels	3 egg whites, beaten
1 tablespoon Nescafe	½ pint heavy cream, whipped
3 egg yolks	18 lady fingers, split

Combine the chocolate morsels and Nescafe in the top of a double boiler and stir over hot (not boiling) water until melted. Allow the mixture to cool about 10 minutes. Then beat in, one at a time, the 3 egg yolks, stirring each time until the yolk is thoroughly blended. Beat the egg whites until stiff but not dry and fold into the whipped cream and the coffee mixture. When blended arrange 12 split lady finger halves on the bottom of a baking dish 10 x 6 x 2. Cover these with ½ the mocha filling. Arrange another 12 lady finger halves on top. Add the rest of the filling and use the last 12 halves of lady fingers to form a design on the top. Chill well before serving.

Teatime Cakes

If you were to travel through the Pacific visiting the islands there, you would encounter sesame seeds in the food over and over again. Usually they are toasted and folded into the recipes; other times toasted and sprinkled over the top as in these tea cookies.

SESAME TWISTS

Makes 3 dozen

3 tablespoons toasted sesame seeds	2 teaspoons baking powder
3 cups enriched flour, sifted	½ teaspoon salt
½ cup butter or margarine	¼ teaspoon nutmeg
½ cup homogenized fat	½ cup milk
½ cup sugar	1 teaspoon vanilla
1 egg	¼ cup heavy cream
	1 egg, beaten

It is a good idea to toast the sesame seeds before beginning to make these cookies. Put them in a skillet along with a teaspoon or two of butter and cook them over low heat stirring constantly until the seeds are browned. Drain on paper towels to make them crisp.

While they cool combine the flour, baking powder, salt and nutmeg and sift together once. Cream the butter and sugar together until well blended and add the egg, milk and vanilla. If you like only butter in your cookies use ¾ cup butter instead of the combination of butter and homogenized fat. Now begin adding the dry ingredients and the heavy cream, a little of each alternately, beating each addition thoroughly before adding another. Roll out the dough in a very different manner than you are used to. Pick up about a tablespoon of the dough at a time and roll between the palms of your hands to form rolls about 8 inches long. Fold ends of these rolls together, pinch to close them and twist to form the figure eight. Place on greased baking sheets, brush the tops with beaten egg and sprinkle with toasted sesame seeds. Bake in moderate oven (350°) 20 to 25 minutes.

You can also roll each bit of dough you pick up into a ball, then roll in the toasted sesame seeds and bake.

CINNAMON TOAST

"Please write about your cinnamon toast," begged writer Blair Niles when she had consumed the sixth portion. "Tell us how you make it."

I know very well that cinnamon toast is not cake, but it is served for tea And this is the way I make it.

Soften 1 stick (¼ pound) of the best quality butter. Add 2 teaspoons ground cinnamon and 4 tablespoons granulated sugar. Stir until blended. Spread heavily *clear to the edge* on thin slices of white bread. Place under the broiler and let the top melt and caramelize. This requires about 5 minutes. Serve immediately. This mixture is a good one to keep in a small jar, ready to be used through the week.

PETITS FOURS

These bite-size cream puffs are gay deceivers. The elegant touch they add to the tea table suggests they are mysterious and difficult to make. The truth is they are great fun to stir up, they bake slowly enough for you to take a shower after they go in the oven and be out by the time the oven timer bell rings.

Cut the recipe in half to make cases to use this week. But use as it is to make a big party supply or to freeze some—unfilled—and to use some right away. But use these tiny puff shells for cocktail time, savory canapes, and for these Petits Fours.

PUFF SHELLS

Makes 24 (2-inch) cases

2 cups boiling water
1 cup (2 sticks) butter
2 cups flour
1 teaspoon salt
8 eggs

Prepare 2 cookie sheets by lightly greasing, before making the batter.

Pour water into a large saucepan, place over high heat. When it begins to boil, add butter, reduce heat and stir until butter is melted. Add salt to flour and dump it—all at once—into the hot mixture. Stir vigorously with a wooden spoon as it continues to cook over low heat. The mixture will turn into a thick batter. When it pulls away from the side of the pan as you beat, remove from heat. Have the eggs and a saucer nearby so that you can break the eggs into it, adding a whole egg, one at a time, to the batter. Beat hard after each egg is added, continuing until all are blended into the batter. This should be done quickly so that the eggs are blended while the batter is hot.

With a rubber spatula, pick up the ball of batter and place in a pastry bag. No metal tip is needed. Squeeze lightly, to form little rounds with a circular motion, on the cookie sheets, remembering to leave 2 inches between each one. Mounds should be no more than an inch across. Bake in preheated 450° oven 5 minutes, reduce heat to 375° and continue baking 40 minutes. Cool, split at side and fill (with pastry tube) with Chocolate Custard. Sprinkle tops with confectioner's sugar, or frost with any cake frosting you like.

CHOCOLATE CUSTARD

- 2 cups hot milk
- ½ cup sugar
- ¼ cup cornstarch
- ½ teaspoon salt
- 1 (6 ounce) package semi-sweet chocolate morsels
- 4 egg yolks, beaten
- 1 teaspoon vanilla

Mix sugar with cornstarch and stir into hot milk in top of double boiler. Cook over hot water, stirring occasionally, until hot but not boiling. Add chocolate and stir until blended. Add beaten egg yolk and continue to cook over hot water until thickened. Remove from heat. Cool and stir in vanilla. Fill the puff cases, and chill before serving.

IRISH GINGERBREAD CAKE

Makes 8-inch square cake

- 1¼ cups sifted enriched flour
- ¾ teaspoon soda
- ½ teaspoon cinnamon
- ¼ teaspoon cloves, ground
- ¼ teaspoon nutmeg, freshly ground
- ¼ teaspoon salt
- ⅓ cup candied fruit, cut into small cubes
- 2 tablespoons candied ginger, chopped
- ¼ cup homogenized shortening
- ¼ cup sugar
- 1 egg
- 7 tablespoons honey or molasses
- ½ cup hot water

Combine dry ingredients and sift them together once before adding the diced fruit and chopped ginger. Stir until the fruit is thoroughly coated. Combine shortening and sugar and cream together well before adding the egg and honey. Beat until thoroughly blended and combine with the creamed mixture. Add dry ingredients and mix thoroughly, adding the hot water and continuing to beat until the batter is smooth. Pour into a well greased and lightly floured 8 x 8 inch pan. Bake in moderate oven (350°) 40 to 45 minutes.

Fruit can be added to a gingerbread mix but stir into the dry ingredients before adding the liquid, otherwise they will all sink to the bottom.

If you want to serve Irish Gingerbread Cake for tea, frost the square with Maple Butter Cream Frosting (*page 237*) and cut into small, dainty squares.

FLORENTINES
Swiss Tea Cakes

Never until I went to Zurich in Switzerland did I eat the delicacy served there at teatime and known as Florentines. These are crisp, thin wafers usually about 3-inches across but sometimes made in 1-inch rounds. They appear to be caramelized and covered with dark, Swiss, bittersweet chocolate. For tea I make them in a 2-inch size. To have bite-size Florentines is a convenience with tea.

Makes 6 dozen 2-inch wafers

- ¾ cup heavy cream
- ¼ cup sugar
- ½ cup slivered almonds, blanched or not as you like
- 1 cup chopped preserved fruit, peel and citron
- 6 level tablespoons all purpose flour
- 1 (6 oz.) package semi-sweet chocolate morsels

Combine heavy cream with sugar. Stir until blended, then add the almonds and chopped fruit. Stir in the flour and when thoroughly blended drop by spoonfuls on a cooky sheet which has been greased with salad oil (do not use butter or the wafers will burn) and lightly coated with flour. Drop teaspoonfuls of batter on this floured cooky sheet, leaving at least 2 inches between each drop. Bake in preheated, slow oven (350°) about 12 minutes. Remove and cool on the cooky sheet. Remove with a spatula and turn upside down on a length of waxed paper. Melt the chocolate morsels in the top of a double boiler over boiling water. With a pastry brush coat the bottom of each cooky with a layer of the chocolate, making a little swirl as you remove the brush so that the chocolate will not be too smoothly spread.

Frostings

WHIPPED CREAM FROSTING

Makes 3 cups

1 cup heavy cream, whipped	Sugar to taste
¼ teaspoon salt	1 cup sweetened berries

Whip the cream and add the salt and sweetened berries. Fold together gently and taste to determine whether or not more sugar is necessary.

Almost any drained berry or fruit you want to use in the whipped cream will combine to make a delicious frosting and filling, but if you want a firmer filling as you might when combining a 3-layer cake here is:

WHIPPED CREAM FILLING

½ envelope unflavored gelatin	juice
2 tablespoons water or fruit	1 cup cream
	Sugar to taste

Soften the gelatin in the water or fruit juice, or flavor by using strong coffee. Do not use the coffee if you are adding fruit. Whip the cream until it is stiff and fold in the dissolved gelatin mixture. At this point additions can be made of vanilla or lemon flavoring, liqueur or more coffee if you wish it stronger, or a combination of melted chocolate and coffee. Any additions should be added without increasing the liquid content more than a couple of teaspoons, although chopped fruits or candies can be folded in in amounts equaling one-half the quantity of whipped cream.

MARBLED WHIPPED CREAM TOPPING

Makes 1 cup

½ cup heavy cream
1 to 2 tablespoons thin chocolate sauce

Chill cream, small bowl and rotary egg beater. Turn cream into bowl and beat rapidly until cream begins to thicken. Then beat slowly until cream holds its shape. Swirl chocolate sauce through whipped cream. Use as topping for cakes.

Add ½ teaspoon peppermint extract for pleasant flavor.

QUICK UNCOOKED FLUFFY FROSTING

Makes 3 cups frosting, or enough to cover tops and sides of 2 (8-inch) layers

1 egg white, unbeaten
¾ cup sugar
¼ teaspoon cream of tartar
1 teaspoon vanilla
¼ cup boiling water

Combine egg white, sugar, cream of tartar and vanilla in small deep bowl; mix well. Add boiling water and beat with rotary egg beater (or at high speed of electric mixer) until mixture will stand in stiff peaks—4 or 5 minutes.

SEAFOAM FROSTING

Fills and covers 1 (9-inch) layer cake

2½ cups brown sugar
½ cup water
2 egg whites, beaten until frothy
Salt
1 teaspoon vanilla
½ cup chopped pecans

Combine sugar and water in a saucepan and stir over medium heat until sugar is dissolved. Reduce heat and allow mixture to boil without stirring until the syrup makes a soft ball when dropped in cold water. Add the salt to the egg whites and beat until they are frothy but not stiff. Pour the hot syrup over the egg whites in a thin stream, continuing to beat constantly until syrup and egg whites are combined. Add the vanilla and place the mixing bowl over the lower part of a double boiler in which water is boiling. Continue to beat until the mixture will hold peaks. Spread immediately on the tops and sides of a 2-layer cake and sprinkle with the pecans.

COFFEE SEAFOAM FROSTING:—When you get the hang of making Seafoam Icing it is so good that you may like to vary it by using coffee flavoring. Simply replace the ½ cup water combined with the brown sugar by ½ cup strong black coffee.

Make this recipe, plus ½ the recipe, for thickly covering and filling a 3-layer 9-inch cake.

SOUR CREAM FROSTING

To frost and cover a 2-layer cake

- 3 tablespoons sour cream
- 3 tablespoons butter
- 1½ cups confectioner's sugar
- ⅛ teaspoon salt
- ¼ teaspoon vanilla

Cream the butter until soft. Add the sugar and blend thoroughly. Add the cream, salt and vanilla, beat well.

CARAMEL SOUR CREAM FROSTING

To join and cover 2 (8-inch) layers

- 1 cup sugar
- 1 cup brown sugar, firmly packed
- ⅔ cup sour cream
- 1 teaspoon vanilla

Combine the white and brown sugar with the sour cream in a saucepan and cook over medium heat, stirring constantly until the sugar is dissolved and a drop of the syrup forms a soft ball in cold water. Remove from heat and cool to lukewarm. Add vanilla and beat with rotary beater until thick enough to spread. Thin with a small amount of cream if it is necessary.

CREAM CHEESE FROSTING

Makes 2 ¼ cups

- 1 (3 oz.) package cream cheese
- 2 cups confectioner's sugar
- ⅛ teaspoon salt
- Sweet Cream

Allow the cream cheese to soften by standing at room temperature, then turn into mixing bowl and stir until creamy. Add the sugar gradually as you beat until it has all been combined. Add salt and the flavoring desired. Since a Cream Cheese Frosting can be tinted from any of the food coloring bottles and flavored according to whim, the amounts stirred into this mixture should depend upon your whim as well. Tinting delicate tints are best; deep ones sometimes are offensive except in tiny flowers or small decorations added to an over-all pale frosting. For flavors use vanilla extract, 2 squares melted bitter chocolate, a spoonful of maple syrup, a little lemon extract or a spoonful of any liqueur you want. After this has been blended use sweet cream in the amount necessary to make the icing the right consistency for piling it onto the top of cup cakes or to frost a larger cake.

SEVEN MINUTE FROSTING

Makes frosting to cover tops and sides of 2 (8-inch) or (9-inch) layers. Or top and sides of 10 x 10 x 2-inch cake or 13 x 19 x 2-inch cake

2 egg whites, unbeaten	⅓ cup water
1½ cups sugar	2 teaspoons light corn syrup
Dash of salt	1 teaspoon vanilla

Combine egg whites, sugar, salt, water and corn syrup in top of double boiler. Beat with rotary egg beater or electric beater 1 minute, or until mixed. Cook over rapidly boiling water, beating constantly with rotary egg beater (or at high speed of electric beater) 7 minutes, or until frosting will stand in stiff peaks. Remove from boiling water. Add vanilla, and beat 1 minute, or until thick enough to spread.

Variations

FOUR MINUTE FROSTING:—Follow directions above, using one egg white and half the amount of other ingredients. Beat over boiling water 4 minutes. Frosts top and sides of 9 x 9 x 2-inch cake or 9-inch tube cake.

COCONUT MARSHMALLOW FROSTING:—Use above recipe; fold in 1 cup marshmallows, quartered, before spreading on cake. Then sprinkle generously with shredded coconut.

MAPLE BUTTER CREAM FROSTING:—Use above recipe, substitute 1 teaspoon maple extract for vanilla.

PINK PEPPERMINT FROSTING:—Use above recipe, substitute ¼ teaspoon peppermint extract for the vanilla. Add red coloring to tint delicately. Especially delicious on a devil's food cake.

PISTACHIO FROSTING:—Use above recipe; decrease the vanilla to ½ teaspoon and add ¼ teaspoon almond extract. If desired, tint a delicate green coloring and garnish with pistachio nuts.

FUDGE FROSTING

Makes 2½ cups frosting, or enough to cover tops and sides of 2(9-inch) layers, or top and sides of 13 x 2-inch cake, or tops of about 3 dozen cup cakes.

3 squares unsweetened chocolate	1¼ cups milk
Dash of salt	3 cups sugar
1 tablespoon light corn syrup	3 tablespoons butter
	1½ teaspoons vanilla

Add chocolate to milk and cook over low heat until smooth, stirring constantly. Add sugar, salt and corn syrup; stir until sugar is dissolved and mixture boils. Continue boiling, stirring occasionally, until a small amount of mixture forms a very soft ball when dropped in cold water (or to a temperature of 234°). Remove from heat; add butter and vanilla. Cool to lukewarm (110°), and beat until of right consistency to spread.

BUTTER CREAM FROSTING

Makes 2⅔ cups, or enough to cover tops and sides of 2 (9-inch) layers

½ cup butter	2 egg yolks, unbeaten
⅛ teaspoon salt	1 teaspoon vanilla
3½ cups (1 pound) sifted confectioner's sugar	2 tablespoons top milk (about)

Cream butter; add salt and part of sugar gradually, blending after each addition. Then add egg yolks and vanilla; blend well. Add remaining sugar alternately with milk, until of right consistency to spread, beating after each addition until smooth.

Variations

LEMON BUTTER CREAM FROSTING:—Use recipe for Butter Cream Frosting, substituting 1 teaspoon grated lemon rind for the vanilla.
COFFEE BUTTER CREAM FROSTING:—Use recipe for Butter Cream Frosting, decreasing vanilla to ½ teaspoon and adding 3 teaspoons instant coffee with the unbeaten egg yolks.
RUM BUTTER CREAM FROSTING:—Use recipe for Butter Cream Frosting, eliminate vanilla and add 1 to 2 tablespoons of rum.

12

Dramatic Desserts

Chocolate and Wonderful Flambés

CHOCOLATE MOUSSE
France

Makes 8 servings

- 2 packages semi-sweet chocolate morsels
- ¼ cup water
- 5 egg yolks, beaten
- 1 cup (6 or 7) egg whites, beaten stiffly
- ¼ teaspoon salt

This is the *Mousse au Chocolat* of France. It is a perfect example of dessert which is so easy to make that the French shrug off the whole procedure as being something for children, while Americans are inclined to be intimidated by it. The French are right. It's easy. This is a dessert to be made a day before you want to use it, and one which will keep well, refrigerated, for several days while you consume it.

Now make it this way: put the chocolate morsels and ¼ cup hot water in top of a double boiler over boiling water. Allow this to stand, stirring occasionally until the chocolate is softened and thoroughly mixed with the liquid. Add the egg yolks and beat until thoroughly blended. Continue cooking over the boiling water for at least 2 minutes stirring constantly. Remove from heat and allow to cool while the egg whites are being beaten.

When separating eggs for this recipe be sure that no bits of yolk get into the white, for this will spoil the meringue. The bowl in which the whites are beaten must not only be big and clean but perfectly dry. Add the salt and beat until the egg whites form stiff peaks with no glisten. When dry and stiff pick up about ¼ of the meringue with the beater and stir it into the chocolate mixture, beating very hard. Turn the chocolate mixture into the egg whites being sure to clean the bowl with a rubber spatula so that all the chocolate mixture is added. Fold in gently until thoroughly blended and turn into a soufflé dish or a crock. Chill 6 to 24 hours before serving.

CHOCOLATE MERINGUE ROLL

Makes 5 to 8 servings

- 7 egg yolks, beaten
- 1 cup granulated sugar
- 1¼ cups (1½ packages) semi-sweet chocolate morsels
- 6 tablespoons water
- ¼ teaspoon salt
- 7 egg whites, stiffly beaten

Prepare a jelly-roll pan by greasing the pan, line with waxpaper leaving a couple of inches of paper extending beyond the pan at each end. Grease the waxed paper and be sure the waxed paper reaches up both sides of the pan.

This heavenly de luxe "Jelly Roll" style Chocolate Roll is another French masterpiece. Notice it is assembled exactly as its twin, the Chocolate Mousse (*page 240*) until the chocolate mixture is added to meringue, then it is *beaten,* not folded in.

Combine semi-sweet chocolate morsels and sugar in top of double boiler. Place over gently boiling water, stirring occasionally until chocolate is melted. Remove from heat, add the beaten egg yolks, and water. Stir thoroughly and return to cook for 2 minutes over boiling water stirring constantly. Remove from heat and set aside to cool.

Add salt to the egg whites, beat until very stiff and dry. Pour cooled chocolate mixture over the meringue using a rubber spatula to scrape all chocolate into the bowl. Beat (don't fold) until thoroughly mixed. Turn into the prepared jelly-roll pan, spreading evenly with a spatula, for this batter is so light it will not spread on its own. Bake on the top shelf in a 350° preheated oven for 15 minutes. Open the oven door and turn off heat, then leave cake in the oven another 5 minutes. Remove and cover with an ice-water soaked cloth which has been wrung almost dry. Allow cake to cool. Remove the cloth, run a knife around the edge of the cake to ease it away from the pan, cover with strip of aluminum foil, invert pan to gently turn the cooled cake onto foil. Remove waxed paper from the top by rolling it gently off the cake. Roll the cake lengthwise, folding over each side once and securing by wrapping the cake in the foil. Place in refrigerator and chill for 1 hour. Remove, allowing the cake roll to open slightly and spread filling down the center. Reroll securely in foil and chill until ready to slice, 1 hour or more.

Serve smooth side up and sprinkle top with unsweetened cocoa.

WHIPPED CREAM FILLING

To fill Chocolate Meringue Roll

1 envelope unflavored gelatin
¼ cup cold water
1½ cups heavy cream, whipped
4 tablespoons sugar
2 tablespoons vanilla

Soften gelatin in cold water in top of double boiler. Whip the cream until it holds soft peaks. Place softened gelatin over boiling water and stir until dissolved. Add sugar, gelatin and vanilla to cream. Fold together and fill roll.

NOREEN'S ENGLISH TRIFLE

Makes 8 to 12 servings

1 round 9-inch layer of white cake
1½ cups heavy cream, whipped
½ teaspoon vanilla
2 cups thick lemon custard
2 cups thick cold applesauce
¼ cup almonds, toasted, slivered
2 tablespoons sugar

Break or crumble the cake into the bottom of a big serving bowl. Sprinkle with the sherry, cover tightly and leave for 2 hours or more. Complete the trifle by adding gelatin to boiling hot liquid, stir until dissolved and pour over the cake. Cool and chill until set. Cover with pear slices, pour warm custard (*page 244*) over to completely cover and cool. Top with sweetened whipped cream. Chill until serving time and garnish with slices of fruit or with berries.

This is a delicious trifle and can't be hurt in the least by increasing the amount of cake or sherry used. Noreen, who originated this, insists its claim to fame lies in a heavy hand when tipping the sherry bottle to sprinkle the cake.

APPLE PYRAMID
Danish

Makes 6 servings

- 1 (9 or 10-inch) layer stale white cake, crumbled or chopped
- 1 cup sherry
- 2 cups hot water (or hot water plus juice drained from pears to make 2 cups)
- 1 package lime-flavored gelatin
- 1 can pear halves, sliced
- 2 cups rum custard
- 1½ cups heavy cream, whipped
- Fresh fruit to garnish

Place the white cake on a platter, cover with the custard and allow it to set for a few minutes before adding chilled applesauce to form a cone-shaped mound in the center. Whip the cream, add sugar to sweeten and vanilla to flavor. Pile over the cake to form a pyramid. Sprinkle with slivered, toasted almonds. Chill at least 30 minutes before serving.
RUM CUSTARD:—Use 1 tablespoon rum with ½ teaspoon vanilla and ½ teaspoon lemon juice.

LEMON CUSTARD FILLING

- 2 cups milk
- 3 egg yolks, beaten
- ⅓ cup sugar
- 3 tablespoons cornstarch
- ¼ teaspoon salt
- 1 teaspoon vanilla

Heat the milk in top of double boiler, but do not allow it to boil. Combine the beaten egg yolks, sugar, salt and cornstarch and stir until blended. Add to scalded milk, stirring constantly and cook in top of a double boiler over boiling water until thickened. Add vanilla, cool and chill.

THE QUEEN'S PUDDING

Makes 12 servings

This pudding is composed of three parts: sweet nut rolls, a sauce to be baked over the top of cold sweet rolls, the meringue to pile high on top. It is an elegantly royal de luxe "bread pudding," first made at the smörgåsbord in Stow, Ohio, when they had a few of the famous nut rolls left over.

Make sweet nut rolls to enjoy a day or two before you make this gorgeous pudding. Hide twelve or you will be out of luck when ready to make it. Here are the recipes you'll need for Sweet Nut Rolls, Sauce, and Meringue.

SWEET NUT ROLLS

Makes 3 dozen, enough for 12 servings

½ cup scalded milk
2 tablespoons sugar
1½ teaspoons salt
3 tablespoons butter
⅓ cup water
1 egg, well beaten
1 cake of compressed yeast (dissolved in 2 tablespoons lukewarm water)
3 cups sifted all-purpose flour
Cinnamon
Brown Sugar
Maple Syrup
Pecans or black walnuts

Scald milk, remove from heat and add sugar, salt and butter. Stir until butter is melted. Add water, egg and dissolved yeast, blend thoroughly, adding flour a little at a time and continuing to beat until a soft dough is formed. Turn onto a lightly floured pastry cloth and knead until dough is satiny, about 5 minutes. Form into ball and store in buttered bowl tightly covered until ready to use.

Roll out into an oblong of ¼-inch thickness, spread generously with melted butter, sprinkle heavily with cinnamon and brown sugar. Fold dough over twice lengthwise and slice into 1½-inch or 2-inch slices.

Prepare pan for baking by greasing heavily. Pour maple syrup in pan to ¼-inch thickness. Place cinnamon rolls in this mixture. Brush tops with butter. Cover and let rise to double in bulk. Bake in preheated (425°) oven until syrup is bubbling and rolls are brown, about 20 minutes.

Invert pan immediately to remove buns and sprinkle while hot with 1 cup finely chopped pecans or black walnuts.

Now begin the pudding.

SAUCE

8 egg yolks, beaten	½ large sweet orange rind, grated
3 cups cream	
½ cup sugar	½ cup orange juice

Cut 12 sweet nut rolls into equal size pieces to make a layer covering the bottom of an 8 x 11-inch pan. Make the sauce by beating egg yolks until light and lemon colored. Add cream, sugar and continue beating until blended. Add orange juice and rind, stir until mixed and pour over the rolls. Bake in preheated (300°) oven until the custard is set but still quivery, about 1 hour.

Remove from oven and reduce heat to 275°, allowing sauced rolls to cool slightly while preparing the meringue.

MERINGUE

1 cup egg whites	2 tablespoons sugar
⅛ teaspoon salt	

Beat egg whites until frothy, add salt. Continue beating, adding the sugar gradually, until the meringue is stiff and of taffy consistency. Spread over top of pudding, forming attractive peaks on top and bake in slow (275°) oven until golden brown, about

20 minutes. Remove and serve while warm or allow it to cool.

The meringue peaks appear to be this queen's tiara—a crown it deserves to wear.

BANANAS FLAMBÉ

Spain

The best Banana Flambé I ever ate was in Madrid where the whole bananas were laid in a large chafing dish, side by side, and completely covered with a buttery liqueur mixture. They cooked this beside us at the table until it was ready to be flamed and served.

Makes 6 servings

6 ripe bananas, peeled and left whole	1 cup rum
½ cup butter	¼ cup granulated sugar
½ cup brown sugar	½ cup brandy, heated

Leave the peeled bananas whole, place in chafing dish as soon as the butter is melted. Sprinkle with the brown sugar and move them slightly, to keep them from sticking, until they are coated with the buttery mixture. Add rum and simmer over medium flame 10 minutes, basting occasionally. Sprinkle granulated sugar over bananas, add hot brandy and ignite the liqueur by touching with a lighted candle. When flame disappears, serve one banana on each plate and spoon sauce over it.

CHERRIES JUBILEE

Cherries Jubilee is easy, elegant and delicious . . . definitely one of those desserts you should serve more often. Decide how large a serving of vanilla ice cream you want for each person, then make enough thin cherry sauce to flame and serve in ½ cup portions for each portion of ice cream. The flaming of a sauce must be done in the top of a chafing dish or any fireproof utensil attractive enough to bring to the table. And the sauce should be spooned out with a long-handled spoon which has a sizable bowl so that a spoonful pretty much covers the ice cream with the individual serving.

The ice cream can be served from a beautiful big bowl or it can be brought in on the dessert plates. You do not use small bowls for this as you would for ordinary ice cream, for you want plenty of room for the sauce. Try this out on the family first and you will see how easy it is, despite its world-wide reputation for elegance.

CHERRY JUBILEE SAUCE FLAMBÉ

Makes 4 cups of sauce

- 2 tablespoons quick-cooking tapioca
- ½ cup sugar
- ¼ teaspoon salt
- 2 cups (No. 2½ can) pitted, drained canned Bing cherries
- Cherry juice plus water to make 1½ cups
- ⅓ cup brandy
- ½ cup rum

Combine in a saucepan all ingredients (except brandy and rum). Cook and stir over medium heat until mixture comes to a boil. Remove from heat. Cool 15 minutes. Stir in half of the brandy. Combine remaining brandy and the rum, place over low heat until warm, pour over the warm sauce and ignite. Spoon the flaming sauce over vanilla ice cream.

This sauce is delicious served over white cake too, or white cake into which you stirred lightly floured pitted cherries before baking.

DRAMATIC DESSERTS
CRÊPES AU KIRSCH

Makes 14 crêpes

- 2 cups pancake mix
- 2¼ cups milk
- 3 eggs, beaten
- ¼ cup sugar
- ¼ pound (1 stick) butter, softened
- ½ cup Kirsch and ½ cup rum, warmed

Make the crêpes, which is pancake in French as you probably know, according to directions on the package. Add 3 eggs and stir until blended. Unless the batter is quite thin, add water a teaspoonful at a time, until batter will spread quickly on griddle to make a very thin pancake.

Combine the butter with the sugar, mix well and put a spoonful in the middle of each pancake after it is cooked. Roll each side to the center and put folded side down in a flameware or chafing dish. When all the crêpes are arranged sprinkle with granulated sugar, then with the warm Kirsch. Use a lighted candle to ignite the heated Kirsch as you serve the crêpes flaming gaily.

MAKING FLAMING PANCAKES FLAME

The secret of making flaming pancakes flame, is to have a little granulated sugar to burn, the liqueur very hot. And to tell the truth, rum burns more brightly and longer than other liqueurs. Its combination with the main flavor helps make your fire burn brightly.

PEACHES FLAMBÉ

Makes 8 servings

- 8 beautiful ripe peaches, peeled and halved
- 1½ cups water
- 1½ cups light brown sugar
- ½ cup rum, heated
- 2 cups vanilla wafers or macaroon crumbs or 8 whole meringue shells

Peel the peaches without removing any of the fruit underneath. Combine the water and sugar in a saucepan and boil until the sugar is dissolved. Add the peach halves to the syrup and allow them to cook for 8 to 10 minutes. Remove peach halves to chafing dish, continue cooking syrup until it is half the original amount, then pour over the peaches.

Prepare the dessert plates with a mound of crushed macaroon or vanilla wafer crumbs or with a meringue shell on each one. Pour the rum over the peaches. Ignite and spoon 2 peach halves with some of the sauce on to each plate.

PEACHES IN CHAMPAGNE

Makes 8 servings

8 beautifully ripened peaches, peeled and halved	⅓ cup brandy 1 bottle chilled champagne

Peaches can be peeled more easily without removing any of the fruit if they are plunged into boiling water for a few seconds as you would do for removing the skins of tomatoes. Peel peaches, halve and remove stones. Place the halves in your most beautiful bowl. Sprinkle with brandy, cover and place in refrigerator to chill for ½ hour or more. When ready to serve cover with chilled champagne; the remainder is intended for the wine glasses.

Serve with a deep-bowled serving spoon which will dip up fragrant liquid with each serving of peaches.

GLACE MELBA PEACHES

Makes 6 servings

12 fresh peach halves 1½ cups sugar	1 quart vanilla ice cream, softened

1½ cups water   2 cups Melba Sauce
2 teaspoons vanilla extract

Peel and halve the peaches removing the stones. Combine sugar, water and vanilla in a large saucepan. Place over medium heat and stir occasionally until sugar is dissolved. Add the peach halves to the vanilla flavored syrup and reduce heat. Cover and allow them to poach for about 10 minutes. Remove peaches to a bowl and cook the syrup until thickened. Pour over the peaches and allow them to continue to steep in the vanilla flavored syrup until ready to serve, placing them on ice when the syrup has cooled.

Serve by placing a layer of vanilla ice cream in an attractive serving bowl, preferably crystal. Scoop up the peach halves to arrange cavity side down over the ice. Cover with the Melba Sauce and serve.

MELBA SAUCE

The quickest way to make this sauce is with an electric blender. Place ½ of 1 package of sweetened frozen raspberries in an electric blender. Turn on machine and run until puréed, then do the same with the other half. If no electric blender is available place the frozen fruit either frozen or thawed in a saucepan, add 1 cup water and cook over medium heat stirring occasionally until blended. Beat vigorously while still hot with a rotary or electric beater for about 5 minutes. Put through a fine strainer and cool before serving.

PEACH AU COGNAC:—Use fresh uncooked peaches for this. Pour the delicious Melba Sauce over vanilla ice cream or over peach ice cream, or cover a mound of ice cream with slices or halves of fresh peaches which have been steeped in brandy in a tightly-covered bowl for at least 1 hour. This is a man's dish.

GINGERED PINEAPPLE IN CHAFING DISH

Makes 4 servings

4 tablespoons butter	¼ cup dark rum
1 can pineapple chunks, drained	½ teaspoon ground ginger
	1 quart vanilla ice cream
Drained juice	2 tablespoons chopped preserved ginger
½ cup brown sugar	

Melt the butter in a chafing dish or similar pan with flame underneath it, add the drained pineapple chunks and stir until lightly browned and heated through. Add the brown sugar, stir until the pineapple chunks are almost caramelized. Add the rum, the juice which was drained off the pineapple chunks, the ground ginger and stir until blended. Spoon over the vanilla ice cream which has been arranged on serving dishes, dividing the fruit and syrup into equal portions. Sprinkle the preserved ginger over the top and serve immediately.

Ambrosias—the Food of the Gods

In classical mythology the food of the gods meant any food which would impart immortality. Most of us would settle for the more modern definition of ambrosias which is "anything imparting the sense of divinity, poetic inspiration. Something especially delicious to taste or smell."

Fruit, fresh fruit, fragrant tree-ripened fruit, poached fresh fruit, are as fragrant as they are delicious to taste. Their appearance suggests divinity, poetic inspiration. Here are a few ideas to remember when fruit and berries are ripe.

DRAMATIC DESSERTS

When It's Fresh Fruit for Dessert

Serve the strawberries from the garden with their stems on, arranged in a circle around a little mound of confectioner's sugar. Dip and eat.

Serve an assortment of berries together on the same plate, 3 or 4 strawberries, a mound of raspberries, a little paper cup filled with blueberries, 3 or 4 cherries with the stems on.

Serve any berries in season in the most beautiful stemmed sherbet glasses you own, topped with sweetened whipped cream, hard sauce or thick sour cream.

Marinate raspberries covered tightly in ½ cup port and ½ cup brandy.

Sweeten berries with ½ orange juice and ½ sugar mixture.

Sweeten them another time with lemon juice added bountifully to a syrup of sugar and water of equal proportions. Cook long enough to make it thick, about 5 minutes. Cool and add lemon juice and serve over fruit.

Serve cherries, dead ripe, warm as when they were picked, with their stems on, heaped into a big glass bowl for people to help themselves after they have posed as a bouquet on the table during the meal.

Add a little lime juice to honey and serve over berries, fresh peaches which have been sliced or juicy ripe pears which have been peeled and halved.

Compose a colorful fresh fruit compote with slices of peaches, chunks of bananas, pitted sweet black cherries, a few berries, either one or several, and orange or grapefruit slices.

Scoop out little melon balls from left-over melon and put in refrigerator to serve as dessert.

Pile an assortment of watermelon, honeydew or canteloupe balls on a large grape leaf and serve as dessert. Add mint leaves to decorate these or the other fruit.

Halve and core large juicy grapefruit. Combine 1 tablespoon confectioner's sugar, 1 tablespoon water and 4 drops of mint flavoring. Stir and sprinkle over the grapefruit halves.

Omit sugar and sprinkle grapefruit halves with Angostura Bitters or with Bitters and sugar.

Sprinkle grapefruit halves with brown sugar, dot with butter and slide under broiler until sugar has melted and formed a crust. Serve hot as a first course.

Remove grapefruit sections, marinate in French Dressing (*page 192*) made with lemon, sprinkle with paprika. Cover. Let stand for at least an hour. Lift wedges from dressing—for it can be used on salad—return them to the grapefruit shells. Serve cold on a lettuce leaf as a salad.

Make an unusual fruit cocktail by combining bananas with black grapes which have been peeled and cut in half and the seeds removed. Add wedges cut from a navel orange. Sprinkle with lemon juice and a little honey. Serve in a beautiful glass dish and sprinkle with sherry.

FROSTED CANADIAN CANTALOUPE

By late August the cantaloupe in some areas in Canada are an enormous deep yellow gold with very small seed centers. The flavor is delicious and the melons need no adornment, but in the event of a party you might like to make these beautiful slices. A thick layer of delicious melon is absolutely necessary, so choose the melons with care.

Makes 8 servings

- 2 very large cantaloupes or 3 medium cantaloupes
- 1 package lime-flavored gelatin
- 2 cups Cream Cheese Frosting (page 236)

Peel the melons and slice a very thin slice off one end so that they will stand upright. Remove a slice from the top which cuts into the melon cavity just enough to enable you to pour the lime gelatin into the center. You can use a funnel to do this, preparing the gelatin according to directions on the package using ¼ cup less liquid than indicated and allowing it to cool a little but not to congeal before filling the centers of the melons. Replace the "lids" and chill in the refrigerator about 30 minutes. Remove then or an hour or two later if it is more convenient and frost the melons with the Cream Cheese Frosting. Chill at least 4 hours. Remove from refrigerator and cut cross-wise into slices and serve on chilled dessert plates.

RHUBARB MOLD WITH SOUR CREAM SAUCE
Danish

Makes 6 servings

3 packages frozen rhubarb	¾ cup sugar
1½ cups water	½ teaspoon vanilla
2 envelopes unflavored gelatin	¼ teaspoon cinnamon
	¼ teaspoon salt

Cook the rhubarb according to directions on the package, omitting sugar, and continuing to cook 2 or 3 minutes longer than directed if necessary until the rhubarb is very soft. Strain through a sieve and then through double cheesecloth to extract the clear juice. If you have a little less than 4 cups after squeezing the double cheesecloth to extract all the juice, add orange juice to make up the quantity you need. Cool.

Soften the gelatin in 1 cup of the juice when it has cooled and dissolve over hot water. Add sugar to the 3 cups of juice remaining and heat until the sugar dissolves but do not allow it to boil. Add the gelatin mixture, vanilla, cinnamon and salt and pour into any mold you like or into 6 individual molds. Garnish with whole ripe strawberries arranged in a circle around the mold. Serve with bowl of chilled thick sour cream.

BANANA COMPOTE

Makes 4 servings

- 4 small, green tipped bananas
- 2 tablespoons butter
- 1 cup dry red wine
- 1 cup sugar
- ½ tablespoon cornstarch
- ½ teaspoon nutmeg
- ⅛ teaspoon salt

Peel the bananas, run a fork down the length of each banana to form ridges. Melt the butter in a large skillet, cut the bananas into ¼-inch slices and place in the butter. This makes very pretty scalloped banana slices. Sauté until the bananas are lightly browned. In a saucepan combine the wine, and the sugar which has been mixed with the cornstarch. Cook over medium heat, stirring constantly until the liquid is slightly thickened and clear. Add the nutmeg and salt and pour over the bananas. Cover and simmer over low heat for about 10 minutes.

PRUNES IN RED WINE

Makes 6 servings

- 1 pound jumbo prunes
- Dry red wine
- ½ cup sugar
- 1 bay leaf
- ½ stick cinnamon
- 1½ tablespoons grated lemon peel

Soak the prunes at least 8 hours in half again as much wine as is necessary to cover them. Be sure they are covered while marinating in the wine, and the longer you leave them in the wine before cooking the better, for they must be thoroughly soft.

Place in a saucepan. Add sugar, spices and lemon peel. Simmer until the prunes are tender and remove them to a serving bowl with a slotted spoon, being very careful not to break the skins. Continue boiling the syrup until it is slightly thick. Strain through double cheesecloth and pour over the prunes.

VERMONT BAKED APPLES

Makes 8 servings

8 firm red apples, cored
2½ cups maple syrup
¼ cup lemon juice
½ cup seedless raisins
½ cup chopped nutmeats

Arrange the apples in a well buttered baking dish. Fill centers of each with a teaspoon of the lemon juice and some of the raisins and nuts. If any of the juice or fillings are left sprinkle them over the top of the apples. Dribble the syrup over the apples until each one is glossy and the bottom of the baking dish well covered. Cover and bake in moderate oven (375°) for 40 minutes, basting occasionally with the syrup. Serve hot with heavy cream and some of the hot syrup.

APPLE PANCAKES STACK

Makes 12 cakes

2 cups sifted all-purpose flour
1 teaspoon salt
1 tablespoon sugar
3 cups milk
6 eggs
3 tart apples, peeled, cored and slivered
¼ cup lemon juice
¼ cup orange juice
2 cups (or 1 package frozen) applesauce, hot
1 cup light brown sugar

Combine dry ingredients and sift together once. Add the milk and stir until blended. Add the eggs one at a time and beat until thoroughly blended before adding the next. Combine the apple slivers with the juices and add to the batter. Bake on hot, lightly greased griddle, browning on both sides and making all the cakes even in size. As each one is browned place on a warm platter, placing pieces of paper towel between cakes to keep them from becoming soft. When all the cakes are done arrange on a hot serving dish making 2 stacks of 6 cakes filled with alternate layers of the hot apple sauce and brown sugar. Sprinkle the top cake with more brown sugar. Cut into wedges, serving 1/4 or 1/6 to each person.

Variations

You can also make these pancakes twice the usual size, about the size of a dinner plate, and make one stack of 6 large cakes filled with alternate layers of hot apple sauce and brown sugar.

Make them either large or small, fill the pancakes with sweetened berries and sprinkle the top pancake with powdered sugar. Cut into wedges and serve.

Frozen Desserts, Ice Creams and Ices

AVOCADO ICE CREAM

Makes about 1 quart

- ⅔ cup mashed avocado
- ½ cup orange juice
- 2 tablespoons lemon juice
- ¼ teaspoon grated orange rind
- ¼ teaspoon salt
- ½ cup granulated sugar
- 1 cup light cream
- 1 cup milk

Cut avocado into halves lengthwise, remove and discard seed and skin. Force avocado through a sieve or combine with the other ingredients in an electric blender and blend until puréed, about 1 minute. Pour into refrigerator tray and freeze. If not blending by machine, combine the sieved avocado with the remaining ingredients, beat until thoroughly blended and pour into refrigerator tray. Place in freezing compartment with controls set at lowest temperature and freeze until firm. Turn into chilled bowl and beat with a rotary beater until smooth and fluffy. Return to freezing compartment and freeze to desired consistency. Reset temperature control to normal for storage.

FRENCH MOCHA ICE CREAM

Makes 1½ quarts

- ½ cup sugar
- ¼ cup water
- ¼ teaspoon cream of tartar
- 4 egg yolks, beaten
- 1 (6 oz.) package semi-sweet chocolate morsels
- 4 tablespoons strong black coffee
- 3½ cups heavy cream
- 1 tablespoon coffee liqueur or *crème de cacao*

Beat the egg yolks until they are thick and lemon colored and set aside. Combine in a saucepan the sugar, water and cream of tartar and cook over medium heat, stirring constantly until the syrup spins a light thread when spoon is lifted from the pan. Pour the syrup over the egg yolks in a thin stream, beating until the mixture is very stiff. Combine the chocolate morsels with the coffee in top of a double boiler, stir over boiling water until thoroughly blended, then add to the syrup and stir in the heavy cream. Pour into mold and freeze until of a mushy consistency. Remove to a chilled bowl. Beat thoroughly, add liqueur, beat until blended, return to mold and freeze until solid. Store at zero.

COFFEE TORTONI

Makes 8 servings

- 1 egg white
- 1 tablespoon instant coffee
- ⅛ teaspoon salt
- 2 tablespoons sugar
- 1 cup heavy cream
- ¼ cup sugar
- 1 teaspoon vanilla
- ⅛ teaspoon almond extract
- ¼ cup toasted almonds, finely chopped
- 8 (2 oz.) paper cups for molding

First set the controls of your refrigerator at the coldest point. Then combine the egg white, coffee powder and salt and beat until the whites are stiff but not dry. Gradually add 2 tablespoons of sugar continuing to beat until the meringue is stiff and satiny. Whip the cream until stiff and fold in the ¼ cup sugar, vanilla and almond extract. Add the egg white mixture and the toasted chopped almonds and fold together till blended. Pour into the paper cups and freeze until firm.

PISTACHIO BOMBE

Makes 3 quarts

- 1 quart pistachio ice cream (page 262)
- 1 quart orange ice
- 1 cup heavy cream, whipped
- ½ cup finely chopped candied peel and citron
- 1 package lime-flavored pudding mix
- Few drops green vegetable coloring
- Whole red cherries and slivered angelica for garnish

Line a melon-shaped mold with the pistachio ice cream which has been softened just enough to handle. Now make another layer of orange ice, leave cavity in center, and place in freezer while whipping the cream. When cream is thickened, but not stiff, add the chopped candied fruit. Whip again for a minute and fill the remaining space in the mold.

Cover with waxed paper which you have oiled lightly, putting the oiled side against the cream. Press the lid down and freeze, at least 4 hours before serving. Unmold and decorate by making the pudding mix as directed on the package, cooking it a little longer to make it very thick. Place in a pastry tube and make lines down the ridges of the melon mold to resemble the darkened areas of a large melon. Cut leaves or diamond shapes out of strips of angelica to form leaves around the red cherry garnish surrounding the mold. This is very fancy, very easy and very, very good to eat. (You can use softened vanilla ice cream in place of whipped cream for filling the final cavity of the mold if you like.)

RICH REFRIGERATOR TRAY ICE CREAM

Makes 1 quart

- 1 envelope unflavored gelatin
- ½ cup cold water
- 1½ cups undiluted evaporated milk, scalded
- 1 cup sugar
- 2 teaspoons vanilla
- 1½ cups heavy cream, whipped

Soften the gelatin in cold water, add to the hot milk and stir until melted. Add sugar and vanilla and stir until sugar is dissolved. Cool and turn into refrigerator trays. Chill until slightly thickened. Turn into chilled mixing bowl and beat until crystals are broken up, then gently fold in the whipped cream. Return to freezing trays and freeze 1 hour, or until crystals begin to form giving it a mushy consistency. Turn into the chilled bowl once more and beat until smooth, but do not allow it to melt. Return to freezing trays and freeze until firm.

Variations

CHOCOLATE ICE CREAM:—Add 2 squares bittersweet chocolate to the hot milk. Stir until the choc-

olate is melted before adding the other ingredients.
LEMON OR ORANGE ICE CREAM:—Reduce evaporated milk to 1¼ cups and add ¼ cup frozen undiluted orange or lemon juice concentrate. Omit vanilla.

PISTACHIO ICE CREAM:—Chop 2/3 cup pistachio nuts and fold into the whipped cream along with 2 or 3 drops of green vegetable coloring. Replace ½ vanilla with 1 teaspoon almond extract.

FROZEN SIERRA

The Sierra Mountains, as you probably know, are those whose snowy peaks are seen in California. This dessert is named after them.

Serves 4

- 2 cantaloupes, halved and seeded
- Mixed fruit and berries to fill cavities, about 2 cups
- ¼ cup sugar
- ¼ cup lemon juice
- Angostura Bitters
- Meringue to cover:
- 2 egg whites, beaten
- ¼ teaspoon cream of tartar
- 6 tablespoons sugar

To make the Melon Sierra fill the cantaloupe halves with a variety of any fruits and berries you like so long as there is contrasting color. Sprinkle 1 tablespoon sugar, 1 tablespoon lemon juice and a dash of Angostura Bitters on each filled half.

Now turn on the oven because you want it very hot (500°). Put the filled cantaloupes on a cooky sheet or in a roasting pan, cover them with sweetened meringue and slide them into the oven for 2 or 3 minutes until the meringue peaks are lightly brown. Serve at once.

To make the meringue beat the egg whites (to which you have added the cream of tartar) until they are fluffy and hold moist peaks. Gradually beat in 6 tablespoons of sugar, adding a spoonful at a time. Beat until the Meringue is stiff and glossy.

NESSELRODE PARTY MOLD

Fills 3-quart mold

- 2 envelopes of unflavored gelatin
- ½ cup cold water
- 1 cup cream or undiluted evaporated milk
- 3 to 4 cups heavy cream, whipped
- 1 cup sugar
- 8 egg yolks, beaten
- 1 cup milk
- 1 cup chopped candied mixed fruit
- ½ cup light or dark rum

Soften gelatin in cold water. Put yolks in top of the double boiler, add sugar and beat until well blended. Combine the milk and cream or undiluted evaporated milk in a saucepan and heat until scalded, but do not boil. When thoroughly hot begin adding slowly to the egg mixture, stirring constantly. When all has been added place over simmering but not boiling water and continue cooking until thickened, stirring constantly. Remove from heat, add softened gelatin and stir until dissolved. Allow the custard to cool, stirring at intervals to prevent a scum forming on top. When the custard is cool whip the cream until it holds soft peaks. Add rum to the chopped fruit, add the fruit mixture to the custard, stir thoroughly and fold in the whipped cream. Turn into a 3 quart mold and chill until firm, at least 3 hours before unmolding.

GRAND MARNIER CREAM

Fills 2-quart mold

- 1 can frozen orange concentrate, thawed
- 1 teaspoon lemon juice
- 1 (6 oz.) can coconut, very finely chopped
- 1 cup cold water
- ¾ cup sugar
- ½ cup cold water
- 1 envelope unflavored gelatin
- 1 teaspoon salt
- 2 cups heavy cream,
- ½ cup Grand Marnier Liqueur

Combine orange juice, lemon juice, 1 cup cold water and the sugar in a large mixing bowl. Beat with rotary beater 1 minute. Soften gelatin in ½ cup cold water, set in hot water and stir until dissolved. Add to orange mixture. Beat cream until it holds soft, but not stiff, peaks. Add salt and liqueur and fold cream and orange mixture together until blended. Cover bowl tightly and chill in freezer 30 minutes. Remove and beat with rotary or electric beater until smooth but not mushy. Pour into melon-shaped mold or any 2-quart container with a cover and freeze for at least 3 hours before serving. Let mold stand at room temperature for 15 minutes before serving.

RASPBERRY ICE À LA CIGOGNE

At La Cigogne restaurant in Paris, this raspberry ice was served in the long-stemmed glasses usually used for serving white wine. The stems were crystal clear, the bowls were pale green, the ice was violet colored. The effect was stunning.

Makes 1 quart

- 2 teaspoons unflavored gelatin
- 2 tablespoons cold water
- 4 cups ripe red raspberries
- ½ cup orange juice
- ½ cup sugar
- 1 teaspoon grated lemon peel
- 2 teaspoons lemon juice
- ½ cup Mirabelle liqueur or port wine
- Few drops violet vegetable coloring (optional)

Soften the gelatin in the cold water, crush berries and put them through a fine sieve or purée in electric blender. Pour orange juice through sieve to clear last bit of berry pulp or add to blender before turning on machine. Combine raspberry mixture, sugar, lemon peel and juice in saucepan and cook over medium heat, stirring constantly until sugar is dissolved. Remove from heat, add gelatin and stir until it dissolves. Add wine and coloring and mix thoroughly. Place in chilled mold or in refrigerator trays, well covered with aluminum foil, and chill in freezer compartment 30 minutes. Remove and beat with rotary beater until mushy but not melted. Cover in container or trays, and freeze until mushy before serving.

For *Blackberry Ice*, use blackberries instead of raspberries. Omit coloring.

FROZEN LEMON PIE

Fills 8-inch pie shell

- 3 egg yolks, well beaten
- ¼ cup lemon juice
- 2 teaspoons lemon peel, grated
- ⅛ teaspoon salt
- ½ cup sugar
- 3 egg whites, stiffly beaten
- 1 cup heavy cream, whipped
- 1 tablespoon sugar
- ¾ cup vanilla wafers, crushed

Combine first 5 ingredients and cook in double boiler until thick enough to coat a spoon. Cool this mixture, and fold in stiffly beaten egg whites; then fold in stiffly beaten whipped cream. Sprinkle crushed vanilla wafers in a freezing tray or pie pan; pour mixture over the crumbs, and add a few crumbs on the top. Place in freezing compartment and freeze. Serve frozen. This pie should not be allowed to become soft before serving.

FROZEN STRAWBERRY PIE:—Is also a good one to freeze.

At the smörgåsbord in Stow, Ohio, they sometimes make Strawberry Pie by substituting orange juice and grated orange peel for the lemon juice and peel. Fold in at the last ¾ cup well-drained frozen strawberries along with the whipped cream. Add 2 drops of red food coloring for a deeper pink.

BAKED ALASKA

There should be nothing forbidding about Baked Alaska despite its being one of the most expensive desserts you can order in a restaurant. Make it for any number you like with whatever flavor of ice cream you like.

Begin with a foundation of one layer of white or chocolate cake. Cover with a layer or mound of ice cream which has been softened enough to handle. Place in freezer long enough to chill while you prepare the Meringue (*page 203*). Coat the ice-cream layer with the meringue and slide under a very hot broiler to brown, or, sprinkle with granulated sugar, drench with heated rum and ignite it. This does the browning at the table and is very attractive.

ICE CREAM CAKES

Again the beautiful combination of layers of thin cake alternating with various flavors and colors of ice cream is one which is most fun when you make it up yourself.

Slice an angel food cake cross-wise or 2, 3 or 4 times depending upon how many ice creams you are going to use between the layers. Or, split baked layers of white or chocolate cake in half. Now frost each layer with a different flavor of ice cream. Here are some combinations if you need them for a starter. Frost sliced layers of round 9 or 10-inch angel food cake with:

1 pint chocolate ice cream   1 pint coffee ice cream
1 pint orange ice

DRAMATIC DESSERTS

Frost the outside with Whipped Cream Frosting (*page 232*). Garnish with chopped pistachio nuts, slivered almonds, grated bitter chocolate or leave it alone. It is quite good enough as it is. After covering the entire cake with the whipped cream frosting and whatever garnish you have decided to use, place in freezer and leave for at least 2 hours before slicing. Serve 10 or 12 persons.

Cheeses from All Over the World Offer Delectable Dessert

ITALY

Parmesan—from Parma. It is a creamy cheese with a slight sting or bite. It is the cheese preferred for many Italian dishes and is perfection for grating on top of all *au gratin dishes*.

Gorgonzola—is not too easily transported but is one of the famous cheeses of the world. Serve it as Roquefort in a wedge, on its side to avoid overexposure and therefore loss of aroma which is part of the attraction of this strong cheese.

Bel Paese—this is one of Italy's most famous cheeses and means "beautiful country." It is a soft, mild, rather sweet table cheese.

HOLLAND

Gouda—with its red crust is one of the most decorative cheeses to be served as an appetizer or on a cheese board for dessert. Cut wedges from it as if cutting a cake. Occasionally forget its beauty and dignity and scoop out the center to be mixed as suggested in Appetizers (*page 12*).

Edam—with its pleasingly mild, rather salty flavor is seen in large sphere-shaped, red-coated balls or spheres which have been pressed and somewhat flattened. The Edam is larger than the Gouda.

Baby Gouda—is oval and red coated and most apt to be found in spheres about the size of a small grapefruit. Slice wedges for serving, as for all the red sphere-shaped cheeses.

SWITZERLAND

Gruyère—a mild, nutty flavor and texture characterizes Gruyère which is one of the ancient cheeses beloved by everyone. Adaptable for every type of cooking, at the table it should be cut from a sizable piece.

Switzerland Swiss—is know in this country as "the cheese with the holes in it." In Switzerland where it is made in the Emmental Valley it bears the name of Emmental cheese and it may easily be the most famous cheese in the world, both because of the tremendous size of Switzerland Swiss wheels, which weigh around 200 pounds, and also because of the rich nutty flavor and velvet texture which is not duplicated by any Swiss-type cheese made in other countries.

FRANCE

Camembert—the dainty wheels of Camembert are no more than 4 inches across and 1 to 1½ inches thick. The inside is creamy and slightly runny. The crust should not be cut away when the cheese is served on a lace paper doily surrounded with fancy pats of butter. Cut wedges from Camembert, as if cutting a cake, when serving it.

Roquefort—made of ewes' milk, is not too easily transported without loss of flavor and coloring. The best way to serve Roquefort is to cut a wedge of the blue veined, moldy-appearing cheese. Serve it on its side for the least air exposure and cut thin slices from the wedge to serve on crisp crackers with butter.

Monsieur Fromage—resembles Camembert, a semi-liquid delicate cheese served as Camembert.

Brie—is similar to Camembert but varies considerably in size and even in flavor. Serve in wedges.

DENMARK

Because of its rich milk and world famous fine butter, the Danes decided after the war to add cheese making to their international industry. As a result they have a variety of cheeses which have been patterned after the famous cheeses of Europe, much as American cheese makers have done.

Danbo—is a mellow flavored, rich rectangular cheese easily sliced.

Molbo—is the Danish ball-shaped Edam in appearance and flavor.

Maribo—is the Danish Gouda.

Mycella—is the Danish Blue cheese and *Esrom* their Port Salut.

Samsoe—is a 30-pound wheel of Danish Swiss-type cheese and their Dana-Blue has a green mold and a sharp buttery flavor which is appealing to anyone who likes Stilton or Roquefort.

UNITED STATES

In the United States the famous cheeses of the world have been duplicated. Most of them are worthy of the names they bear. Two cheeses are typically American-originated and are extremely popular throughout the country. One is *Cream Cheese* which is an uncured rich cheese used for spreading on sandwiches or canapés. The other is *Cottage Cheese* and *Pot Cheese*, also uncured and unaged, made from milk and produced in delicious curds.

ENGLAND

Cheddar—was first made in England in the sixteenth century and was the first type of cheese made in America. Its popularity is so great that 75 per cent of all he cheese made in this country is Cheddar or Cheddar-type. The wheels of Cheddar are usually about 14-inches across and 12-inches thick and they weigh around 75 pounds. For a dessert cheese board or for a Rabbit, aged Cheddar, at least 2 years old, is preferred.

Stilton—is one of the most famous cheeses in the world and considered by many the finest cheese of England. It is a mild flavored, blue-veined cheese which puts it in the group of French Roquefort and Italian Gorgonzola. Its flavor is rich and mellow and it has a piquant flavor which is memorable and milder than either the French or Italian blue-veined cheeses.

CANADA

Oka—is a Port Salut-type cheese, lots of odor, lots of fine flavor, not to be missed.

GERMANY

Münster—is known in this country as Muenster. It is a semi-soft cheese brick with a mild flavor and small openings throughout the cheese. In Europe it is always served with caraway seeds and often a cheese similar to Münster is made with caraway seeds in the loaf of cheese.

13

Planning Fabulous Meals

Serving Buffet

Plan buffet meals to be easy on yourself; easy and inviting for your guests to help themselves:

Keep the menu simple.

Serve it dramatically.

Improve on your recipes, your serving arrangements or choice of dishes in order to make conversation pieces. How do you achieve this? . . . in the following ways:

Serve the *first course* on the canapé tray along with the welcoming beverage. Cups of hot coffee or soup are welcome in bitter cold weather. More often vegetable crisps, dips and canapés available with a cold drink are a pleasantly filling beginning.

The *main course* should be something made in advance and kept hot on a burner, or in your automatic deep-fat fryer which is a dream of a hot-food server. Or select a main course to make in a chafing dish while everyone looks at the miracle.

The *salad* should be one that won't fall down! Tossed salads are marvelous but not on your best dress or on the carpet. A soufflé salad or a superb molded salad which will stay where it is put is the salad to accompany a buffet meal.

272 PLANNING FABULOUS MEALS

Dessert should be easy to serve and eat but look as impressive as all get out, and be just as delicious.

All the recipes in this book have been offered with these points in mind, knowing that most of you will cook, serve and usually do the clearing of the tables without benefit of the starchy maid of yesteryear. With an easy but elegant menu, you are going to like it . . . especially if you have adequate burners to keep your food warm, generous-size bowls and spoons for serving, and a steady cart to use for serving the first course of appetizers and beverages, to roll used dishes out of sight, to wheel in the dessert.

INTERESTING INTERNATIONAL DINNERS

Potted Duckling Spread
(page 11)
Melba Toast
Coq au Vin **(page 145)**
Peas De Luxe **(page 94)**
Country Fried Potatoes
(page 80)
Green Beans with Almond
Butter Sauce **(page 99)**
Peaches in Champagne
(page 250)
Demitasse

Vegetable Madrilene
Filet Mignon **(page 106)**
Artichoke Bases **(page 84)**
Crisp Corn Fritters
(page 87)
Stuffed Mushrooms
(page 90)
Grand Marnier Cream
(page 263)
Demitasse

Minted Fruit Cup
Beef Tenderloin in Aspic
(page 105)
Toasted Soft Rolls
Butter
Chocolate Mousse
(page 240)
Demitasse

Dry Sherry
Crisp Fried Fish Sticks
Paella Riscal **(page 34)**
Lettuce and Parsley Salad
with Tart Dressing
Bananas Flambé
(page 247)
Demitasse

Dry Sherry
Bengal Curry Lamb
(page 117)
Condiments—Rice
(page 148)
Buttered Spinach
Cranberry Mousse Salad
(page 186)
Orange Ice Cream
(page 262)
Demitasse

Pumpkin Soup (page 31)
Surrey Fowl with Cream
Sauce
(page 151)
Whipped Potatoes with
Pimiento (page 80)
Brussels Sprouts with
Chestnuts
(page 84)
Onions with Chopped
Peanuts
(page 92)
Noreen's English Trifle
(page 243)
Demitasse

Gazpacho (page 30)
Crown Roast of Lamb
(page 116)
with Danish Sour Cream
Gravy (page 296)
Purée of Turnips
(page 97)
Asparagus
Roast Potatoes

Chicken Mexicaine
(page 152)
Chili Stuffed Eggplant
(page 89)
Little Boiled Potatoes in
Parsley Butter
Corn Bread Squares
Avocado Ice Cream
(page 258)
Demitasse

Melon Balls
Roast Chicken in Paper
Bag
(page 142)
Gourmet Stuffing
(page 143)
Cabbage with Peanut
Butter
Sauce (page 103)
Beets Sauterne (page 85)
Chocolate Brazilian
Chiffon Cake
(page 221)
Demitasse

Clear Consommé
Roast Duck with Oriental
Plum Sauce
(page 160)
Broccoli Espagnole
(page 84)
Carrots Vichy (page 87)
Finger Rolls
Butter Balls
Gingered Pineapple in

Chocolate Meringue Roll
Demitasse

Chafing Dish
(page 252)
Demitasse or Tea

Cranberry Cocktail
Lamb Pie with Poppy
Seed Crust
(page 118)
Louisiana Salad Bowl
(page 188)
Rhubarb Mold with Sour
Cream Sauce **(page 255)**
Demitasse

Shrimp Tempura
(page 63)
Pork Sukiyaki **(page 119)**
Pistachio Ice Cream
(page 262)
Tea

MEALS YOUR GUESTS WILL LIKE

Little Suppers

Menus are made to be changed—to suit your taste, the season, your way of life. Even the time of serving can be changed to suit you, for these menus offer interest and abundance: dishes you can serve instead of the usual fried chicken or steak and receive compliments but nary a complaint; dishes that can make their appearance for luncheons, "little suppers" either at dusk or at night after cards and frolicking, or for Sunday dinner if you add a soup or a vegetable.

Spiced Tongue with Curry
Sauce **(page 41)**
Potato Herb Casserole
(page 79)
Spinach with Olive Cream
Sauce **(page 102)**
Picture Salad Bowl
(page 173)
Orange Slice and Black
Grapes

Lobster au Champagne
(page 40)
Mixed Greens Salad with
French Dressing
(page 192)
Melba Toast Rounds
Sweet Butter
Cointreau Parfait Pie
(page 204)
Coffee

Compote (page 254)
Coffee

Ham in Vermouth Sauce
(page 38)
Green Noodles (page 55)
Crusty Whole Wheat
Italian Loaf
Broccoli—Lettuce Salad
with Cottage Cheese
Dressing
Coffee Tortoni (page 260)
Espresso

Sausage Gastronome
(page 40)
Artichokes à la Mireille
(page 83)
Chocolate Rainbow Pie
(page 207)
or
Peach Melba (page 250)
Coffee

Sweetbreads and Ham
(page 42)
Baked Pineapple Rice
(page 51)
Marinated Onions and
Tomatoes
Mocha Refrigerator Cake
(page 227)
Coffee

Chicken or Turkey Mornay
(page 39)
Waldorf Jewel Salad
(page 185)
Crisp Hot Rolls
Cherries Jubilee
(page 247)
Coffee

Veal Stroganoff
(page 114)
Buttered Broccoli—Fluffy
Brown Potato Balls
(page 77)
Thin Slices Pumpernickle
Crêpes au Kirsch
(page 249)
Demitasse

Veal Aspic Loaf
(page 114)
Thin White Bread
Butter Balls
Dream Boat Fruit Platter
(page 185)
Hot Tea or Coffee

Soup and Salad Luncheons

Soup leads to salad, often as not. The pair make a "Little Meal." Try these combinations for beautiful, delicious fare with little fuss but with big effect ... before or after bridge ... T.V. parties ... Sunday snacks ... for "Winter Warmers."

Banana Vichyssoise (page 23)
Chef's Salad (page 187)

Bisque (page 22)
Green Salad in Mincemeat Ring Mold (page 178)

Cherry Soup (page 28)
Salade Niçoise (page 187)

Chicken Soup Oriental (page 24)
Coconut Pineapple Slaw (page 174)

Pink Velvet Soup (page 27)
Chicken Salad in Aspic Ring Mold (page 179)

Hot Apple Soup (page 27)
Tuna Soufflé Salad (page 182)

Chilled Shrimp Soup (page 26)

English Trifle Salad (page 186)

French Onion Soup (page 31)
Shepherd's Hour Salads (page 187)

Quick Gazpacho (page 30)
Fruit Soufflé Salad (page 182)

Pumpkin Soup (page 31)
English Trifle Salad (page 186)

Borsch (page 28)
Frozen Cheese and Date Salad (page 191)

When It's "Dessert and Coffee"
Serve these desserts before bridge or for a shower party:

Exotic Cake (page 218)
Canadian Cup Cakes (page 225)

Lime Meringue Pie in Coconut Shell (page 208)
Coffee Velvet Cream Pie (page 214)

Planning Fabulous Meals

Banana Butterscotch Pie **(page 213)**

Chocolate Mousse **(page 240)**

Frosted Canadian Cantaloupe **(page 254)**

Lemon Cream Pie **(page 212)**

Noreen's English Trifle **(page 243)**

For the Sewing Circle

Make it a luncheon by preceding one of those colorful desserts with one of these:

Coconut Rice **(page 51)**

Vegetable Shortcakes **(page 74)**

Macaroni and Cheese with Peanuts **(page 56)**

Raisin Spaghetti with Ham Balls **(page 57)**

Crabmeat Mousse Salad **(page 186)**

Creamed Seafood in Rice Ring Mold **(page 49)**

Creamed Chicken in Mushroom Ring Mold **(page 177)**

Hot Potato Salad with Hot Toast **(page 189)**

After Theater Suppers

Highballs or coffee or both would be offered as guests arrived, and would continue to be served until they leave. The filling part could be any of the supper dishes for main courses, with Jellied Meat Loaf (*page 129*), a Venison Loaf (*page 168*), or any of the cold loaves for slicing. These add decoration as well as variety to the table.

Soufflés or Ring Molded Salads are pretty on the table and are easy to handle through buffet service. Two or three salads are better than one, more attractive on the table. Same with desserts.

Dessert? One of the dramatic desserts, or one of several of the fruit or berry suggestions. A cake too, if you like. Or choose a dessert suggesting the nationality of the rest of the meal.

Ham in Vermouth Sauce **(page 38)**
with Green Noodles
Apple Jelly Salad Mold **(page 180)** or
Dreamboat Platter **(page 185)**
Chocolate Mousse **(page 240)**

Curried Chicken Breasts **(page 153)**
Orange Rice **(page 47)**
Artichokes à la Mireille **(page 83)**
Celery Olives Radishes
Exotic Cake **(page 218)**
Fresh Peaches au Cognac **(page 251)**

Paella Riscal **(page 34)**
Tiny Hearts of Lettuce
French Dressing **(page 192)**
Peaches Flambé **(page 249)**

Veau à la Suisse **(page 291)**
Rösti **(page 78)**
Cranberry Ring Mold **(page 178)**
Frozen Strawberry Tarts **(page 265)**
Parfait Pies or Tarts **(page 204)**

Ham Rolls Glacé **(page 129)**
Baked Whole Oranges **(page 134)**
Chicken Ring Mold **(page 180)** or
Turkey Mornay **(page 39)**
Coconut Slaw **(page 174)**
Lemon Banana Molds **(page 136)**
Grand Marnier Ice Cream **(page 263)**

Abbie's Curried Chicken **(page 146)**
Condiments
Fluffy Rice **(page 46)**
Tropical Freeze Garnishes **(page 136)**
Fresh Fruit Salad **(page 183)**
Brazilian Chiffon Cake **(page 221)**

Roast Loin of Pork
(page 123)
Sauerkraut Mold **(page 181)**
with Sour Cream Dressing

Sliced Avocado Garnish
Buttered Rolls
Noreen's English Trifle
(page 243)

MEN IN THE KITCHEN

The kitchen is one place where men are just as good as they think they are. When men like to cook, they originate recipes, sauces, short-cuts and often show off with a little fun abacadabra surrounding the serving.

Some men are experienced; some must have lots of help; others are inspired chefs whose every dish is a challenge which has been met with skill. And every one of them likes steak. But here are some fine meals which reveal that great variety is included in their kitchen whimsies and it is not always a 3-inch sirloin. These meals suggest faraway places and fine-flavored imagination. Select a first course and beverage suitable to the weather and the way the meal is served. Add coffee or the beverage you prefer.

Steak and Kidney Pie
(page 108)
Tossed Green Salad
(page 171)
Roquefort Dressing
(page 193)
Raspberry Ice à la Cigogne
(page 264)

Brisket of Beef
with Horseradish Sauce
(page 108)
Broccoli with Sour Cream
Sauce
Baked Potatoes **(page 75)**
Fresh Fruit Bowl
(page 253)

Crown Roast of Lamb
(page 116)
Caramelized Potatoes and
Carrots **(page 79)**
Asparagus **(page 81)** with

Crisp Country Fried
Chicken **(page 154)**
Corn Pudding or Baked
Ears in Husks **(page 88)**
Country Fried Potatoes
(page 80)

Lemon Butter Sauce
  (page 102)
Bananas Flambé (page
  247)

Bowls of Sweetened Raspberries (page 253)

Roast Pork (page 123)
Whole Baked Oranges
  (page 134)
Cabbage with Peanut Butter Sauce (page 103)
Beets Sauterne (page 85)
Frozen Lemon Pie
  (page 265)

Beef Burgundy Casserole
  (page 109)
Sweet Potato, Cecilia
  (page 81)
Zuccini—Red Cabbage
  Slaw (page 175)
Baba au Rhum (page 219)

Large Summertime Buffet

Peanut Loaf (page 53)
Venison Loaf (page 168)
Jellied Meat Loaf (page 129)
Broccoli Espagnole (page 84)
Chili Stuffed Eggplant (page 89)
Soufflé Salads (pages 181-82)
Assorted thin bread slices
Assorted relishes—Kumquats
  (page 135)
Molds of Marjoram Jelly (page 139)
The Queen's Pudding (page 245)
Cheese Board
Crackers—Butter curls
Hot Coffee—Iced Drinks

Tree Trimming or Holiday Suppers

Swedish Pot Roast (page
  110)
Hard Crisp Rolls
Soufflé Salad (pages 181-82)
Sour Cream Apple Pie
  (page 208)
Coffee—Chocolate

Shrimp Bisque (page 26)
Herbed Croutons (page
  19)
Apple Pyramid Cake (page
  244)
Coffee

Swiss Cheese Fondue **(page 35)**
Crusted French Bread Cubes
Meringue Loaf **(page 224)** or Baked Alaska **(page 266)**
Kirsch (optional)
Black Coffee or Tea

Chicken Burgundy **(page 150)**
Herbed Wild Rice **(page 49)**
Broccoli with Hot Sour Cream Sauce **(page 103)**
Petite Layer Cake
French Mocha Ice Cream **(page 259)**

Shrimp and Ham Jambalaya **(page 64)**
Mincemeat Salad Ring **(page 178)** with Whipped Cream Dressing
Beaten Biscuits
Snow Berry Cake **(page 222)**
Cranberry Pie **(page 206)**
Coffee

Bavarian Beef Stew **(page 111)**
Hot Biscuits
Coconut Pineapple Slaw **(page 174)**
Eggnog Parfait Pie **(page 205)**
Coffee

Boneless Duck with Mushrooms **(page 160)**
Brazilian Rice **(page 52)**
Cloverleaf Rolls
Pistachio Bombe **(page 260)**
Coffee or Mulled Wine

New Year's
Shepherd's Hour Salad **(page 187)**
Ham Loaf with Tomato Horseradish Sauce **(page 44)**
Vegetable Soufflé **(page 73)**
Tray of Relishes
Pumpkin Pie with Pecan Crust and Meringue Topping **(page 209)**

14

When It's a Party

The more famous people are the more inclined they are to be at ease about serving simple, but delicious and easily prepared food. They know a party depends upon the people invited, and upon their being happily wined and dined with whatever menu the hour of entertaining recommends. Abundance, certainly. Each dish very hot or very cold as it should be, and served with attractive, but not necessarily expensive accessories.

Every host learns from experience what is most suitable for his friends, what can be most beautifully served in the equipment he has, and which dishes are most popular. Neither your favorite menus nor your colorful tableware become tiresome to your friends. Instead they offer comfortable familiarity and hospitality which is reliably yours—not changing too frequently in this changing world.

It is a help to know what other people do, in other cities, in other circumstances or in those similar to our own. You are always reading what Mrs. Smart does and how she does it—from *Oeufs en Gelée* to the *Bombe Glacée*. But take a look at how men entertain. Men inevitably show daring and flair in their own cooking or in their planning. When they entertain, they do it because they think it wonderful fun. Here are the Weissberger recipes together with the name of the celebrity whose pleasure in these dishes caused them to be chosen for inclusion.

AFTER THEATER

At the Weissberger's

MENU

Hot Cinnamon Punch
Baked Beans Channing
Macaroni Harrison
Pot Roast Noel
Meat Loaf Hildegarde
De Luxe Cheese Cake Evelyn
Coffee

L. Arnold Weissberger is a counselor-at-law whose clients compose a *Who's Who* of the theater. It is his pleasure to have in his home all of the approximately five hundred famous people who are friends or clients or both. This is handicapped by his life which takes him hopping back and forth between Europe and New York. But the schedule of entertaining his friends is softened by the presence of his mother, whose pleasure it is to repeat those dishes some of their favorite actors and actresses hope to find on the heavily laden Weissberger Supper Table.

Here is a selection of the food which might appear on the table at midnight for the Weissbergers and their hungry theater friends, who make it a practice to dine lightly before the theater and enjoy a *filling* hospitality afterward. These, and the other dishes served, are favorites of various celebrities.

Mr. Weissberger entertains about forty guests at his "After Theater Parties," spaced about six weeks apart during the whole year, either in New York or at his summer home in Westhampton. To insure inviting everyone at least once, he keeps a card file, and it is well known that the names are "graded," indicating the standing and tastes of the celebrity, as carefully as Cartier grades fine gems. Mr. Weissberger's special contribution to arranging these affairs, is his skill in assembling his guests. He privately enjoys using his home as a setting to bring famous clients together in a provocative assortment. It is an opportunity for "setting off sparks and making things happen." Here are the Weissberger recipes:

HOT CINNAMON PUNCH

This is a favorite of Faye Emerson's. The recipe makes one-half gallon, and is to be served in tiny cups.

Squeeze juice of 4 large oranges and 3 large lemons. Boil the orange and lemon peels in 4 cups water for 10 minutes. Strain, add juices and 3 cinnamon sticks. Toss in 6 cloves, bring the mixture to a boil once more, cool and cover, for it should stand over night. Next day add 1 bottle of claret and sugar to taste. Boil about 10 minutes and serve over warmer which will keep it piping hot.

BAKED BEANS CHANNING

This favorite of actress Carol Channing's is easy to make for any number you like. You merely empty cans of pork and beans into the mixing bowl until you have enough for everyone to have about 1 cup each. For each No. 2 can of the pork and beans, add ½ cup catsup, ½ cup molasses, 1 teaspoon salt and 1 cup grated raw potato. Salt to taste, stir thoroughly and turn into a buttered baking dish which has been sprinkled with cracker crumbs. Bake in 300° oven 2 hours. If you like a bit of a nip, add ¼ teaspoon Tabasco sauce to the beans. For a crusty top, sprinkle before baking with brown sugar.

BAKED MACARONI HARRISON

The internationally famous actor Rex Harrison is devoted to Mrs. Weissberger's Baked Macaroni. Prepare by boiling according to macaroni time chart (*page 55*), drain and for each package of macaroni add 1 cup of grated Cheddar cheese and 1 cup of thick sour cream. Add 2 cups milk, stir lightly, add salt if necessary, and pour into a well buttered, shallow baking dish. Spread top with coarse bread crumbs well coated with melted butter, and pour any remaining butter over the top. Bake in preheated (350°) oven until the top is an even golden brown, about 45 minutes.

POT ROAST NOEL

Maybe it's because he's English, but playwright Noel Coward adores this beef dish. The roast is seasoned, the night before it is cooked, with garlic, salt and paprika and a generous sprinkling of freshly ground pepper. Next day, chicken fat is melted in an iron pot and the meat is turned in the fat over a hot flame until crusty brown. For a 6-pound chuck or other roast, add 3 cups beef broth and 2 cups chopped or slivered onions. Cover and simmer over low heat until tender, about 3 hours, or bake in 300° oven 3 hours. Add 1 cup sherry wine and 4 tablespoons catsup after first 2 hours of cooking.

MEAT LOAF HILDEGARDE

Songbird Hildegarde is content if she finds this meat loaf. It is made with half ground veal and half ground beef. For each pound of meat add 1 egg, 1 teaspoon salt and ½ teaspoon each of paprika and black pepper. Fry a slice of bread in butter, after soaking it in milk and pressing the milk out of it. Crumble this into the meat, add ½ cup tomato soup. Mix well, form into a loaf and roll it in coarse bread crumbs. Place in a greased pan, drench the loaf with melted butter, brown in a preheated fairly hot oven (400°) for 5 minutes, reduce heat to 325° and continue baking 25 minutes.

DE LUXE CHEESE CAKE EVELYN

Makes 8 to 10 servings

- ¾ cup finely crushed graham cracker crumbs
- 1 tablespoon sugar
- 2 tablespoons butter, melted
- 1 package vanilla pudding
- ½ cup sugar
- 1 cup light cream
- 1 pound (2 cups) cottage cheese, at room temperature
- ½ pound cream cheese, at room temperature
- 4 egg yolks
- ¼ teaspoon salt
- ¼ teaspoon nutmeg
- 1 teaspoon dark rum, rum extract or vanilla
- 4 egg whites, beaten to soft peaks

Combine crumbs, 1 tablespoon sugar and butter, mixing well. Press mixture on bottom of 9-inch spring form pan or 3-quart casserole. Combine pudding mix, ½ cup sugar and light cream in a saucepan. Cook and stir over medium heat until mixture comes to a *full* boil. Remove from heat. Combine cottage cheese and cream cheese and mix well. Add egg yolks one at a time, mixing well after each addition. Add salt, nutmeg, vanilla and cooked pudding; blend well. Fold in beaten egg whites. Pour over crumb mixture in pan. Bake in slow oven (300°) 1 hour. Cool to room temperature, then chill thoroughly.

Variation

LEMON CHEESE CAKE:—Use lemon pudding mix instead of vanilla. Increase sugar to 2/3 cup, omit rum and use 1 teaspoon lemon extract flavoring.

HEARTY DINNER

Ted Barclay's Cornish Rock Hen Dinner

MENU

Extra Dry Gibsons
(served on the rocks)
Fresh Vegetable Hors D'Oeuvres (*page 8*)
Cornish Rock Hens
Wild Rice
Green Salad
Tossed in French Dressing
Cherries Jubilee (*page 247*)
Coffee
Brandy

The gentleman who frequently prepares this meal is a business man with two hobbies: antiques and cooking. He gets the Cornish hens from dramatist-pianist-comedian Victor Borge, who thinks anyone of good mind and health would want a whole hen at a meal. However, this menu recommends 2 hens for each 3 persons and no complaints yet.

Scotch or Bourbon occasionally replaces the extra dry Gibsons before this dinner, but the dessert is always a flamed one which is the most suitable ending for such a dramatic dinner.

CORNISH HENS

Makes 6 servings

- 4 Cornish Rock hens, dressed
- 8 sheets aluminum foil
- ½ cup olive oil
- Salt
- Pepper
- Paprika
- 8 teaspoons Worcestershire sauce
- 8 tablespoons dry red wine
- 1 teaspoon thyme
- 1 teaspoon poultry seasoning
- 4 tablespoons chopped parsley
- Parsley flowerette garnish

Split a Cornish hen down the back and open wide. Flatten on cutting block with the flat side of a cleaver. Place two sheets of aluminum foil out flat. Pour two tablespoons of olive oil on top sheet of aluminum. Rub the hen around in the olive oil to cover the meat side well and at the same time spread the oil over the foil. Sprinkle with salt, pepper and paprika. Place hen meat side down and put the following in the cavity of each hen.

- 2 teaspoons Worcestershire sauce
- 2 tablespoons red wine
- ¼ teaspoon thyme
- ¼ teaspoon poultry seasoning
- 1 tablespoon chopped parsley

Grind pepper and salt to taste and shake paprika over before folding in foil.

Fold the first sheet tightly around bird, being careful not to break foil. Then fold the second sheet of foil around to make a steam-tight package. Place on a cooky sheet in preheated (300°) oven for 45 minutes. At this point you can vary the time you serve by several hours if you care to by turning the oven down or up. I have held dinner two hours and the hen was just as good. Remove and have broiler hot and ready for the last operation.

Unwrap the package and be very careful to save the juice that has formed around the hen. Pour it into a cup to use for basting. Put one of the sheets of foil on the broiler pan if you are a tidy cook. Place the bird *meat side up* under a hot broiler and watch for desired color (some like a light brown, others dark). Keep basting with the juice and save all the juice from the broiler pan to serve with the wild rice. Garnish with chopped chives and parsley.

Prepare the wild rice as indicated on the package. (Some of the wild rice being offered today requires just about one-half the cooking time of others.) Steam the rice to a dry, fluffy consistency and serve around the Cornish hens on a platter. Garnish with parsley. Serve with juice from the Cornish hen.

MAN ABOUT TOWN SUPPER

George H. Doran's Rabbit

MENU

Welsh Rabbit
Green Salad (*page 170*)
Beer

George H. Doran, one of the great names in book publishing, lives in Toronto. There was a time when his fragrant "Rabbit" was an after-theater sensation in New York City and in London. His adventures in the writing world are told in his *Chronicles of Barabbas,* but the "Rabbit" recipe has been revealed *only* to us, along with the philosophy which made it extraordinary.

"I have always thought there should be a certain degree of courage in the matter of seasoning," he explains, before warning that his "Rabbits" were always made with aged Cheddar no less than 2 years—and preferably 3 years—old. His seasonings required no addition of salt.

WELSH RABBIT

Makes 6 servings

Condiment:

2 tablespoons Worcestershire sauce
3 teaspoons dry mustard
3 tablespoons butter
Freshly ground black pepper

Cheese:

- 1½ pounds chopped sharp Cheddar cheese
- 6 ounces of ale
- 2 eggs, slightly beaten
- Paprika

Combine seasonings in top of double boiler. Stir over boiling water until blended. Cover and let stand while you grate the cheese.

Add cheese by handfuls, one at a time, stirring vigorously each time until cheese is melted; repeat stirring and adding cheese only after each addition has become smooth.

When cheese is melted, add ale. Stir. Add beaten eggs, continue to stir 2 minutes. Serve immediately over buttered toasted triangles of bread.

Some people add a clove of garlic to the seasoning, and remove it when the "rabbit" is served.

Service was to arrange bread triangles, which had been toasted and buttered, on a large serving plate, spoon the "Rabbit" over it and sprinkle with paprika. Tossed green salad and mugs of beer, ale or burgundy is good company for "Rabbit."

SEVEN MEN AND THEIR FAVORITE FEASTS

Dr. Irving's Swiss Menu

MENU

Veau à la Suisse
Rösti (*page 78*)
Buttered Asparagus
Soft Rolls
Butter
Fresh Strawberry Tarts
Coffee

VEAU À LA SUISSE

Makes 6 servings

- 2 pounds loin of veal, slivered
- 1 medium-sized onion, finely chopped
- ⅛ pound (½ a stick) butter, melted
- 3 tablespoons flour
- 1½ teaspoons salt
- ½ teaspoon freshly ground pepper
- ½ to 1 cup dry white wine
- 1 cup chicken broth

With a very sharp knife cut the veal into the smallest possible slivers. It must not be ground but *cut*. Chop the onion and set aside until the butter has been melted in a skillet. When it is very hot add the slivered veal and cook until the meat turns white, only 2 or 3 minutes, stirring constantly. Remove the meat to a warm serving dish, add the onion to the skillet and stir over low heat until it is translucent but not brown. Add the flour and seasonings, stirring constantly. Add the wine and chicken broth, continue to stir and when lightly thickened add the veal to the gravy and cook over low heat stirring frequently for 15 minutes, until the veal is tender but not browned.

The resulting dish should be pale and the sauce around the veal slivers thick. Garnish with finely chopped parsley.

Dr. Irving, who specializes in this dish, uses a Moselle wine and serves the remainder of the bottle with the meal.

Bill Kimball's Seafood Feasts

MENU

Steamed Clams in Butter Sauce
Trout (cooked in foil)
Country Fried Potatoes (*page 80*)

Mixed Vegetable Tossed Salad
Parfait Pie (*page 204*)
Coffee
Armagnac Liqueur

This is a meal which goes from extraordinary to elegant, most of it prepared-in-advance food.

For this feast, scrubbed clams in their shells are placed in a steamer, accompanied by freshly caught trout. The trout have been cleaned (leave heads on, please), brushed with melted butter, sprinkled with salt and pepper and wrapped in aluminum foil. Steam by laying foil-wrapped trout on rack high enough to prevent water touching them. Add clams. Steam 15 minutes, remove clams, pour off juice into bowls, add 2 cups boiling water to pot, recover and continue steaming trout another 10 to 20 minutes, depending upon size.

The pie and salad were made in advance, except for adding salad dressing. Potatoes for frying were cooked in their jackets the night before.

BAKED SPANISH MACKEREL

This meal is varied depending upon the season and opportunity for securing mackerel by replacing a baked Spanish mackerel for the steamed clams and trout of Kimball's meal.

The cleaned mackerel is brushed with olive oil inside and out and then brushed with tomato paste and stuffed with chestnut dressing. If any basting is done during the baking he uses sauterne and the fish is baked, naturally, according to the size of your fish.

Sarge's Quiche Lorraine

MENU
Quiche Lorraine

Tossed Green Salad
Warm Apple Pie
Wine
Coffee

QUICHE LORRAINE

Fills 6 tart shells or 1 (9-inch) pie shell

- 6 tart shells or 1 (9-inch) shell, unbaked
- 2 cups light cream, scalded
- 4 eggs, slightly beaten
- ¼ cup chopped onion
- 2 tablespoons chopped chives
- 2 tablespoons finely chopped parsley
- 1 teaspoon salt
- ½ teaspoon pepper
- ⅛ teaspoon nutmeg
- 6 slices crisp bacon, crushed

Prepare the pie pastry and bake it until only partially done, 10 minutes.

To prepare the filling scald the cream, sauté the onion in butter, stirring in the chives, parsley and seasonings as the onion cooks until a pale golden color. Add the beaten eggs and the onion mixture to the cream which has been heated to the boiling point but not allowed to boil. Stir until thoroughly blended. When the pie shells are removed from the oven scatter the crisp bacon bits over the bottom of the pastry shells and fill with the hot cream mixture. Return to the oven and bake at 325° until the custard is set, about 40 minutes.

A variation of the menu including this famous French Quiche Lorraine was to sometimes serve Niçoise Salad *(page 187)* made with tomato wedges, black olives, capers, a few chopped anchovies, snap beans and diced cooked potatoes all tossed together with any salad dressing you like so long as it is flavored with mustard. When this salad was served Berries in Liqueur or Meringue Loaf *(page 224)* were the dessert. Because Sarge lived in Paris he never thought of a cocktail. Apéritif and thirst quenchers through the meal were always *vin ordinaire*, inexpensive vermouth or table wine.

Ben Lucien Burman's Shrimp Tolliver

MENU

Shrimp Tolliver
Saffron Rice (*page 50*)
Avocado and Tomato Wedges Salad
Hot Garlic Bread
Cold Ale
Pistachio Bombe (*page 260*)

Ben Lucien Burman and his artist wife Alice Caddy were being wined and dined when his story about *Mundy Tolliver* was published. For the occasion Ben shared a shrimp recipe which everyone at the party wanted for his own, and this is it.

SHRIMP TOLLIVER

Makes 4 servings

- 1 cup marinade
- 2 pounds little shrimps, shelled
- 2 tablespoons butter
- 1 clove garlic
- 1 cup blanched almonds, slivered
- Generous dash of Tabasco sauce
- ½ cup dry vermouth

Prepare 1 cup French Dressing (*page 192*) with lemon juice instead of vinegar and add the shelled or canned, drained shrimps to marinate for 2 hours or over night. Melt the butter in a large skillet. Add the garlic and the shrimp, dipping them out of the marinade and saving it to use later in this recipe. Cook over medium heat until the shrimp are dusky pink. Remove the garlic and remove the shrimps to a hot platter. Add the slivered almonds to the hot butter and pour the marinade into the skillet along with the seasonings and vermouth. If you like you can brown the almonds in the butter a few minutes before adding the marinade and seasonings to allow them to brown. When blended and very hot, pour this sauce over the shrimp and serve with Saffron Rice (*page 50*) which has had a sprinkling of chopped chives or finely chopped green onion tops stirred into the rice after it was cooked.

This platter is so good that the only thing any man would want with it is the right company—which is hot garlic bread, and a green salad or a salad with tomato wedges and avocado tossed with the greens.

Lazy Gentleman's Chicken Dinner

One gentleman I know, who shall be nameless, is a masterly cook but he is just as clever at saving himself trouble in both serving and cleaning up after cooking. This is a recipe for his

CHICKEN BAKED IN FOIL

Makes 6 servings

Chicken—6 breasts
          6 drumsticks or thighs
          1 pound of chicken livers
1 cup flour
½ teaspoon thyme
2 teaspoons salt
½ teaspoon pepper
1 teaspoon MSG *
1 teaspoon paprika
½ cup bacon drippings and butter or margarine
½ cup melted butter or margarine
6 pieces foil, 16 to 18 inches in length

Rinse and dry chicken pieces. Combine flour and seasonings in paper bag, shake to blend. Add few pieces of chicken at a time, shake to coat, continue

* See footnote, page 92.

until all are coated. Melt fat in large heavy skillet and add floured chicken to brown. Cook, turning to brown evenly, about 30 minutes.

On each piece of foil place breast and drumstick or thigh and 2 or 3 livers, sprinkle with 1 tablespoon melted butter, bring edges of foil together and fold over to seal. Arrange in shallow pan. Bake in 400° oven 1 hour. Serve in foil packages or not, but they are fun.

This is a gravy the clever gentleman made to make vegetables he served extraordinary.

DANISH SOUR CREAM GRAVY

Makes 1 cup

- 2 tablespoons butter or drippings
- ½ cup vegetable stock
- ½ cup sour cream
- ¼ teaspoon freshly ground pepper
- 2 tablespoons flour
- ¼ teaspoon salt
- ¼ teaspoon freshly ground nutmeg

Add flour mixed with seasonings to melted butter or drippings. Stir well and gradually add hot vegetable stock. Allow this to thicken before adding the cream.

This is also extra good with chicken, but he served it over fried tomatoes, kale, spinach or green beans.

Monsignor Bela Varga's Hungarian Feast

MENU

Cocktails
Cheese Board
Small Hot Sausages
Székelygulya's
Boiled Potatoes in Butter Sauce
Thim Dark Bread Slices
Pastry
Coffee

When It's a Party

Monsignor Bela Varga, the last freely elected President of Hungary, has found refuge in the United States since 1945. On one occasion recently he invited the press to gorge themselves on Hungarian *Székely-gulya's*. Whether or not you can pronounce it, you will welcome his recipe when you have a crowd—or try it out by making a third of the recipe first, if you like.

SZEKELYGULYA'S

(say-kay-goo-yosh)

Makes 40 servings

- 15 pounds shoulder of pork, lean and cut in small dices
- 10 medium-sized onions, sliced
- 1 cup sweet paprika
- 3 large green peppers, sliced
- 3 large ripe tomatoes
- 15 pounds sauerkraut
- 2 pounds lard
- 2 tablespoons salt
- 2 cups water
- 5 large containers sour cream

Start working with very large kettle. Heat lard in large deep kettle. Add sliced onions to hot lard and fry until light golden brown. Stir with wooden spoon constantly over low heat. Add paprika, green peppers and tomatoes. Mix well and let simmer 10 minutes. Salt meat and add to mixture, stir to mix thoroughly. Add water, cover and continue to cook. While ingredients are cooking use wooden spoon, as you toss a salad, to keep ingredients well mixed. After 1 hour add sauerkraut. Mix well, continue to cook over low heat until meat is tender, about 2 more hours. When ready to serve add sour cream. Stir and serve.

Charlie Marshall's Last Meal

"When I am in the death cell," said Charlie Marshall who is a publisher, not a gangster, "I don't want steak before they take me to the chair. I want Shad Roe Amandine and Pumpkin Pie." So here it is.

MENU

Whiskey Sours
Shad Roe Amandine
Lettuce Salad with Tart French Dressing (*page 192*)
Pumpkin Pie (*page 209*)
or
Camembert Cheese—Hot Saltines
Iced or hot coffee

SHAD ROE AMANDINE

Makes 2 servings

- 1 pair shad roe (about 1 pound)
- Bouillon to cover
- 2 tablespoons lemon juice or vinegar
- 4 strips bacon, cooked and drained
- 4 tablespoons butter
- ½ cup slivered, toasted almonds

Shad roe is a great delicacy, and is treasured by many people who do not enjoy the superb but bony shad from which it comes. I must disillusion you and say, that a very good quality canned shad roe is easily presented as fresh roe, so you can have this dish the year round.

Rinse roe, drop into boiling bouillon and add lemon juice or vinegar. Cook 5 minutes over medium heat. Pour off bouillon and save to eat later, for it is even better after latching on to the flavor of the roe. Rinse roe in cold water, remove center vein.

Cook bacon over slow heat while shad roe is parboiling. Remove to drain on paper towel, and drain off all fat except 2 tablespoons which you leave in the pan. Add butter, and sauté the roe over low heat, turning to brown on all sides, until cooked through, about 15 minutes. Remove to hot platter. Add slivered almonds to skillet and stir over high heat to heat through. Pour almonds and butter sauce over the roe and serve with lemon wedges and strips of bacon.

SLIVERED ALMONDS

Blanch almonds by dropping them into boiling water. Cover and remove from heat. Set timer and drain them exactly 5 minutes later. Slip their coats off with thumb and finger. Put on chopping board and chop, or carefully sliver lengthwise, or leave whole. Put on cooky sheet with 2 tablespoons butter for each cup of almonds, and toast in a 350° oven, stirring every few minutes to insure even browning, about 30 minutes. When toast brown, drain on paper towel, sprinkle with salt, use or store extra supply in covered jars in refrigerator for use on vegetables, such as green beans, when you are not having roe.
BLANCHED WALNUTS:—Are prepared the same way. Leave them covered 10 minutes with boiling water before slipping off their skins.

Or make another favorite of Charlie's, whose wife is also a good cook and may spoil him with:

LIQUEUR WHIPPED CREAM AMANDINE

Makes 4 servings

- 1 cup heavy cream, whipped
- ⅓ cup sugar
- ¼ teaspoon salt
- 3 tablespoons Grand Marnier or any liqueur
- ¼ cup toasted slivered almonds

Whip cream until it holds soft peaks. Add all other

ingredients, fold together, pour into serving dishes, cover with aluminum foil and let stand 20 minutes at room temperature before chilling.

> Remember now, use your timer to cook exactly the correct number of minutes. Ten minutes before putting the dish into the oven, turn your oven on to the exact required temperature for anything you intend to bake.
>
> Use level measurements, measuring (not tea) cups, and measuring spoons to get perfect results. With these habits on your part and the recipes in this book, you have my blessing.
>
> *Carolyn Coggins*

TO MEASURE RECIPE INGREDIENTS ACCURATELY:

Use measuring cups and spoons.
Level tops with spatula or knife.

THESE ARE THE MEASUREMENTS (Always Level):

1 cup	16 tabsp.	4 quarts	1 gallon (16 cups)
4 tabsp.	¼ meas. cup	1 tabsp.	3 teaspoons
2 cups	1 pint	2 tabsp.	1 oz. butter, sugar
1 quart	2 pints		½ ounce flour
		1 teasp.	60 drops

THE QUANTITY YOU BUY MEANS THIS:

Butter

1 pound	16 ounces	2 cups	4 sticks
½ pound	8 ounces	1 cup	2 sticks
¼ pound	4 ounces	½ cup	1 stick

Sugar or Flour

1 pound granulated sugar	2 cups
1 pound powdered sugar	2 ⅔ cups
1 pound brown sugar	2 ⅔ cups
1 pound flour	4 cups

TIMES AND TEMPERATURE FOR ROASTING MEAT
(Home and Garden Bulletin No. 1. Dept. of Agriculture)

Oven temperature: 325 degrees F.

Meat	Weight in Pounds	Cooking Time Minutes per Pound	Temperature of Meat When Done
Beef:			
Standing ribs	6 to 8		
rare		16 to 18	140
medium		20 to 22	160
well done		27 to 30	170-180
Boned and Rolled		add 15 min. per lb.	
Veal:			
Loin	6 to 8	30 to 35	170-180
Lamb:			
Leg	6 to 7	25 to 30	⎫
Shoulder	4 to 6	25 to 30	⎬ 175-180
Loin	4½ to 5	30 to 35	⎭
Boned and Rolled		add 10 min. per lb.	
Pork:			
fresh			
Loin, piece	4 to 5	35 to 40	⎫
Loin, whole	12 to 15	15 to 20	⎬
Shoulder	4 to 6	35 to 40	⎬ 185
Boned and Rolled		add 10 min. per lb.	⎬
Ham, fresh	10 to 14	30 to 35	⎭
Spareribs, 1 side	1½ to 2½	40	
smoked			
(not pre-cooked)			
Ham, whole	15 and over	15 to 20	170
	10 to 12	18 to 20	160 for
Ham, half	6 to 8	25	precooked
Shoulder	5 to 8	28 to 35	ham

TIME TABLE FOR BROILING STEAKS
(Home and Garden Bulletin No. 1. Dept. of Agriculture)

Steak	Total time (minutes)
1 inch thick	
rare	about 10
medium	about 15
well done	20 to 25
2 inches thick	
rare	about 25
medium	about 25
well done	45 to 50

THESE ARE THE TEMPERATURES YOU USE IN COOKING:

Oven

Slow	300-325 degrees F.
Moderate	350-375 degrees F.
Hot	400-450 degrees F.
Very Hot	475-550 degrees F.

Top of Stove

Simmering	180-200 degrees F.
Boiling (sea level)	212 degrees F.

THESE ARE THE PANS YOU USE FOR BAKING:

Cakes, cookies, pies or tarts

9" square, 2" deep cake pan
cookie sheet
muffin tins
9"x5"x3" loaf pan
15"x10"x1" jelly roll pan
13"x9"x2" flat pan
8" spring form pan, 3" deep
9" spring form pan
melon mold with lid
two 9" pie pans
three 9" cake pans
8 cup ring mold
Angel cake tube pan

KITCHEN AIDS FOR THE COOK:

Electric blender—does in 1 minute what you might do by beating for 15 minutes. Secures velvet texture impossible except with blender.

Electric beater and mixer—does hard work for you in mixing batters.

Wire Whisk—achieves greatest volume and dry meringue for French Meringue recipes.

Measuring spoons—available in sets for accurate measurement of ¼ teaspoon up to 1 tablespoon.

Measuring cups—available in ¼ cup—1 cup sets, level to top of container for dry measurements.
Cups for liquids have brim above cup marker. 1 quart measuring cup great convenience and time-saver.

Automatic deep fat fryer—Removes hazard from quick crisper cooking of French fried foods. Have heat control dial checked for accuracy.

Dutch Oven—Heavy pot, usually iron, with cover for slow-baking or top-of-stove simmering of many foods.

TO COOK SUCCESSFULLY:

Use range timer or a portable timer to cook exactly right amount.

Turn oven on 10 minutes before putting food in oven to bake. Then bake in preheated oven as directed.

Use low temperature for roasting all meats or fowl or game—325 or 300 degree oven.

Use slow oven for meringues, except meringue pie topping, which is tenderest browned in hot 450 degree oven.

Index

Alaska, Baked, 266
Almond Butter Sauce, 99
Almonds, Slivered, 299
Aloha Chiffon Pie, 211
Anchovy Dressing, 193
Appetizer Crisps, 6
Appetizers
  Cottage Cheese Dip, 7
  Crisps, 6
  Deviled Crab Dip, 7
  Dips, 6–8
  Dunking Sauce, 6
  Egg-Parsley Dip, 6–7
  Guacamole Dip, 7
  Mill Reef Club Dip, 8
  Spicy Chili Dip, 8
  Tomato-Sour Cream Dip, 7
  See also Hors D'Oeuvres and Canapes
Apple Jelly Salad, 180–81
  Pancakes Stack, 257–58
  Pyramid, 244
  Soup, Hot, 27–28
  Stuffing, 158
Apples, Vermont Baked, 257
Artichoke Bases, 84
Artichokes, 83
  à la Mireille, 83
Asparagus, 81–82
  serving ideas, 82
Aspic Jelly, 105–06
  Jelly, Clear, 179
Avocado Ice Cream, 258–59

Baba Au Rhum, 219–20
Bacon, Canadian, with Sherry, 45
Baked Alaska, 266
Baked Beans Channing, 284
Baked Macaroni Harrison, 283–84
  Pineapple Rice, 51

Baked (*Cont.*):
  Spanish Mackerel, 292
Banana Butterscotch Pie, 213–14
  Compote, 256
  Vichyssoise Soup, 23–24
Bananas Flambé, 247
Barbecued Swordfish, 66
Bass, Baked Striped, 60–61
  Stuffed Baked Striped, 61
Bavarian Beef Stew, 111–12
Béarnaise Sauce, 132–33
Beef
  Brisket of, with Horseradish Sauce, 108
  Burgundy Casserole, 109–110
  Filet Mignon, 106
  Hamburger, Superb, 112
  in Aspic Jelly, 104
  Rib Roast of, 111
  Steak and Kidney Pie, 108–109
  Stew, Bavarian, 111–12
  Swedish Pot Roast, 110–11
  Tenderloin in Aspic, 105–106
  Tournedos, 106–107
Beets, Buttered Boiled, 85
  Sauterne, 85
Bengal Curry Lamb, 117–18
Bisques, *see* Soups
Blackberry Ice à la Cigogne, 265
Blanched Walnuts, 299
Borsch Soup, 28
Bouillon, Court, 65
Brazilian Chocolate Chiffon Cake, 221
  Rice, 52–53
Broccoli Espagnole, 84
Brown Rice, French Fashion, 48
Brussels Sprouts with Chestnuts, 84–85
Buffet Turkey, 156–57

305

INDEX

Butter Cream Frosting, 238–39
Butterfly Shrimp, 63–64

Cabbage with Caraway Seeds, 86
Cake, 217–32
  Baba Au Rhum, 219–20
  Brazilian Chocolate Chiffon, 221
  Canadian Cup Cakes, 225
  Caraway Ring, 226
  Cheese, Evelyn, De Luxe, 286
  Cinnamon Toast, 229
  Exotic, 218–19
  Florentines, 232
  Hazelnut Torte, 223–24
  Ice Cream, 266–67
  Irish Gingerbread, 231
  Lemon, 217–18
  Lemon Cheese, 286
  Meringue Loaf, 224
  Mocha Refrigerator, 227
  Petite Layer, 221–22
  Petits Fours, 229
  Puff Shells with Chocolate Custard, 229–30
  Sesame Twists, 228
  Snow Berry, 222–23
  Teatime, 227–32
Cake Fillings
  Chocolate, 225–26
  Chocolate Custard, 230–31
  Lemon Custard, 244
  Rum Custard, 244
  Whipped Cream, 233
Cake Frostings
  Butter Cream, 238–39
  Caramel Sour Cream, 235–36
  Cinnamon Glaze, 226–27
  Coconut Marshmallow, 237
  Coffee Butter Cream, 239
  Coffee Seafoam, 235
  Cream Cheese, 236
  Four Minute, 237
  Fudge, 238
  Lemon Butter Cream, 239
  Maple Butter Cream, 237
  Marbled Whipped Cream, 234
  Pink Peppermint, 237–38
  Pistachio, 238
  Quick Uncooked Fluffy, 234
  Rum Butter Cream, 239
  Seafoam, 234–35
  Seven Minute, 237
  Sour Cream, 235
  Whipped Cream, 233

Canadian Bacon with Sherry, 45
  Cup Cakes, 225
Canapés
  Clam Puffs, 13–14
  Mushroom Deviled Eggs, 15
  Party Mix, 16–17
  Peanut Butter Dreams, 14
  Savory Melba Toast, 17
  Stuffed Mushroom Caps, 14–15
  Swiss Cheese Caraway Squares, 16
  See also Appetizers and Hors D'Oeuvres
Cantaloupe, Frosted Canadian, 254–55
Caramel Sour Cream Frosting, 235–36
Caramelized Potatoes, 79
Caraway Ring Cake, 226
Carrots, 86
  Vichy, 87
Celery Sauce (for Salmon), 43–44
Cheese
  As dessert, 267–70
  Cake Evelyn, De Luxe, 286
  Cake, Lemon, 286
  Cream, Dressing for Tart Fruit Salads, 195
  Cream, Frosting, 236
  Edam, Bowl, 12–13
  Pie Crust, 199–200
  Rice, 47–48
  Sauce, 99
  Swiss, Caraway Squares, 16
  Swiss, Fondue, 35–37
  Swiss, Sauce, 100–01
  Welsh Rabbit, 289–90
Chef Salad, 187
Cherries Jubilee, 247–48
  Pickled, 138
  Stuffed Bing, 136
Cherry Jubilee Parfait Pie, 205
  Jubilee Sauce Flambé, 248
  Soup, 28–29
Chicken
  Baked, in Cream, 144–45
  Baked in Foil, 295–96
  Bonne Femme, 151
  Burgundy, 150
  Chinese Roast, 143
  Chinese Walnut, 149
  Coq au Vin, 145–46
  Curried Baked, Breasts, 153–54
  Curry, Abbie's, 146–47

Chicken (*Cont.*):
  Fried, Crisp Country, 154–55
  Guinea Hen Fricassee, 155
  Hawaiian, 145
  Livers in Sour Cream, 42
  Mexicaine, 152–53
  or Turkey Mornay, 39
  Ring Mold, 180
  Roast, 142–43
  Salad, 190
  Soup Oriental, 24–25
  Sub-Gum-Gai-Pen, 149
  Surrey Fowl with Cream Sauce, 151–52
  Tarragon, 144–45
Chiffonade Dressing, 193
Chili Rice, 48
  Stuffed Eggplant, 39
Chinese Duck Soup, 29–30
  Roast Chicken, 142–43
  Walnut Chicken, 149
Chives Rice, 48
Chocolate Coconut Pie Crust, 202
  Custard, 230–31
  Filling, 225–26
  Ice Cream, 261–62
  Meringue Roll, 241–42
  Mousse, 240–41
  Rainbow Pie, 207
Cinnamon Glaze, 226–27
  Toast, 229
Clam Puffs, 13–14
Clams, Steamed in Butter Sauce, 291–92
Coconut Marshmallow Frosting, 237
  Nutmeg, 184
  Pie Crust, 202–203
  Pineapple Slaw, 174
  Rice, 51–52
  Soup, 24
  Toasted, 184
Coffee Butter Cream Frosting, 239
  Seafoam Frosting, 235
  Tortoni, 260
  Velvet Cream Pie, 214–15
Cointreau Parfait Pie, 204–205
Cole Slaw, De Luxe, Plate, 188
Colonial Beer Glaze (for Ham), 127
Condiments for Curried Dishes, 148–49
Coq au Vin, 145–46
Corn
  Baked Ears of, in Husks, 88

Corn (*Cont.*):
  Fritters, 87–88
  Pudding, 87
Cornflake Crumb Pie Crust, 201–202
Cornish Hens, 287–88
Cottage Cheese Dip, 7
Court Bouillon, 65
Crab and Avocado Ring, 179–80
  Bisque, Quick, 25
Crabmeat Salad, Hongkong, 189
Crabs, Deviled, in Shells, 61
Cranberry Crabmeat Mousse Salad, 186
  Pie, 206–207
  Ring, 178–79
Cream Cheese Dressing for Tart Fruit Salads, 195
  Cheese Frosting, 236
Cream of Vegetable Soup, 22
Crêpes au Kirsch, 249
Croutons, 19–20
Crumb Pie Shells, 200–201
Crumbs
  Dutch, 101
  Herbed, 101
Cucumber Mold, 179
  Soup, 25–26
  Stuffing (for Fat Fish), 70–71
Cucumbers in Sour Cream, 190
Curried Baked Chicken Breasts, 153–54
  Tongue Sauce, 41–42
Curry
  Abbie's Chicken, 146–47
  Condiments for, 148–49
  Mayonnaise, 195

Danish Sour Cream Gravy, 296
Deep Dish Peach Pie, 211–12
Desserts, 240–70
  Apple Pancakes Stack, 257–58
  Apple Pyramid, 244
  Apples, Vermont Baked, 257
  Banana Compote, 256
  Bananas Flambé, 247
  Cheeses, 267–70
  Cherries, Jubilee, 247–48
  Cherry Jubilee Sauce Flambé, 248
  Chocolate Meringue Roll, 241–42
  Chocolate Mousse, 240–41
Crêpes au Kirsch, 249

INDEX

Desserts (*Cont.*):
  Frosted Canadian Cantalope, 254–55
  Fruit, Fresh, 252–54
  Gingered Pineapple in Chafing Dish, 252
  Noreen's English Trifle, 243–44
  Peach au Cognac, 251–52
  Peaches Flambé, 249–50
  Peaches, Glacé Melba, 250–51
  Peaches in Champagne, 250
  Prunes in Red Wine, 256–57
  Queen's Pudding, The, 244–46
  Rhubarb Mold with Sour Cream Sauce, 255–56
  See also Ice Creams and Frozen Desserts
Deviled Crab Dip, 7
  Crabs in Shells, 61
  Eggs Ring Mold, 179
Dips, *see* Appetizers
Duck Bigarde, 161–62
  Boneless, with Mushrooms, 160–61
  Gravy, 159–60
  Roast, 159
  Roasted, with Oriental Plum Sauce, 160
  Wild, 164
Dunking Sauce, 6
Dunking Sauce (for Shrimp), 62

Edam Cheese Bowl, 12–13
Eggnog Parfait Pie, 205–206
Egg-Parsley Dip, 6–7
Eggplant Provençale, 88
  Chili Stuffed, 89
English Trifle Salad, 186
Exotic Cake, 218–19

Filet Mignon, 106
Fillings for Cake, *see* Cake Fillings
Fish Dips, 10–11
  Pudding with Mushroom Sauce, 69
Florentines, 232
Fondue Neuchâteloise, 35–37
Four Minute Frosting, 237
French Dressing, 192
  Dressing, Garlic, 192–93
  Dressing, Quick, 193
  Fried Onion Rings, 92
  Mocha Ice Cream, 259

French Dressing (*Cont.*):
  Rice, 47
Frikadeller (Viggo Hansen), 121
Frosted Canadian Cantaloupe, 254–55
Frostings for Cake, *see* Cake Frostings
Frozen Cheese and Date Salad, 191
  Lemon Pie, 265–66
  Peanut Butter Salad, 192
  Sierra, 262
  Strawberry Pie, 265–66
Fruit, Fresh, 252–54
  Juice Glaze (for Ham), 127
  Platter Salad (Dream Boat), 185
  Salad Dressing (with French Dressing), 193
  Salad Dressing (with Mayonnaise), 196
Fudge Frosting, 238

Garlic French Dressing, 192–93
  Mayonnaise, 195
Garnishes for Meat, 133–34
  Cherries, Pickled, 138
  Cherries, Stuffed Bing, 136
  Jeweled Rings, 137
  Kumquats, Abbie's, 135
  Lemon Banana Molds, 136
  Marjoram Jelly, 139
  Orange Stuffing Patties, 137–38
  Oranges, Baked Whole, 134–35
  Pineapple Marmalade, Quick, 139
  Sweet Potato Orange Cups, 136
  Tropical Freeze, 136–37
  Watermelon Preserves, 140
  Wine Jelly, 139–40
Gazpacho, 30
  Quick, 30–31
German Potato Cakes, 77
Ginger Pork with Pears, 119
Gingered Pineapple in Chaffing Dish, 252
Glacé Melba Peaches, 250–51
Glazes
  Fruit (for Ham), 127
  Mustard (for Ham), 126–27
  Wine (for Ham), 127
Goose, Wild, Roast, with Cranberry Stuffing, 166–67
Gourmet Stuffing, 143–44
Graham Cracker Pie Crust, 201

INDEX 309

Grand Marnier Cream, 263–64
Green Salad, 170–71
Grouse, Broiled, 164–65
Guacamole Dip, 7
Guinea Hen Fricassee, 155

Ham
  Baked, in Wine, 128
  Baking, 124–25
  Balls, 57–58
  Fruit and Wine Glazes for, 127
  Hawaiian, Pie, 128
  How to cook, 124–25
  How to decorate, 127
  in Vermouth Sauce, 38
  Jellied Meat Loaf, 129
  Loaf with Tomato Horseradish Sauce, 44–45
  Mustard Glazes for, 126–27
  Paprika, 127–28
  Ring Mold, 180
  Rolls Glacé, 129–30
  Spicy Tenderized, 125–26
Hamburger, Superb, 112
Hawaiian Chicken, 145
  Ham Pie, 128
Hazelnut Torte, 223–24
Herb Flavoring for Vegetables, 97–98
Herbed Crumbs, 101
Hollandaise Sauce, 101–102
Hors D'Oeuvres
  Edam Cheese Bowl, 12–13
  Fish Dips, 10–11
  Fresh Vegetable, 8–9
  Marinated Mushrooms, 89–90
  Potted Duckling Spread, 11–12
  Swedish Fish, 9–10
  Unusual ideas for, 17–18
  Welsh Rabbit Spread, 11
  See also Appetizers and Canapés
Hot Cinnamon Punch, 284

Ice Cream Cakes, 266–67
Ice Creams and Frozen Desserts, 258–67
  Avocado, 258–59
  Baked Alaska, 266
  Blackberry Ice à la Cigogne, 264–65
  Chocolate, 261–62
  Coffee Tortoni, 260
  French Mocha, 259

Ice Cream and Frozen Dessert (*Cont.*):
  Frozen Sierra, 262
  Grand Marnier Cream, 263–64
  Ice Cream Cakes, 266–67
  Lemon, 262
  Nesselrode Party Mold, 263
  Orange, 262
  Pistachio, 262
  Pistachio Bombe, 260–61
  Raspberry Ice à la Cigogne, 264–65
  Rich Refrigerator Tray, 261
  Strawberry Pie, Frozen, 265–66
Irish Gingerbread Cake, 231

Japanese Rice à la Luise, 35
Jellied Meat Loaf, 129
Jellies
  Marjoram, 139
  Wine, 139–40
Jeweled Rings, 137

Kumquats, Abbie's, 135

Lamb, 116
  Bengal Curry, 117–18
  Crown Roast of, 116–17
  Pie with Poppy Seed Crust, 118–19
  Roast Leg of, 116–17
Lattice-Top Pie Crust, 198
Lemon Butter Cream Frosting, 239
  Butter Sauce, 102
  Banana Molds, 136
  Cake, 217–18
  Cheese Cake, 286
  Cream Pie, 212–13
  Custard Filling, 244
  Ice Cream, 262
  Pie Crust, Quick, 200
  Pie, Frozen, 265
Lime Meringue Pie in Coconut Shell, 208
Liqueur Whipped Cream Amandine, 299–300
Lobster au Champagne, 40–41
Lobster, Broiled Rock, Floridian, 65
Louisiana Salad Bowl, 188

Macaroni and Cheese with Peanuts, 56–57

INDEX

Macaroni (*Cont.*):
  Baked, Harrison, 285
  Salami, Toss-up, 58
Mackerel, Baked Spanish, 292
Madeira Sauce, 131-32
Maple Butter Cream Frosting, 237
Marbled Whipped Cream Topping, 234
Marinated Bermuda Slices, 93-94
  Mushrooms, 89
  Onions (Red), 93
  Whole Onions, 190-91
Marjoram Jelly, 139
Marmalade, Pineapple, Quick, 139
Mayonnaise, 193-94
  Blender, 194-95
  Curry, 195
  Garlic, 195
Meat Loaf Hildegarde, 285-86
  Loaf, Jellied, 129
Meat Platter Garnishes, 133-34
Melba Sauce, 251
Melon Gingerale Salad, 185
Menus
  After Theater Suppers, 277-79
  Buffet, 271-72
  "Dessert and Coffee," 276-77
  Interesting International Dinners, 272-74
  Little Suppers, 274-75
  Men in the Kitchen, 279-81
  Sewing Circle, 277
  Soup and Salad Luncheons, 275-76
  See also under Parties
Meringue, 203-04, 246-47
  Loaf, 224
  Shells, 203
Mill Reef Club Dip, 8
Mincemeat Salad Ring, 178
  Sauce, 131
Mocha Ice Cream, French, 259
  Refrigerator Cake, 227
Mornay Sauce, 101
Mushroom Caps, Fresh, 90
  Deviled Eggs, 15
  Ring Mold, 177
  Sauce (for Fish Pudding), 69
Mushrooms, Marinated, 89
  Stuffed, 90-91
  with Thick Cream, 90
Mustard Glazes (for Ham), 126
Nesselrode Party Mold, 263

Noreen's English Trifle, 243-44

Olive Cream Sauce, 102-103
Onion Rings, French Fried, 91
Onions, 91
  à la Arabian Nights, 94
  Bermuda Slices, Marinated, 93-94
  (Red) Marinated, 93
  with Chopped Peanuts, 92-93
Onion Soup, 31
Orange-Flavored Ginger Pie Crust, 198-99
  Ice Cream, 262
  Rice, 47
  Sauce, 135
  Stuffing Patties, 137-38
Orange Rice, 47
Oranges, Baked Whole, 134-35
Oriental Plum Sauce, 160

Paella Riscal, 34-35
Paprika Ham, 127-28
Parsley Rice, 48
Parties, 282-300
Partridge, 165
Partridges, Hunter Style, 165-66
Party Mix, 16-17
Pasta, 53-54
  How to cook, 54-55
  Italian, 55-56
  Macaroni and Cheese with Peanuts, 56-57
  Raisin Spaghetti with Ham Balls, 57
  Salami Macaroni Toss-Up, 58
  Salmon Puff, 58-59
  Time Chart for, 55
Peach au Cognac, 251-52
  Pie, Deep Dish, 211-12
Peaches Flambé, 249-50
  Glacé Melba, 250-51
  in Champagne, 250
Peanut Loaf, 53
  Butter Dreams, 14
  Butter Salad Dressing, 195-96
  Butter Sauce, 103
Peas De Luxe, 94-95
Petite Layer Cake, 221-22
Petits Fours, 229
Pheasant, 162-63
  in Pressure Cooker, 164
  Roast, au Vin Blanc, 163
  Roasted, in Paper Bag, 163-64

INDEX 311

Pickled Cherries, 138
Pies, 197–216
  Aloha Chiffon, 211
  Banana Butterscotch, 213–14
  Cherry Jubilee Parfait, 205
  Chocolate Rainbow, 207
  Coffee Velvet Cream, 214–15
  Cointreau Parfait, 204–205
  Cranberry, 206–207
  Crust, Cheese, 199–200
  Crusts, Chocolate Coconut, 202
  Crusts, Coconut, 202–203
  Crusts, Cornflake Crumb, 201–202
  Crusts, Flaky, 197–98
  Crusts, Graham Cracker, 201
  Crusts, Lattice-Top, 198
  Crusts, Orange-Flavored Ginger, 198–99
  Crust, Quick Lemon, 200
  Crusts, Stir and Roll, 199
  Deep Dish Peach, 211–12
  Eggnog Parfait, 205–206
  Freezing, 215–16
  Lemon Cream, 212–13
  Lime Meringue, in Coconut Shell, 208
  Meringue, 203–204
  Meringue Shells, 203–04
  Parfait Liqueur, 204–05
  Pineapple Meringue, 207
  Pineapple Pumpkin, 210
  Pumpkin, 209–210
  Shells, Crumb, 200–201
  Sour Cream Apple, 208–209
Pineapple Marmalade, Quick, 139
  Meringue Pie, 207–208
  Pumpkin Pie, 210
Pink Peppermint Frosting, 237–38
Pink Velvet Soup, 27
Pistachio Bombe, 260–61
  Frosting, 238
  Ice Cream, 262
Pork, 119
  Burgundy Chops, 122
  Frikadeller (Viggo Hansen), 121
  Ginger, with Pears, 119
  Roast Loin of, 123
  Scrapple, 122–23
  Spareribs, Quick Barbecued, 123–24
  Sukiyaki, 119–20
  Sweet and Sour, 120–21
  Székelygulya's, 297

Pork (*Cont.*):
  Potato Balls, Fluffy Browned, 77
  Cakes, German, 77
  Herb Casserole, 79–80
  Sweet, Cecilia, 81
  Salad, Hot, 189
  Sweet, Orange Cups, 136
Potatoes, Baked, 75–76
  Boiled, New, 76
  Boiled New, with Sour Cream, 76–77
  Caramelized, 79
  Fried, Good Country, 80–81
  Lumpless Mashed, 76
  Rösti, 78–79
  Scalloped, 78
  Stuffed, 76
  Whipped, with Pimiento, 80
Pot Roast Noel, 285
  Roast, Swedish, 110–11
Potted Duckling Spread, 11–12
Poultry and Game, 141. *See also* Name of Fowl
  Cornish Hens, 287–88
  Preparation of, 141–42
Preserves, Watermelon, 140
Prunes in Red Wine, 256–57
Puff Shells with Chocolate Custard, 229–31
Pumpkin Pie, 209–10
  Soup, 31–32
Punch, Hot Cinnamon, 284

Quail, 166
Queen's Pudding, The, 245–47
Quiche Lorraine, 293–94
Quick Uncooked Fluffy Frosting, 234

Raisin Sauce, 130–31
Raisin Spaghetti with Ham Balls, 57
Raspberry Ice à la Cigogne, 264–65
Red Cabbage Slaw, 175
Rhubarb Mold with Sour Cream Sauce, 255–56
Rhum Sauce, 220–21
Rice, 46–47
  Baked Pineapple, 51
  Brazilian, 52–53
  Brown, 48
  Cheese, 47
  Chili, 48
  Chives, 48
  Coconut, 51–52
  French, 47

INDEX

Rice *(Cont.)*:
  Orange, 47
  Parsley, 48
  Peanut Loaf, 53
  Ring, 49
  Rosy, 47
  Rosy Cheese, 47–48
  Saffron, 50–51
  White, 47–48
  Wild, Herbed, 49–50
Rich Refrigerator Tray Ice Cream, 261–62
Roast Beef and Sherried Mushrooms, 39
  Canadian Goose with Cranberry Stuffing, 166–67
  Chicken, 142–43
  Duck, 159
  Leg of Lamb, 117
  Leg of Venison with Sour Cream, 167–68
  Loin of Pork, 123–24
  Pheasant au Vin Blanc, 163–64
Roquefort Dressing, 193
Rösti, 78–79
Rosy Cheese Rice, 47–48
  Rice, 47
Rum Butter Cream Frosting, 239
  Custard Filling, 244
Rutabagas, *see* Turnips

Saffron Rice, 50–51
Salad, 169–96
  Apple Jelly, 180–81
  Chef, 187
  Chicken, 190
  Chicken Ring Mold, 180
  Clear Aspic Jelly, 179
  Coconut Pineapple Slaw, 174
  Crab and Avocado Ring, 179–80
  Crabmeat, Hongkong, 189
  Cranberry Crabmeat Mousse, 186
  Cranberry Ring, 178–79
  Cucumber Mold, 179
  Cucumbers in Sour Cream, 190
  De Luxe Cole Slaw Plate, 188
  Deviled Eggs Ring Mold, 179
  Dream Boat Fruit Platter, 185
  English Trifle, 186
  Frozen, 191
  Frozen Cheese and Date, 191
  Frozen Peanut Butter, 191–92
  Fruit, 183–84
  Green, 170–73

Salad *(Cont.)*:
  Ham Ring Mold, 180
  How to serve, 170
  How to unmold, 176–77
  Louisiana, Bowl, 188
  Marinated Whole Onions, 190–91
  Melon Gingerale, 185
  Mincemeat, Ring, 178
  Mixed Vegetable Tossed, 173
  Mushroom Ring Mold, 177
  Niçoise, 187
  Picture Bowl, 173–74
  Potato, Hot, 189
  Red Cabbage Slaw, 175
  Ring Molded, 175–77
  Sauerkraut Mold, 181
  Shepherd's Hour, 187–88
  Shrimp and Avocado, 187
  Soufflé, 181–83
  Soufflé, flavoring of, 182–83
  Vegetable Ring Mold, 180
  Waldorf Jewel, 185–86
  With an International Reputation, 186
Salad Dressings, 192–96
  Anchovy, 193
  Chiffonade, 193
  Cream Cheese, for Tart Fruit Salads, 195
  French, Garlic, 192–93
  French, Garlic, 192
  French, Quick, 193
  Fruit, 196
  Fruit Salad, 193
  Mayonnaise, 193–94
  Mayonnaise, Blender, 194–95
  Mayonnaise, Curry, 195
  Mayonnaise, Garlic, 195
  Peanut Butter, 195–96
  Roquefort, 193
Salami Macaroni Toss-Up, 58
Salmon Loaf, 43
  Puff, 58–59
  Soup, 26
Sauces (for Meat, Fish, and Fowl)
  Béarnaise, 132–33
  Celery (for Salmon), 43–44
  Curried Tongue, 41–42
  Dunking (for Shrimp), 62
  Madeira, 131–32
  Mincemeat, 131
  Mushroom (for Fish Pudding), 69
  Oriental Plum Sauce, 160
  Raisin, 130–31
  Supreme (Chicken), 147–48

Sauces (Cont.):
  Tomato Horseradish (for Ham), 44–45
  Vermouth (for Ham), 38
Sauces (for Vegetables), 99–103
  Almond Butter, 99
  Cheese, 99
  Crumbs, Dutch, 101
  Crumbs, Herbed, 101
  Hollandaise, 101–102
  Lemon Butter, 102
  Mornay, 101
  Olive Cream, 102–103
  Peanut Butter, 103
  Sour Cream, Hot, 103
  Swiss Cheese, 100–01
  White, 99–100
  Wine Butter, 102
Sauerkraut Mold, 181
Sausage Gastronome, 40
Savory Melba Toast, 17
Scalloped Potatoes, 78
Scallops, Broiled Savory, 66
Scrapple, 122–23
Seafoam Frosting, 234–35
Seafood
  Bass, Baked Striped, 60–61
  Bass, Stuffed Baked Striped, 61
  Deviled Crabs in Shells, 61
  Fish Pudding with Mushroom Sauce, 69
  Lobster, Broiled Rock, Floridian, 65
  Scallops, Broiled Savory, 66
  Shad Roe Amandine, 298–99
  Shrimp and Ham Jambalaya, 64–65
  Shrimp, Beer-ded, 62
  Shrimp, Butterfly, 63–64
  Shrimp Scampi, 62–63
  Shrimp Tempura, 63
  Shrimp Tolliver, 294–95
  Spiced Noodles à la Neptune, 67–68
  Stuffing, Cucumber, 70–71
  Stuffing for Large Baked Fish, 70
  Swordfish, Barbecued, 66
  Tuna Soufflé, 67
  Tureen, 68–69
Sesame Twists, 223
Seven Minute Frosting, 237
Shad Roe Amandine, 298–99
Shepherd's Hour Salad, 187–88
Shortcakes, Vegetable, 74
Shrimp and Avocado Salad, 187

Shrimp (Cont.):
  and Ham Jambalaya, 64–65
  Beer-ded, 62
  Butterfly, 63–64
  Scampi, 62–63
Slivered Almonds, 299
Snow Berry Cake, 222–23
Soufflé Salad, 181–82
Soufflés
  Tuna, 67
  Vegetable, 73–74
Soup, Chilled, 26–27
  Tempura, 63
  Tolliver, 294–95
Soups
  Amount of Servings, 20
  Banana Vichyssoise, 23–24
  Bisques, 22–23
  Borsch, 28
  Cherry, 28–29
  Chicken Oriental, 24–25
  Chinese Duck, 29–30
  Coconut, 24
  Crab Bisque, Quick, 25
  Cream of Vegetable, 22
  Croutons, 19–20
  Cucumber, 25–26
  Gazpacho, 30
  Gazpacho, Quick, 30–31
  Hot Apple, 27–28
  Hungarian Tomato, 32–33
  Ideas for, 21–22
  Onion, 31
  Pink Velvet, 27
  Pumpkin, 31–32
  Pumpkin, Cream of, 31–32
  Salmon, 26
  Shrimp, Chilled, 26–27
Sour Cream Apple Pie, 208–209
  Cream Frosting, 235
  Cream Gravy, Danish, 296
  Cream Sauce, Hot, 103
Spaghetti, Raisin, with Ham Balls, 57
Spareribs, Quick Barbecued, 123–24
Spiced Noodles à la Neptune, 67–68
Tongue with Curry Sauce, 41–42
Spicy Chili Dip, 8
Spiedeno Romano, 37–38
Steak and Kidney Pie, 108–109
Steamed Clams in Butter Sauce, 291–92
Stew, Bavarian Beef, 111–12
Strawberry Pie, Frozen, 265

Stuffed Mushroom Caps, 14–15
Stuffings (for Fish and Fowl)
  Apple, 158
  Cucumber, 70–71
  for Large Baked Fish, 70
  Gourmet, 143–44
  Wild Rice and Sausage, 158–59
Sub-Gum-Gai-Pen, 148
Sukiyaki
  Pork, 119–20
  Vegetable, 75
Surrey Fowl with Cream Sauce, 151–52
Swedish Fish Hors D'Oeuvres, 9–10
  Pot Roast, 110–11
Sweet and Sour Pork, 120–21
Sweetbreads and Ham, 42–43
Sweet Nut Rolls, 245–46
Sweet Potato Cecilia, 81
Swiss Cheese Caraway Square, 16
  Cheese Fondue, 35–37
  Cheese Sauce, 100–101
Swordfish, Barbecued, 66
Székelygulya's, 297

Tarragon Chicken, 144–45
Tomatoes, Fried, 95
Tomato Horseradish Sauce, 44–45
  Soup, Hungarian, 32–33
  Sour Cream Dip, 7
Tournedos
  Béarnaise, 107
  Gabrielle, 107
  Mistral, 107
  Montmorency, 107
  Rossini, 107
Tropical Freeze, 136–37
Tuna Soufflé, 67
Turkey
  How to carve, 155–56
  Buffet, 156–57
  Mousse, 157
Turnips, 96–97
  Purée of, 97

Unusual Supper Dishes
  Canadian Bacon with Sherry, 45
  Chicken Livers in Sour Cream, 42
  Chicken or Turkey Mornay, 39
  Ham in Vermouth Sauce, 38
  Ham Loaf with Tomato Horseradish Sauce, 44

Unusual Supper Dishes (*Cont.*):
  Japanese Rice à la Luise, 35
  Lobster au Champagne, 40–41
  Paella Riscal, 34–35
  Roast Beef and Sherried Mushrooms, 39
  Salmon Loaf, 43
  Sausage Gastronome, 40
  Spiced Tongue with Curry Sauce, 41
  Spiedeno Romano, 37–38
  Sweetbreads and Ham, 42–43
  Swiss Cheese Fondue, 35–37

Veal, 113
  Aspic, 114–15
  Breast Stuffed with Sauerkraut, 115–16
  Steaks, Sautéed, 113
  Stroganoff, 114
  Veau à la Suisse, 291
Veau à la Suisse, 291
Vegetable (Fresh) Hors D'Oeuvres, 8–9
  Ring Mold, 180
  Shortcakes, 74
  Soufflé, 73–74
  Sukiyaki, 75
Vegetables, 72–98. *See also* Name of Vegetable
  Herb flavoring for, 97–98
  Sauces for, 99–103
Venison Loaf, 168
  Roast Leg of, with Sour Cream, 167–68
Vermouth Sauce, 38
Vichy Carrots, 87

Waldorf Jewel Salad, 185–86
Walnuts, Blanched, 299
Watermelon Preserves, 140
Welsh Rabbit, 289–90
Welsh Rabbit Spread, 11
Whipped Cream Amandine, Liqueur 299–300
  Cream Filling, 233
  Cream Frosting, 232–33
White Rice, 47–48
  Sauce (for Vegetables), 99–100
Wild Duck, 164
Wild Rice and Sausage Stuffing, 158–59
  Rice, Herbed, 49–50
Wine Butter Sauce, 102
  Glaze (for Ham), 127
  Jelly, 139–40
Woodcock, 166